THE INTERNATIONAL
PSYCHO-ANALYTICAL
LIBRARY
No. 39

THE INTERNATIONAL PSYCHO-ANALYTICAL LIBRARY
EDITED BY ERNEST JONES, M.D.
No. 39

TRENDS IN PSYCHO-ANALYSIS

BY

MARJORIE BRIERLEY

THE HOGARTH PRESS LTD.
40-42 WILLIAM IV STREET, LONDON, W.C.2
AND THE INSTITUTE OF PSYCHO-ANALYSIS
1951

PUBLISHED BY

The Hogarth Press Ltd.

and

The Institute of Psycho-Analysis

LONDON

★

Clarke, Irwin & Co. Ltd.

TORONTO

PRINTED IN GREAT BRITAIN

BY R. AND R. CLARK, LTD., EDINBURGH

ACKNOWLEDGEMENTS

GRATEFUL acknowledgement is made to the Hon. Editors of the *International Journal of Psycho-Analysis* and the *British Journal of Medical Psychology* for permission to reprint papers issued in these journals. Also to the following authors and publishers for permission to quote from their publications: to Dr. Ernest Jones for passages from *Essays in Applied Psycho-Analysis*, to Mrs. Melanie Klein for quotations from *The Psycho-Analysis of Children* and *Contributions to Psycho-Analysis*, and to the Hogarth Press for these and numerous quotations from the translations of Freud's works and other volumes in the International Psycho-Analytical Library; to Professor Flugel and Gerald Duckworth & Co. Ltd., for quotations from *Man, Morals and Society*; to Longmans Green & Co. Ltd., for extensive passages from *Collected Papers of Evelyn Underhill*, edited by Lucy Menzies; to Methuen & Co. Ltd., for quotations from the late Evelyn Underhill's *Man and the Supernatural*; to Dr. S. L. Frank and Jonathan Cape Ltd., for passages from *God With Us*; and to Miss Vita Sackville West and Michael Joseph Ltd., for extracts from *The Eagle and the Dove*. For certain other quotations not exceeding 150 words permission has not been formally requested, but acknowledgement is hereby tendered to the several authors and to the publishers of their works.

My personal thanks are due to Mr. Leonard Woolf of the Hogarth Press for helpful suggestions regarding the arrangement of the book; to Dr. Sylvia Payne and the Publications Committee of the British Psycho-Analytical Society, and to a number of friends who helped at various times. I am particularly grateful to the late Ella Sharpe for her long-standing friendship and encouragement, and to Dr. Edward Glover, not least for the training which preserved to me the ability to think for myself; above all, I am grateful to my husband, whose help has been invaluable, and to whom I therefore inscribe this book.

MARJORIE BRIERLEY

READING
11 July 1949

CONTENTS

INTRODUCTION

THE title of this book, *Trends in Psycho-Analysis*, requires a brief comment. The title describes the subject-matter of the book but the contents are more selective than the title, since many trends have been and are operative in psycho-analysis which find little or no mention in these pages. More precise description could have been given only by some unwieldly title such as 'Some Trends in Psycho-Analytical Theory with Notes on the Implications of Psycho-Analysis'.

The book is based on, and includes, papers written by the author between 1934 and 1947; some of these are reprinted almost in their original form, while others have undergone more extensive revision and rearrangement. The contents fall naturally into three sections: first, an introductory review of theory up to the year 1934, with a supplementary chapter on affects (Chapters I and II); second, a middle section, dealing with the work of Melanie Klein and with some issues raised by it (Chapter III); third, a final section discussing the nature of psycho-analytical theory and the wider relationships of psycho-analysis with some of its more general implications for human life (Chapters IV, V, and VI).

Chapter I indicates the historical background against which later contributions to theory may be viewed; it is reprinted almost exactly as it appeared in 1934 and is a digest of Lectures delivered to Candidates (student psycho-analysts) in training at the London Institute of Psycho-Analysis. The chapter is over-condensed, although much of importance is omitted, but it may serve to indicate the general pattern followed by the development of theory up to 1934. Even in a science with so short a history as psycho-analysis, it is of value to establish historical perspective in relation to new hypotheses.

Chapter II rather interrupts the continuity between Chapters I and III but affects are too vital a topic to be omitted from the introductory section. The subject raises a number of points which recur later in the book.

Chapter III expresses no final judgments and makes no pretence of being an exhaustive critical examination of the work of Melanie Klein. It represents chiefly the author's share in the prolonged discussions in the British Psycho-Analytical Society of the divers problems which arose in connection with this work. Contact with fledgling analysts and with Candidates in training and their not-infrequent bewilderment by current debates, persuaded the author of the need to help in promoting in the Society as a whole a 'scientific attitude' towards differences of opinion and a clarification of the nature of theory, its relation to consulting-room practice, etc. Hence it will be evident that this section is as much concerned in advocating a constructive approach to controversial issues as in examining specific problems. Further, it will be clear that two themes are commingled, namely, consideration of the general methods of evaluating new contributions and consideration of particular aspects of Melanie Klein's work. Some of this material is better suited to a theory-seminar audience than to a wider public, but it would be difficult to omit it without breaking the double thread which runs through the chapter, although this may not always be obvious to readers unfamiliar with the local climate in which the papers were first written.

It will also be evident that two personal attitudes underlie the 'controversial' discussions, one general and one particular. The general attitude is that of the paramount necessity of considering all hypotheses, new and old, on their merits rather than on their authorship. It was inevitable that, in its early years, psycho-analysis should be identified with its creator. Further, in view of the incomparable quality of Freud's work in this field, it is only natural that this identification should die hard, both in the psycho-analytic and in the public mind. Nevertheless, psycho-analysis should no longer be identified with Freud any more than the theory of evolution is now identified with Darwin, although this also happened for a time and had to be outgrown. The validity of Melanie Klein's work cannot be decided by the answer to the question: Do the views of Melanie Klein agree in every detail with the views of Freud? The only relevant question is: Are her views consonant with the basic principles of psycho-analysis as hitherto confirmed by clinical experience, *i.e.* do they represent, in whole or in part, a valid expansion of theory or an aberrant growth?

The second, more specific attitude is that the work of Melanie Klein should not be regarded as an independent theory, complete in itself. Treated as an independent theory it could easily become, in fact, the magical cult-substitute for psycho-analysis which some opponents already insist that it is. On the contrary, her work can justly be assessed only as a contribution to psycho-analysis, a contribution whose value in aiding the legitimate growth and expansion of theory is still in process of determination. Just and impartial assessment requires time; it cannot be effected by logic alone but must be put to the test of clinical experience, and thus many years may be needed to stabilize judgment. Any correlation would almost certainly demand some modification of both old and new views and would eventuate in a restatement including the positive values of both. No science can remain alive if it ceases to grow and, if the theory of psycho-analysis does not continue to develop, psycho-analysis itself will degenerate into a stereotyped cult. The writer accepts the basic principles of psycho-analysis established by Freud; but theory is, for her, a series of working-hypotheses, which can and should be modified as knowledge advances, and not a creed to be espoused. Her intention is to adhere to the expressed aim of the British Psycho-Analytical Society, 'the furtherance of the science of psycho-analysis': this aim, by definition, excludes both partisan attack upon, and partisan defence of, any 'teaching', whether of its founder or any later comer, since the relativity of scientific knowledge is axiomatic.

The stimulus of controversy compelled the author to reconsider her views on the essential nature of psycho-analytical theory and the general status, relationships, and implications of psychoanalysis. The third and final section of the book embodies the outcome of this reconsideration. There is a certain amount of overlap between Chapters IV, V, and VI, but in view of their schematic and highly condensed form, it was thought that some repetition might be found more helpful than irritating.

Chapter IV is a discussion of the nature of psycho-analytical theory and of its bearings on research and public relations, with particular reference to metapsychology. It is pointed out that theory has two aspects, subjective or personal and objective or impersonal; it comprises two series of hypotheses, which differ, not in the data from which they are inferred but in the mode of approach to the data and in the 'reference' of the ensuing generalizations. The data for both series are the same, i.e. in the main, the recounted experiences and observed behaviour of living persons undergoing psycho-analysis. Subjective theory remains personal, and expresses its conclusions in terms of experience which have reference to persons and human relationships. Objective theory, on the other hand, infers from the same data impersonal conclusions regarding mental function, which are expressed in abstract terms and no longer have direct reference to personal experience. The words 'subjective' and 'objective' being still too ambiguous, the term 'personology' was later borrowed from Smuts and the two aspects distinguished as 'personology' and 'metapsychology'.

Metapsychology is a theory of mental processes and their organization and of the distribution of energy between psychic systems. It is therefore suggested that it should be recognized more explicitly that it belongs to the category of 'process' theories familiar to modern scientists. Such recognition in no way alters the content of metapsychology, it merely 'places' it in more evident relationship to current trends in thought. The dynamic and economic view of mental life which metapsychology affords is the kind of over-all conception to which other psychologies and human sciences are tending to converge. It is partly the failure of psycho-analysts to appreciate the nature of metapsychology that makes it possible for statements like the following to be made about psycho-analysts: 'It might be a question whether they are genuine psychologists at all, or only able and often successful "empirics", standing to the genuine psychologist much as an ingenious and practised mechanic without any training in theoretical physics does to the physicist' (Taylor, 1945, footnote to p. 44).

Chapter V discusses the relation of metapsychology to personology, and the nature and scope of the latter. It then considers the relation of psycho-analysis to other branches of knowledge and its potential contribution to a more adequate and more integrative *Lebensanschauung*. The attitude to life that appears to the writer to be implicit in psycho-analysis is termed 'neo-realistic humanism', because this phrase gives a succinct description. This term naturally suggests the kind of philosophical outlook with which psycho-analysis would be consonant, but it should be understood that no intention of fabricating any closed system of psycho-analytical philosophy is thereby conveyed.

Chapter VI considers first the problem of personality types and the difficulties in the way of their adequate classification. Optimal integration being taken as the goal of personality development, it is suggested that a personal, as distinct from a social, standard of normality may be found in adequacy of integration. The plan or mode of integration offered by Christianity is then examined and compared with the type of integration furthered by psycho-analysis. The contribution of psycho-analysis to a realistic ethic is discussed under the sectional heading 'Ethics as the Principles of Integrative Living'. Reference is involved to such topics as 'Psi' phenomena and the nature of mystical experience. In attempting to describe the latter as accurately as possible in a brief sketch, the spiritual authorities have been allowed to speak for themselves in the first place; hence, the free use of quotations in the sections on mysticism.

Attention has also been given to the 'present state' of Christianity because it is far from evident that assumptions of its rapid demise are correct. On the contrary, if world conditions permit their survival, it may be that Christianity and the human sciences will continue side by side for many years to come. Some readers may consider that the writer over-estimates the vitality of Christianity, but it seems to her that the conviction of Christians that their religion will endure is not merely 'wish-fulfilling' but psychologically justifiable. Prevalent modes of solving infantile life-problems, especially the common tendency to resort to mechanisms of idealization-denigration as a means of surmounting Oedipal conflict, are likely to perpetuate religious needs rather than to diminish them. We should not close our eyes to the fact that there are people who can develop their capacities for love and work only in relation to a divine ideal. The desire to worship and adore is not a minor aberration but one of the strongest human passions, and 'faith' is likely to be proportionate to 'need to believe'. If people who need religion, and who are drawn to God, generally find Him, liberty of conscience might appear to be the sufficient answer. A form of religion which tolerated liberty of thought and conscience would put no barriers in the way of continued research into, and dissemination of knowledge of, human nature, though it would naturally assimilate such knowledge to its own faith. Tolerance would seem to be on the increase among Protestants to-day, but it is difficult to see how it could ever become an official attitude in the Catholic Church. Unfortunately, it may be that the Roman Church is more 'catholic' in its unconscious appeal than are its 'protestant' derivatives. In any case, the mode of personal integration offered by Christianity is inherently unstable; as Ernest Jones (1948, p. 325) remarks: 'It was born in conflict and it lives in conflict'.

The Christian mode of integration, which, at any rate until quite recently, is the mode which tends to be favoured or 'selected' by Western civilization, is unstable because it tends to perpetuate civil war within the personality. It is based upon an alliance of reality-self and conscience against instinct and infantile selves, particularly against infantile erotism and aggressiveness. This Christian conscience in its post-Oedipal pattern, is dominated by identifications with idealized and de-sexualized parental imagos; the 'bad' sexual and hostile aspects of the parents are correspondingly denigrated and repressed along with the young child's own erotic and aggressive impulses. The erotic impulses may subsequently find expression in sublimations or symptoms and in adult sexuality, but the repressed hostility to the parents finds a way through conscience which directs it against the reality-self. It is difficult to see how these organizational trends can be effectively modified until the facts of infantile sexual and emotional development become as well known and as taken for granted as the phenomena of somatic development.

The mode of integration implicit in psycho-analysis and actually furthered, to some extent, in successful therapy, is a mode which tends, not to subjective civil war, but to the greater harmonization of the total personality, through the development of a higher degree of psychological reality-sense and ego-toleration of hitherto intolerable components of the psyche. The degree of integration attainable naturally varies from person to person, but if processes of re-integration are once initiated they tend to continue. The integrity achieved is always relative, but even an uneasy armistice is better than open war.

A major implication of psycho-analysis which directly affects the sphere of ethics is that the only efficient method of personal and social instinct-control is control by use. Frustrations are inevitable at all periods of life, but the sanity-promoting method of dealing with frustrated impulses and desires is to provide them with personally and socially acceptable alternative outlets. It is necessary to overcome our irrational fear of instincts and to recognize and respect them as the mainspring of our lives, but we are abundantly justified in fearing all such impulses as have succumbed to repression but have not found a route back to motility through satisfying 'symbolic' activities.

The difference between the attitude to life implicit in psychoanalysis, here called, for convenience of reference, 'neo-realistic humanism', and all forms of materialism which deny the existence of psychological realities, will be self-evident. Neo-realistic humanism does not share the illusion of the older humanisms that man is fundamentally good. It recognizes that all men are both good and bad: that they are impelled by ineradicable instincts which are themselves pre-moral, moral values being the product of a human type of mental organization. Hate and love are both 'normal' sentiments.

The difference between neo-realistic humanism and all forms of idealism and perfectionism is equally definite. The standard of reality which obtains in the consulting-room is applicable in the wider world; it is the acceptance of things as they are, in human nature and in world affairs, in so far as we are able to assess them. Leaving aside the problem of how far the individual can improve his reality-sense without specialist aid, the immediate personal application can be stated very simply. One should not concern oneself primarily with what one thinks one ought to be, or with what one thinks it most desirable to be for some extrinsic reason, *e.g.* social approval, etc., nor should one adopt a rôle in life which is a pretence of being something that one is not. One should try to form an objective estimate of one's personal character and abilities and to shape one's life accordingly. It is necessarily more difficult to arrive at an objective appreciation of oneself or one's intimates than of strangers, just as it is usually easier to deceive oneself than other people. Where it can be done (temperament and character permitting) it is often an aid to realism to look upon oneself temporarily as a third person, *e.g.* in the case of a difficult decision, to ask oneself what advice one might be tempted to offer to another person in similar circumstances. Any decision, if it is to be integrative in its effects, should take into account the three directions in which adaptation is required, namely, environment, personal capacity and inclination, and attitude of conscience. Three types of question need to be asked: one, is the decision reasonable in view of the external circumstances, *i.e.* does it appear to answer to the requirements of external reality; two, does it appeal to already known interests and inclinations or seem to offer new and desirable opportunities, *i.e.* to what extent is it likely to receive adequate instinctual support; three, will conscience permit and co-operate, *i.e.* is it a decision on which inclination and conscience can agree and reinforce one another? A decision which is reasonable in given circumstances and in accord with natural inclination may be personally undesirable if the specific conscience in question strongly objects to it. The adult has to accept his conscience, like his other realities, as he finds it; this is often annoyingly irrational, rather than rational. Anyone is able, on occasion, to flout his conscience, but should not be surprised if he has subsequently to pay for this privilege. Conscience-revenge is the liability to which our inescapable morality exposes us.

A realist, having acquired by experience a working knowledge of himself and his potentialities, will seek to do the best he can with himself as he is, and will no longer try to be a different kind of person. To use a crude analogy, a pony, suitably employed, may be a useful and happy creature and a source of profit and pleasure to others, but his owner would be accounted very ill-advised if he used him as a cart-horse or attempted to train him for the Derby. Yet this is precisely the type of mistake very commonly made by adults in regard to themselves, and by parents and teachers in regard to children and adolescents, if they do not take pains to estimate personality objectively. All this may seem very trite, but the discussion of the implications of psycho-analysis in the text of the book is necessarily so very general that it seemed that it might be advisable to give some indication of the way in which they can be applied in simple matters of daily life. Decisions, of course, affect not only the person who takes them but all the other people with whom he is associated in varying degrees of intimacy. These people and the probable effects on them constitute part of the external reality situation, and humane realism requires a just assessment of mutual advantages and disadvantages. It may be very difficult to strike a balance which is fair to oneself and to other people, but the intention to do so is a safeguard against both undue self-immolation and excessive exploitation of other people.

Consideration of the wider implications of psycho-analysis is not a substitute for the step-by-step advance of precise knowledge by detailed and often laborious research. Research is indispensable, but consideration of its implications is also necessary. Until very recently, Freud's own dislike of the pretensions of philosophy, together with the youthfulness of the movement, the concentration of personal energy demanded, and the time-requirements of clinical practice, have combined to prevent more than a very few psycho-analysts from paying attention to the second task, the consideration of implications. Thus, Professor Waddington (1947, p. 125) feels justified in asking psycho-analysts 'whether they can truthfully say that they devote enough time to discussing the most fundamental implications of their studies'. The position is that mainly negative implications, deduced by non-analysts, will continue to hold the field unless the more positive implications are worked out by psycho-analysts themselves and stated with whatever degree of precision can be attained.

Psycho-analytical views are now very widely disseminated and are continuing to spread, but this very process has itself been adduced by critics as a sign of the nihilistic trend of the times. The initial impact of psycho-analysis on human thought was undoubtedly 'revolutionary': it has, therefore, incurred its full share of the blame attributed to modern science for destroying traditional values without offering new ones in their place. This situation has been exacerbated by popular misunderstandings and undesirable kinds of publicity. In consequence, whilst negative implications have frequently been ventilated, the more creative and positive implications are only beginning to be recognized. Not even genius is free from the limitations of specific human personality, and it is the equation of a personal trait of Freud with the character of psycho-analysis that enables Reinhold Niebuhr (1941, p. 26) to write with sincere conviction: 'One of the modern fruits of Nietzschean thought is Freudian pessimism'. At the same time, Reinhold Niebuhr himself appreciates that psycho-analysis has other, more positive, implications, though he naturally expresses these in terms of his own theological conceptions.

A considerable amount of new work has been published since the contents of this book were first written. Much of this is not referred to in these pages, but in revising the original papers certain additions have been made to bring the illustrations more up to date. It should be remembered, however, that the intention has not been to compile a treatise or to review the whole literature of the subjects discussed. The aim has been to present in broad and tentative outline the general conception of human nature and the attitude towards life, with its consequences for behaviour, which appear to the writer to be inherent in psycho-analysis. Any such general estimate can only be selective and personal, but it is hoped that, in spite of their inevitable subjective co-determination, the conclusions reached have a measure of objective validity.

CHAPTER I

TRENDS IN PSYCHO-ANALYSIS [1]

I. INTRODUCTION

THE theory of psycho-analysis expanded very rapidly during the decade which elapsed after Freud recognized aggression as a primary instinct and published his revised views of psychic organization in *The Ego and the Id* in 1923 (1927). In this country in particular, this expansion was further stimulated by the findings of child analysts using the play-technique. One result of this fertile growth has been to make the present state of theory somewhat confusing and difficult to grasp. It may be a comforting reflection that this difficulty is by no means confined to non-analysts but is experienced by analysts themselves. A relatively easy way to orientation among present tendencies would appear to be to approach them in the light of their historical perspective. If we bear in mind the developments which led up to the turning-point represented by the concepts of a primary instinct of aggression and of super-ego formation, we shall be in a better position to understand the changes which have resulted from their introduction and the main points at issue at the present time. I propose, therefore, to begin by reminding you of the state of theory as it existed in 1905, when Freud first published the *Three Contributions to Sexual Theory* (1930a), to follow this by a very brief survey of the main advances between 1905 and 1923, and then to consider more recent developments. I hope to be able to show you that there is a pattern or sequence in theory, that modern theory is the result of a natural expansion of earlier views, an organic growth and not a chaotic jumble of ideas, and that the clue provided by this pattern is available to analysts and non-analysts alike.

II. EARLY THEORY

In his *Interpretation of Dreams*, first published in 1899, Freud described the psyche as an apparatus for the regulation of

---

[1] Reprint, slightly amended, of 'Present Tendencies in Psycho-Analysis', *Brit. J. Med. Psychol.* (1934), vol. xiv, Part iii.

instinct tension (1932a, p. 520). Assuming that instincts have an organic basis, he characterized instinct, in contradistinction to stimuli of external origin, as a constant source of stimuli arising from within the organism itself which cannot therefore be mastered by flight. One may flee from a wild beast but one cannot run away from one's own hunger or rage. The psychic tension produced by instinctual need, felt as pain or unpleasure, 'Unlust', must therefore be reduced by discharge, or gratification, felt as pleasure, or 'bound' by intrapsychic mechanisms, by the so-called instinct defence-mechanisms, which are directed to the avoidance of pain. This is essentially the view which we still hold to-day. We continue to regard the psyche as the mediator between inner and outer reality, between the individual's instinctual needs and the possibilities of their gratification in the external world. We regard all psychic activity as inspired and sustained by instinctual drives, and as directed either to securing the gratification of instinctual aims or to the resolution of the tension associated with instinctual frustration, that is, in modern terminology, to the mastery of anxiety.

To begin with, Freud accepted the current biological distinction between instincts of self-preservation and instincts of race-preservation, between hunger and love, and made these the basis of his first classification, ego-instincts and sex-instincts (1915a, *C.P.* iv, p. 60). The libido is the psychic sexual drive. Analysis of dreams and psychoneurotics led him to the conception of conflict between ego and sexual drives, which might issue in the repression, the rendering unconscious, of the sexual drives. Failure of repression resulted in the return of the repressed in disguised form, for example, as a dream or symptom (1932a). The nature of the repressed impulses, as brought to light by analysis, led to the revolutionary conception of the adult sexual impulse as the end-product of a long process of development, an integration of drives active in the individual from earliest infancy and not, as previously supposed, a simple reproductive urge which emerged full-blown at adolescence (1930a). Infantile sexuality revealed itself in a number of relatively independent component or partial impulses, originating in erogenous zones, that is in regions of the body such as the mouth or anus which seem to behave like genitals as well as performing self-preservative functions. The variety of infantile impulses and their similarity to perversions caused Freud to label them 'polymorphous perverse'. He defined them as objectless or auto-erotic. At this time, he considered that full co-ordination of sexual impulses under the primacy of the genital zone and true object-choice only occurred at puberty. A proportion of the infantile impulses continue to find direct gratification in the form of fore-pleasure associated with the adult genital act, and the remainder undergo repression and displacement and reappear as sublimations or symptoms, or, if they escape repression, as perversions. Hence the dictum that 'the neurosis is the negative of the perversion'.

The psyche at this early stage therefore appeared as a twofold system, consciousness (including the preconscious or potentially conscious) and the unconscious, equated with the repressed. It could be described topographically as a series of levels, as for instance in the iceberg metaphor, a small part above and a larger part below the threshold of consciousness. Mental life could be described dynamically in terms of the urgency and conflict of instinctual drives. A big advance had been made in knowledge of the sexual instincts, though genital impulses were still held to be relatively unimportant in infancy, but the ego was still unexplored and the psychic mechanisms so far recognized, such as repression and displacement, were chiefly those revealed by the analysis of hysteria and the study of dreams.

III. 1905-1923

In the next twenty years it became clear that infantile sexuality was not the chaos it at first appeared, but that it exhibited a more or less orderly series of pre-genital organizations, centring first about mouth-interests and giving rise to an oral primacy, and later about the anus and excretory processes, giving rise to an anal-sadistic primacy (Freud, 1913, *C.P.* ii, p. 122; 1930a). These primacies were further subdivided by Abraham (1924). It was not until 1923 that Freud became really convinced that a genital primacy was also established in infancy. He considered even then that only the male genital was recognized, that the vagina was undiscovered by both sexes until puberty, and that the primacy reached was therefore "not a primacy of the genital, but of the phallus" (1923, *C.P.* ii, p. 245). This exclusively phallic conception of infantile genitality dies hard, but the modern work of Horney (1926, 1932, 1933), Jones (1933), Klein

(1932), and others, strongly supports the view that the undiscovered vagina of Freud's phallic phase is a vagina previously known but denied by both sexes from motives of anxiety connected with the imaginary dangers of copulation.

It also became clear that infantile sexuality is not only more orderly than at first appeared but that it is not auto-erotic in the sense Freud at first supposed; that is, objectless, and that its aims are not limited to the attainment of organ-pleasure. Even the suckling has an object in the external world, his mother's breast, and he exhibits a variety of reactions towards this object which show that very early in his life it means something to him, i.e. that it is an object in the psychological sense. Abraham called the type of organ-object represented by the nipple a part-object, to distinguish it from whole-person objects, such as the complete father or mother. Personal object-choice is also achieved in infancy; Freud thought somewhere between the ages of three and five, 'in such a manner that all the sexual strivings proceed in the direction of one person in whom they wish to attain their aims' (1930a, p. 58). This object situation, which is related to the phallic phase and associated with castration anxiety, is the now universally familiar Oedipus complex, the nuclear complex of the neuroses (1929, lecture 21). The notion that fixation in the Oedipus phase was the precondition of neurosis became firmly established during these years, and Abraham (1924) made the first attempt to classify mental diseases by the relative depth of regression behind the Oedipus phase, a classification on the basis of specific fixations at pregenital stages.

This period also saw the beginnings of ego psychology in the form of character study, Ferenczi's classical essay on the development of reality sense (1916), and the concept of narcissism (Freud, 1914, C.P. iv, p. 30). The co-existence of megalomania with loss of interest in the outer world characteristic of paraphrenics led Freud to suppose that the megalomania came into being at the expense of object-libido. 'The libido withdrawn from the outer world has been directed on to the ego, giving rise to a state which we may call narcissism' (op. cit. p. 32). This led on to the supposition that all libido was at first accumulated in the ego which put forth and withdrew object-cathexes much as an amoeba puts forth and retracts pseudopodia. Freud writes: 'We perceive also a certain reciprocity between ego-libido and object-libido. The more that is absorbed by the one, the more impoverished does the other become' (*op. cit.* p. 33). Normal sleep on this view is a recurrent state of narcissism. The introduction of this concept is an important turning-point for two main reasons. In the first place, we here pass from the older conception of a simple antithesis between ego-instincts and sex-instincts, between ego and libido, to the notion of the distribution of a quantum of libido between ego and objects. In other words, the economic canon of description has been added to the topographic and dynamic and we are now definitely in the field of what Freud termed metapsychology (see Jones, 1923, p. 54). In the second place, we have learnt something very important about the hitherto unexplored ego, namely, that it is itself regularly cathected with libido, that self-love exists side by side with object-love. Moreover, Freud thought that infantile narcissism or self-love was later transmuted by the formation of an ego-ideal into love of this ideal. In this conception of an ego-ideal we have the first hint of the existence of a differentiating grade in the ego itself which was to issue later in the concept of super-ego formation.

Meanwhile analysis of obsessional neurotics (Freud, 1913; Jones, 1923, p. 553) and of psychotics (Abraham, 1924) had been bringing to the fore the importance of hate and sadism in infantile life, and the ambivalence, the mixture or alternation of love and hate, in most infantile object-relations. Hatred and aggression were considered to be secondary phenomena, the result of frustration. Certain observations on play, the repetition by children in their games of painful situations such as medical examinations, the anxiety dreams of traumatic neuroses in which the shock is re-lived over and over again, and the transference revivals during the analysis of painful situations in patients' lives, led Freud to assume the existence in the psyche of a tendency older and more fundamental than the pursuit of pleasure or the avoidance of pain, namely, a compulsion to repetition (1922a). Inasmuch as repetitions can be shown to be directed towards the mastery of painful situations, which is often the case, this tendency would appear to be only another method which the psychic apparatus can employ in its work of reducing instinct-tension. But Freud sees in it far more than this. He considers it to be an expression of a 'conservative' character of instinct hitherto overlooked, 'a tendency innate in living organic matter impelling it towards the reinstatement of an earlier condition' (*op. cit.*, p. 44), the inorganic or death. These lines of thought, which are biological rather than psychological, issued in the new bipartite classification of life-instincts and death-instincts. The antithesis is no longer between ego-instincts and sex-instincts, nor between ego-libido and object-libido, but between Eros and Thanatos, libido and aggression. The death-instinct is not easily recognizable, it is for the most part 'mute', and becomes manifest only when turned outwards as aggression and when fused with libido in sadism and masochism. The first line of defence against the death-instinct is its externalization by means of the musculature and the mechanism of projection with which we first became familiar in paranoia. The second line of defence is fusion with libidinal impulses. Freud inclines to the view that 'we never have to deal with pure life-instincts and death-instincts at all, but only with combinations of them in different degrees. Corresponding with the fusion of instincts there may under certain conditions occur a defusion of them' (1924a, *C.P.* ii, p. 240). In *Civilization and its Discontents* he writes: '... I can no longer understand how we could have overlooked the universality of non-erotic aggression and destruction' (1930b, p. 99). This passage suggests the existence of 'pure' impulses. If all impulses are mixed, or if they are mostly mixed, we must be careful to define sadism and masochism as fusions in which aggressive or death-instinct components predominate, if these terms are to retain a distinctive, clinically useful meaning. The third line of defence, which is defence against aggression rather than against the death-instinct itself, is turning against the self. The self-reproaches of melancholics were recognized by both Freud and Abraham to be reproaches against a former external object now identified with the self as the result of introjection, phantasied in these cases as an oral incorporation of the object (Abraham, 1924). This mechanism of introjection was soon to prove to be the most important agent in super-ego formation. Defence against aggression, by turning it on the self, has the immense disadvantage of re-internalizing aggression.

There are two points which should be remembered in regard to the status of the death-instinct. The first is that the concept need not stand or fall with the crediting or discrediting of the compulsion to repetition as a fundamental tendency beyond the pleasure principle, that is, on what Freud has described as biological evidence; there is, for instance, a considerable amount of purely psychological evidence to be drawn from the study of masochism. It must be admitted, however, that a stronger case exists, that is, evidence is more easily available, for the hypothesis of a primary instinct of aggression or destruction than of primary self-destruction. On the other hand, every physiologist takes for granted that life depends upon a nice adjustment between anabolic and katabolic processes in the body cells, and there seems no reason why psychologists should be unduly disturbed by the suggestion that this antithesis may have its instinctual or psychic parallel.

The concepts of the ego-ideal and of the death-instinct appear to have been the immediate precursors of the views put forward by Freud in *The Ego and the Id*, from which all distinctively modern theory dates. He there writes: '. . . In every individual there is a coherent organization of mental processes, which we call his ego. This ego includes consciousness and it controls the approaches to motility' (1927, p. 15). Repressions proceed from the ego, but since we know from analytic experience that they may give rise to resistance, of which the patient is completely unaware, it follows that some part of the ego itself is unconscious. Therefore 'We recognize that the Ucs. does not coincide with the repressed; it is still true that all that is repressed is Ucs. but not that the whole Ucs. is repressed' (*op. cit.* p. 17). Further, the unconscious (Ucs.) is to be regarded as the source of all instinctual drives. To this wider conception of the unconscious, the unconscious as an instinct reservoir including the repressed, Freud applies Groddeck's term the 'Id'. The ego now becomes 'that part of the Id which has been modified by the direct influence of the external world' (*op. cit.* p. 29). But 'The ego is first and foremost a body-ego' (*op. cit.* p. 31), that is, derived from bodily sensations. The differentiating grade in the ego, the ego-ideal or super-ego, for the most part unconscious, arises through the substitution of identifications for object-cathexes through introjection, the process first recognized in melancholia but now known to occur frequently. The origin of the super-ego lies in the identifications with the parents which follow the dissolution of the Oedipus complex (Freud, 1924b, *C.P.* iii, p. 262). The relative intensity of the father and mother identifications will depend on the preponderance of the positive or negative aspects of this complex, but its 'broad general outcome' will be 'the forming of a precipitate in the ego, consisting of these two identifications in some way combined together' (1927, p. 44).

The super-ego is in free communication with the id, and as the representative of the parents it assumes the functions of instinct scrutiny or instinct testing, leaving the ego free to concentrate on reality testing, but at the cost of loss of direct control of id impulses (Glover, J., 1926). The super-ego thus exercises both self-observing and self-judging functions (Freud, 1933, p. 82), and the results of its activities are experienced by the ego as the promptings of conscience. The relations between ego and super-ego are even yet by no means fully explored. They appear to range from confluence with co-operation to sharp demarcation with acute conflict and hostility. The sense of guilt, or super-ego anxiety, is the expression of tension between ego and super-ego. The super-ego is the instigator of repression, and inhibitions are the effect of super-ego prohibitions. The super-ego tends to be a harder taskmaster than the real parents, and there is evidence from the first that its so-called severity is dependent upon the strength of the individual's own aggression rather than on the actual behaviour of the real parents; it is equivalent to the child's hatred of the parents, now turned against himself. Freud has recently suggested that it may be related also to the severity of the parental super-ego (1933, p. 90), but he has often reaffirmed the reciprocal relation which appears to exist between the amount of aggression which is repressed by the individual and the strength of his sense of guilt (1930b, p. 116).

IV. IMPLICATIONS OF NEW CONCEPTS

What now are the chief implications of these modern views and in what do they differ from earlier conceptions?

First of all, the psyche has become a threefold system consisting of a reservoir of instinctual impulses, the id, a conscious or potentially conscious ego-system, concerned with reality testing and the adaptation of impulse to reality conditions, and an unconscious ego-system, concerned in the internal adaptation and regulation of instinctual impulses. In other words, the id represents the unorganized reservoir of instinctual impulses and the ego and super-ego the organized systems through which these operate and by which they are controlled. The ego proper now appears as 'a poor creature owing service to three masters and consequently menaced by three several dangers: from the external world, from the libido of the id, and from the severity of the super-ego' (Freud, 1927, p. 82).

Secondly, though our knowledge of libidinal impulses has increased, especially our knowledge of the comparatively orderly development and of the object-relations of infantile sexuality, it is evident that we can no longer study libidinal impulses by themselves. In future we must always take into consideration the relations between libido and aggression. Whether we accept aggression as a primary instinct or whether we still prefer to regard it as evoked by frustration, we have to recognize that it is invariably evoked. That is to say, we have to recognize a phylogenetically entrenched reaction which comes into operation very early in life, and that this infantile aggression, especially in the various forms of sadism in which it is blended with libidinal impulses, is a factor of primary importance in development.[1]

Thirdly, the defence-mechanisms of introjection and projection have shown themselves to be important not only in the production of pathological syndromes such as melancholia and paranoia but as general or normal mechanisms of defence against aggression and as agents in libido-distribution. Moreover, they appear to be mechanisms which come into operation earlier than true repression. Thus Freud, in speaking of externalization as the first defence against the death-instinct, really gives priority to projection as a method of dealing with instinct tension. The time-relations of repression are still, however, rather obscure. Freud posited a primal repression which can be thought of in two ways: in the first place it amounts to a primary tendency to ignore or not to become aware of painful impressions, which precedes their positive negation and could be also considered as perhaps preceding any attempt to deal with them by projection (Freud, 1925, 1936); in the second place, primary repression would appear to be an emergency measure which the primitive ego can employ when tension becomes intolerable, that is, in traumatic or shock situations where there is a sudden quantitative increase of tension. Repression proper, or secondary repression, the type associated in our minds with the production of hysterical symptoms, seems to be a later method of

[1] For a survey of the development of instinct theory, see Bibring, 1941.

defence, though Freud suggests that it may always take place along lines previously laid down by primal repression. It is recognized that the super-ego becomes the instigator of repression: Freud writes cautiously on the subject; he says (1936, p. 26): 'We cannot at present say, for instance, whether it is the emergence of the super-ego which provides the line of demarcation between primary repression and secondary expulsion'; but he also says: 'Nevertheless we shall bear in mind for future consideration the possibility that repression is a process which has a special relation to the genital organization of the libido, and that the ego resorts to other methods of defence when it has to secure itself against the libido on other levels of organization' (*op. cit.* p. 84). Freud's description of the process of repression as the separation of an idea from its preconscious verbal image suggests a relatively late origin, since verbal images can hardly occur prior to the development of at least an understanding of words.[1]

Further, though the original conception of conflict between impulses is not lost sight of, and is, indeed, inherent in the antithesis between libido and aggression, nevertheless conflict between impulses is now to a great extent superseded by notions of tension between psychic systems. Control is effected by the distribution of energies between systems, and is a result of the combined reaction of the ego-systems to impulses, rather than of any direct action of impulse on impulse.

Fourthly, though the sequence of stages in development represented by the series of libidinal primacies worked out by Freud and Abraham can still be accepted with certain reservations, it is evident that we can no longer study development in terms of a theory of impulses alone. We must at every stage be prepared to take into account the type of ego-organization through which they operate and the mechanisms by which they are controlled, including the degree of ego-differentiation and of reality-sense development which obtains. That is to say, the theory of development in terms of libidinal stages has to be expanded into a theory of developmental stages of the whole psyche, or, as Alexander (1930) phrased it, the 'total personality'. All modern work concerns the further differentiation of old, or the creation of new hypotheses, coming under one or other of these four heads.

[1] Anna Freud's detailed study, *The Ego and the Mechanisms of Defence* (1937), had not been published when this paragraph was written.

V. RECENT DEVELOPMENTS

The most immediate consequence of the new views was the stimulation of inquiry into the relations of the psychic systems and, in particular, into the rôle of the super-ego both in pathogenesis and in so-called normal life. There is a mass of literature on the subject of the sense of guilt and the need for punishment, into which I will not attempt to enter here. As Freud says in his *New Introductory Lectures*: 'The problems raised by the unconscious sense of guilt, its relation to morality, education, criminality and delinquency, is at the present moment the favourite field of investigation for psycho-analysts' (1933, p. 142). We must note, however, that there exists a tendency against which Freud himself has recently warned us (*op. cit.* p. 105), a tendency namely to treat the ego-organizations as sharply defined structures. Alexander's structural theory of neurosogenesis (1930) is perhaps the most outstanding example of this tendency, though he has lately rectified his views in some important respects (1933). He, however, originally introduced such anthropomorphic terms as 'secret alliance' between the super-ego and the id, and corruption of the super-ego by ego-bribery. The temptation to personify is insidious, but it is desirable to resist it and to treat the psychic systems impersonally as relatively stable organizations of impulse and not as entities in the animistic sense. From the point of view of metapsychological theory the so-called 'severity' of the super-ego is simply the amount of aggression at its disposal or the amount of sadism with which it is charged.

His new views led Freud himself to revise the concept of anxiety (1936). In the beginning he regarded anxiety as transformed libido, that is, as painful affect produced by frustration or repression. Closer study of symptom formation revealed that, so far from being a result of repression, anxiety usually precedes repression. It is a 'signal' to the ego that danger is threatening. Freud sees the prototype of all anxiety experience in the uncomfortable tensions of the birth trauma; according to him, outbreaks of anxiety after birth occur mainly when the child is either alone, in the dark, or with strangers, that is, where the essential condition is the absence of the loved person. The suckling longs for the presence of the mother because he is helpless without her and only she can gratify his needs. He fears the frustration-tension which may develop in her absence, against which he is himself powerless. Since her presence is the guarantee of safety, her absence comes to be a danger in itself because it may lead to helpless discomfort. Thus the infant may at first cry only when he is intolerably hungry, and later, if he finds himself alone, for fear, so to speak, that he may become intolerably hungry, and later still, if he thinks his mother is about to leave him. The traumatic situation which is ultimately dreaded, and in which the anxiety is quantitatively related to the degree of frustration, is represented by the intolerable hunger, the danger situation, whose quality evokes anxiety, by the absence of the mother, which may lead to trauma. This shift forward from the trauma to the danger situation represents the stride in development from the automatic reproduction of anxiety in an actually traumatic situation to its use as a signal or warning to the ego that there is a danger that an intolerable situation may develop if not warded off. In both cases anxiety is the product of the psychic helplessness of the infant, the correlate of its biological helplessness.

Every phase of development appears to have a type of anxiety appropriate to it. None of these is necessarily relinquished in the course of development, the older may co-exist alongside the later types. Thus neurotics may be said to be dominated by anxieties natural in infancy but outmoded in the adult. Castration anxiety is the natural development of separation anxiety appropriate to the genital phase. Castration anxiety can no longer be regarded as the sole motive for repression. With the development of the super-ego, castration anxiety passes into super-ego anxiety of which the latest development is the fear of death. All defence-mechanisms aim at the avoidance of anxiety, and symptoms may be said to be constructed in order to avoid danger situations. Loss of parental love and castration are indeed external dangers, but they would not threaten us were it not for our forbidden desires. Instinctive impulses therefore condition external dangers, and these can be overcome by regulating instinct. In the *New Introductory Lectures* Freud reverts to the view 'that frightening instinctual situations can in the last resort be traced back to external situations of danger' (1933, p. 117); he says, however, '. . . what is feared, the object of the anxiety, is always the emergence of a traumatic factor', that is, a mental 'condition of tense excitation, which is felt as pain, and which cannot be mastered by discharge' (*op. cit.* p. 122). '. . . These traumatic factors create their own anxiety anew, though in accordance with the pattern of the birth situation. . . . But I can see no objection to postulating a twofold origin of anxiety, first as the direct effect of a traumatic factor, and secondly as a signal that a traumatic factor of this kind threatens to recur' (*op. cit.* p. 123). He reaffirms that the ego is the only seat of anxiety and that 'the three main varieties of anxiety—objective anxiety, neurotic anxiety and moral anxiety—can so be easily related to the three directions in which the ego is dependent, on the external world, on the id and on the super-ego' (*op. cit.* p. 112).

VI. DEVELOPMENTS ASSOCIATED WITH CHILD ANALYSIS

So far anxiety has been considered chiefly in relation to libidinal frustration, but Freud has recognized that super-ego anxiety, the sense of guilt, is intimately dependent upon aggression. Thus he suggests that 'when an instinctual trend undergoes repression, its libidinal elements are transformed into symptoms and its aggressive components into a sense of guilt' (1930b, p. 132). Moreover, it is the pathogenic rôle of anxiety which has been chiefly elaborated. It is to child-analysis that we owe, in the first instance, our present recognition of the interdependence of anxiety and aggression and of its importance in normal development. Melanie Klein considers that the child's reaction to frustration is always in part one of rage, and that what it fears is its own aggression. She writes: 'Thus anxiety would spring from aggression. But since, as we know, libidinal frustration heightens the sadistic instincts, ungratified libido would, indirectly, liberate anxiety or increase it. On this theory Freud's suggestion that the ego senses a danger in abstinence would be a solution of the problem after all. My only contention is that it is the destructive instincts which give rise to that danger which he calls "psychological helplessness in the face of instinctual danger" ' (1932, p. 183). 'The gradual overcoming of sadism and anxiety is a result of the development of the libido. But the very excess of his anxiety also impels the individual to overcome it. . . . That very anxiety which is pre-eminently an inhibiting agency in the development of the individual is also a factor of fundamental importance in promoting the growth of his ego and of his sexual life' (*op. cit.* p. 200). There is perhaps an 'optimum' degree of anxiety (varying from individual to individual) which favours development; more or less than this optimum may hinder it. The clinical relations between sadism and anxiety are well established, but it is still of course arguable that aggression is only the major or most constant stimulus to anxiety and that other instincts may be contributory stimuli. The wary may regard anxiety as ego-experience of instinct tension which may be of mixed origin, or they may continue to suspect that all forms of fear are intrinsically self-preservative. Clinically speaking, whenever anxiety occurs, an aggressive factor will usually be found at work, though it sometimes appears that the aggression has been evoked by anxiety and not vice versa.

Melanie Klein's views on anxiety are intimately related to her conceptions of infantile sadism and of early Oedipus and super-ego formation. Frustration in relation to the breast during the sucking stage stimulates sadism, leading to the second oral biting or cannibalistic phase, with its further increase of sadism, which 'reaches its climax during and after weaning and leads to the fullest activation and development of sadistic tendencies flowing from every source' (1932, p. 185). This mixture of oral, urethral, anal, and muscular impulses is all at first directed against the mother's breast, but soon, possibly via phantasies of scooping and sucking out the breast and experiences of hungry emptiness, comes to be directed to the inside of the mother's body. Phantasies relating to the inside of the mother's body had been registered in the literature, but it had not been realized that such phantasies were possibly of general occurrence at a certain stage of development. The evidence from early analyses is to the effect that such phantasies regularly accompany the later oral and early anal stages of development, and that sadism reaches its maximum during these phases (*op. cit.* p. 187).

According to Melanie Klein oral frustration not only heightens sadism: it also releases genital impulses and initiates Oedipus conflict and super-ego formation. In both sexes the loss of the nipple appears to institute a compensatory search for the penis and a desire to incorporate it. It is located at first inside the mother's body. In the girl the desire to incorporate the father's penis constitutes her first positive Oedipus wish, and the attacks she makes in imagination on the body of the frustrating mother in order to obtain this coveted organ are the foundation of the major feminine anxiety, namely, the fear of some mysterious internal damage to her own body. In the boy the hatred of the mother's body is mitigated sooner than in the girl through the awakening of genital impulses towards it, and the hatred becomes concentrated on the penis which he wishes to destroy inside her. Only later, when the parents have become recognized as separate individuals, does anxiety regarding the penis inside the mother give place to fear of castration by the father, and it is dread of the internalized penis, the combined parent imago, which is at the root of most male anxieties regarding intercourse. Melanie Klein writes: 'I do not think that a sharp distinction can be made between the early stages of the Oedipus conflict and the later ones. Since, as far as my observations show, the genital impulses set in at the same time as the pregenital ones . . . and since, as a result of this early association, they themselves bear traces of certain pregenital impulses even in later stages of development, the attainment of the genital stage merely means a strengthening of the genital impulses' (1932, p. 192).

Further, Melanie Klein holds that the control of aggression by turning against the self dates not from the passing of the Oedipus complex but from the earliest oral phantasy incorporations, '. . . the incorporated object at once assumes the functions of a super-ego' (*op. cit.* p. 184). The so-called cruelty of the early super-ego is to be ascribed to the fact that the object introjected is an image of the real object distorted by the child's hatred of it. Fear of the internalized 'bad' object leads to attempts to expel it, and produces a continuous alternation of projection and introjection. Sadism is gradually diminished by the development of libidinal relations to objects with corresponding correction of their sadistic distortion and the introjection of 'good' objects. Both mastery of anxiety and development of reality sense are furthered by the spread of interest over a number of objects by way of symbolism, a path which leads, on the one hand, to phobia formation and, on the other, to sublimation. 'Viewed in this light, super-ego formation, object-relations and adaptation to reality are the result of an interaction between the projection of the individual's sadistic impulses and the introjection of his objects' (*op. cit.* p. 209).

Melanie Klein's views have obtained wider recognition in

this country than they have as yet on the Continent. Thus Fenichel (1931), while admitting that children form attachments to their parents much earlier than the classical Oedipus phase, still insists that the aims connected with them are not yet genital, and calls them, therefore, pre-genital antecedents of the Oedipus complex. He ignores the considerable weight of evidence which exists as to the occurrence of true genital impulses and phantasies alongside the pre-genital from a very early age. Freud himself (1932b) has recently come to attribute great importance to what he calls pre-Oedipal fixation to the mother, especially in women. He recognizes that the true Oedipus complex may be prematurely awakened, but objects to its systematic backward displacement on various grounds. Edward Glover writes (1932a, p. 306): 'I agree that interpretations of a nuclear complex existing prior to the mainly genital Oedipus phase are to a certain extent suspect, that they are subject to the charge of being "ruck-phantasieren" products. . . . But I cannot find any adequate explanation of drug-addiction which does not assume an active Oedipus situation at a stage when object-relations are little more than the psychic reflection of organ relations.' Fenichel (1931) again distinguishes pre-genital 'precursors of the super-ego' from what he regards as the true post-Oedipal super-ego. Freud still believes that small children 'have no internal inhibitions against their pleasure-seeking impulses. The rôle which the super-ego undertakes later in life is at first played by parental authority' (1933, p. 84). Edward Glover says: 'I believe, however, that any psychic imprint which is sufficiently permanent, and which leads to the subdivision of instinctual energies within the ego (Freud's turning on the self), is entitled to claim super-ego status. . . . Nevertheless, opponents of Mrs Klein's view may continue to insist that the only super-ego worth calling a super-ego is that derived from the final frustration of genital impulses towards complete parental objects. But at this point argument becomes fruitless. Mrs Klein insists that true genital frustration exists from the first year, and opponents cannot escape the task of re-examining their clinical material on this basis' (1933a, pp. 123-4).

The emphasis laid by Melanie Klein on the reciprocity of super-ego formation and object-finding reminds us that we must not overlook the nature and functions of the primitive ego itself. The adult has a strong prejudice in favour of regarding himself as a unified personality, hence the primitive ego is usually treated as an entity, the ego. Nevertheless, in 1914 Freud wrote: 'It is impossible to suppose that an entity comparable to the ego [that is, the adult ego] can exist from the start; the ego has to develop' (1914, *C.P.* iv, p. 34), but he envisages this development as the growth from weakness to strength of a unitary ego. In *The Ego and the Id* he says that while the ego is weak, the cathexis of objects takes place directly from the id (1927, p. 65). But even the first impulse to suck must be felt and must be carried into effect through the musculature, that is, it must surely be rated as an ego experience which provides not only a basis for the establishment of at least an organ or part-object relationship, but also what one might call an oral contribution towards the formation of a body-ego. Edward Glover first suggested that the primitive ego may not be a unity at all, but a variety of relatively independent ego-nuclei associated with different impulse-reaction systems whose progressive integration ultimately produces a unified ego. He writes: 'Any psychic system which (*a*) represents a positive libidinal relation to objects or part-objects, (*b*) can discharge reactive tension (*i.e.* aggression and hate against objects), and (*c*) in one or other of these ways reduces anxiety, is entitled to be called an ego-system or ego-nucleus. Thus an oral system gratifies instinct on a part-object (the mother's nipple); it can exert aggression towards the nipple (sucking, pulling, biting), and it is able to prevent some degree of anxiety . . . the earliest ego tendencies are derived from numerous scattered instincts and gradually converge until, probably about the age of two, a coherent anal-sadistic organization is established' (1932c, p. 8). 'Oral primacy is much more relative than we have supposed, and it is capable of more detailed subdivision' (1933a, p. 123). On the development of reality sense, he writes: 'As a result of alternating processes of projection and introjection, brought about by frustration of instinct, the child's relation to what the observer would call objective reality becomes distorted and unreal. Nevertheless the child during this phase has some primitive objective reality of its own. . . . Adult objective reality, self-preservation apart, is not so much something we come to recognize, as an inheritance from infancy, something we maintain possession of and expand after it has passed through screens of fear, libidinization and sublimation. In some respects it is indeed a residue, a view which is in keeping with the fact that in many ways adults are less objective than children. This expanded inheritance or residue functions to a large extent as a guarantee of the absence of fear. It is manifestly limited in accordance with the range of individual interest plus the range of interest of individuals we either love or hate' (1933b, pp. 498-9).

This brings us to the question of what is to be regarded as normal development. The distortion of reality produced by projection would seem to justify the description of early infancy as a period of pan-psychosis. According to Melanie Klein (1932), all children pass through psychotic and neurotic phases. Ernest Jones says: 'the typical phallic stage is a neurotic compromise rather than a natural evolution in sexual development' (1933, p. 15). 'It is a deviation from the direct path of development, and it is a response to anxiety, but nevertheless, for all we know, research may show that the earliest infantile anxiety is inevitable and that the phallic defence is the only one possible at that age' (*op. cit.* p. 33). On this view psychotic and neurotic phases are to be considered as normal phases of infantile development, though there must be many differences between infantile or proto-psychic phases and adult psychotic states. Both Melanie Klein and Freud agree as to the multiplicity of infantile anxieties and their tendency to persist in later life. They are perhaps not so much overcome or outgrown in the successfully adapted adult as continuously liquidated. According to Edward Glover: 'Adult normality is a state in which infantile psychotic views concerning the external outer world have been so reduced that they do not interfere with the possibilities of adult gratification' (1932b, p. 162), and 'Efficient reality-testing, for any subject who has passed the age of puberty, is the capacity to retain psychic contact with the objects that promote gratification of instinct, including here both modified and residual infantile impulse' (1933b, p. 486).

VII. CONCLUSION

The difficulties which confront us at the present day are many. (This is as true in 1949 as in 1934.) There has not yet been time to test all the newer hypotheses nor to effect the systematic revision of theory which they call for. Old and new concepts exist side by side and overlap each other. Thus the original concept of narcissism relates to the notion of a unitary primitive ego, and many narcissistic phenomena now can be described as effects of introjection. Further, in our enthusiasm for new and useful conceptions we have to be on our guard lest we undervalue or lose sight of older notions which we should do well to retain. Just as we used to regard aggression as secondary to libidinal frustration, so we are now possibly in danger of regarding libidinal development as a means to the mastery of anxiety connected with aggression. But it is upon the interaction of libido and aggression that development depends. There seems little doubt that the child's erotic development is enormously stimulated by anxiety and that the infant will exploit his love impulses to their limit in the effort to master his anxieties and to overcome hatred with love. But it would be as much out of proportion to regard infantile sexuality as a secondary effect of anxiety as it would be to regard adult sexuality as nothing but a means of allaying residual infantile anxieties or a compensation for difficulties encountered in reality adaptation. The adult genital impulse may, and does, subserve both these purposes, but it is none the less a valid impulse in its own right. Moreover, in our interest in the antithesis of libido and aggression we tend to overlook Freud's earlier distinction between self-preservative and erotic impulses. But we must continue to find room for self-preservative impulses. We are particularly interested in the libidinal and aggressive components of oral impulses, but we ought not to forget that they contain hunger-components too, though this will not invalidate our clinical inference that suckling is an erotic as well as a nutritive experience. As Freud says: 'Libido participates in every instinctual experience but not everything in that experience is libido' (1930, p. 101). We suffer also from lack of clarity in definition and from laxity in our use of terminology. Apart from the tendency to personification mentioned earlier, it is important to distinguish between psychic systems and the processes affecting them, that is, between institutions and mechanisms. It is equally necessary to distinguish between processes and the phantasies in terms of which they occur. The introjection of a part-object may, in a given instance, correspond with a phantasy of swallowing a penis, but from the point of view of conceptual thinking the phrase 'introjected penis' is a bastard term. Many present divergences of opinion

CHAPTER II

AFFECTS IN THEORY AND PRACTICE[1]

I. THE RELATIVE NEGLECT OF AFFECT IN THEORY

IN the early days of psycho-analysis affect played a leading rôle in theory and in practice. Freud's first hypotheses were framed in terms of ideas rendered dynamic by their emotional charges. Thus, the hysteric was said to suffer from repressed painful memories, and cure was held to follow the recovery of these memories, together with the adequate discharge of the associated feelings. The essence of cure by catharsis was abreaction of affect. Psychic tension appeared first as feeling-tension, and conflict as conflict between ideas with incompatible feeling-charges. Soon, however, Freud's investigation of the repressed unconscious brought him up against problems of instinct. With the formulation of the libido theory and the conception of conflict as conflict between ego and sexual instincts, the ideo-motor terminology lapsed into disuse. To-day the language of instinct holds the field in theory. Thus, we speak of cathexes of objects rather than of the emotional charges of ideas, and tend, in practice, to regard these two expressions as synonymous, though the precise relation between instinct and affect is by no means fully understood as yet. The modern concept of the threefold structure of the mind is a concept of an unorganized id-reservoir of instinct out of which organized ego and super-ego systems are differentiated. We regard instinct as the source and stimulus of psychic activity. We regard mind as an apparatus for the regulation of instinct-tension and as the mediator between instinct and the outer world. We think of the development of mind as progressive organization, adaptation, and modification of instinct. Nevertheless, we are also accustomed to think of development as progressive mastery of anxiety, an affect concept, and we do not hesitate to equate instinct-defence with defence against the emergence of intolerable affects. But, until quite recently, very little attention has been paid in theory to

[1] Reprinted, with minor alterations, from the *Int. J. Psycho-Anal.* (1937), xviii, p. 256.

affects as such, apart from anxiety and from some studies of special emotions such as pity and jealousy. Indeed, Federn's last paper (1936) contains the first systematic theory of affect in the literature.

In spite of this temporary eclipse in theory, affect has never lost its importance in practice. Whatever differences of opinion exist as to principles of technique, no psycho-analyst fails to pay attention to his patient's feelings. Diagnosis, prognosis, and criteria of cure all involve some estimation of affectivity. Indeed, patients themselves leave us in no doubt here. With few exceptions, they one and all complain of some disorder of feeling and tend to estimate their own progress by changes in their feelings and in their ability to cope with them. In practice we find our way only by following the Ariadne thread of transference affect, and go astray if we lose contact with this. It is time that we restored affects to a place in theory more consonant with their importance in practice. This paper is an attempt to clear the ground by reviewing briefly some of the cardinal problems of affect.

II. AFFECT AND INSTINCT; PROBLEMS OF DEFINITION AND CLASSIFICATION

Probably every psycho-analyst would agree with the general statement that affects have a peculiarly intimate relation with instincts but that they are essentially ego-experiences. As Freud said years ago: 'It is surely of the essence of an emotion that we should feel it, *i.e.* that it should enter consciousness' (1915b, *C.P.* iv, pp. 109, 110). Further, we should probably agree that affects constitute a specific kind, or mode, of ego-experience; that they vary both in quality and quantity, and that individuals differ markedly both in the range and in the intensity of their affectivity. It is when we try to make these general statements more precise that we encounter difficulties.

In the first place it may be argued that, since affect is so closely related to instinct, it is putting the cart before the horse to attempt to arrive at a theory of affect before we have achieved a complete theory of instinct. Recent literature offers abundant evidence that our theory of instinct is still in the melting-pot. But, if we consider this welter of discussion, we perceive that it does not tend to any discarding of the primary working hypotheses formulated by Freud but, rather, to the re-examination and re-casting of these hypotheses in forms more consonant with our growing knowledge, particularly of the early stages of development. For instance, the libido theory is not wrong; it is only that, as originally stated, it now appears in some respects to be inadequate and, in others, to be too rigid. Further, it need make little difference to our study of affects as such whether we accept the death instinct or its variants 'Destrudo' (Weiss, 1935) and 'Mortido' (Federn, 1936, p. 6), or whether we lean to the more readily demonstrable instinct of aggression. For instance, the inter-relationships of fear, guilt, and hate traced by Ernest Jones (1929) are not altered whichever view we take. So far from waiting on the theory of instinct, we might reasonably expect that a closer study of affect would contribute to the solution of some of the problems of instinct. The layering of affects described by Ernest Jones corresponds to their genetic sequence. Fuller knowledge of these sequences, and of what Edward Glover calls the compounding of affects (1935, p. 139), might provide a useful index to the stages, phases, or positions of mental development.

Our notion of the relation between instinct and affect will vary according to whether we believe that impulses can themselves be conscious or not. Freud writes: 'If the instinct did not attach itself to an idea, or manifest itself as an affective state, we could know nothing about it' (1915b; C.P. iv, p. 109). This notion, that instinct can be represented in the mind either as an idea or as an affect, is also expressed by Nunberg (1932, p. 174). He describes affects as the most direct derivatives of instinct in the psyche, where they easily combine with the other representatives of instinct, images, and ideas. This alternative representation calls to mind Freud's description of consciousness as a sensory organ having a double surface of perception (1932a, p. 528), external and internal, and suggests that ideas are external surface phenomena, whereas affects arise from stimulation of the internal surface. This tends to align affects with organic sensations, and is getting very near to the James-Lange theory, criticized in our literature by Kulovesi (1931). Actually, we recognize that affects are very closely linked with organic sensation, but we usually differentiate between the sensory and emotional elements of an affective experience. Freud distinguishes anxiety from other affects by the fact that stereotyped organic reactions seem to form an integral part of it (1936, p. 75). Certainly, in his earlier papers, he ranged affects on the efferent rather than on the afferent side of the instinctual arc. Thus, he writes in 1915, 'ideas are cathexes—ultimately of memory-traces —whilst affects and emotions correspond with processes of discharge, the final expression of which is perceived as feeling' (1915b; *C.P.* iv, p. 111). And also, 'Affectivity manifests itself essentially in motor (*i.e.* secretory and circulatory) discharge resulting in an (internal) alteration of the subject's own body without reference to the outer world; motility, in actions designed to effect changes in the outer world' (*op. cit.* p. 111, footnote). This discharge idea is still present in *Inhibitions, Symptoms and Anxiety* in the suggestion that affects may be the normal equivalents of hysterical attacks but in a much wider connection. Freud there defines anxiety as a precipitate but not necessarily a complete reproduction of birth experience, and queries whether all affects may not be such precipitates, possibly of phylogenetic experiences (1936, p. 76). This is a notion not far removed from his earlier definition of instincts themselves as being, 'at least in part, the precipitates of different forms of external stimulation, which in the course of phylogenesis have effected modifications in the organism' (1915a; *C.P.* iv, p. 64). All our modern conceptions of the relation of anxiety to symptom-formation and of its rôle in development contradict the idea that affect is itself a discharge, and support the view that it is a tension-phenomenon impelling to discharge either in the outer or the inner world. Both the fact that affect is a mode of consciousness and clinical experience incline us to place affect, both topographically and in time-order, in the middle of the instinct-reaction arc.

However, there are still differences of opinion about the nature of affect, as may be seen from views expressed since the initial publication of this paper in 1937. Thus Landauer (1938, p. 388) regards affects as 'typical responses to typical demands, responses handed down from one generation to another in the form of potentialities', and he concludes (*op. cit.* p. 415) 'that the individual passes through an infinitely complicated evolution of his affects, which repeats in part the history of the race'. Edward Glover thinks (1939, p. 302) 'the most useful classification of affects seems to be that into tension affects and discharge affects'. He isolates a 'psychic feeling of disruption' as 'a typical and very early tension affect, which in course of development may become fixed in different forms ("canalized" by association with phantasy systems) according to the experiences and unconscious ideations of different developmental periods'. In *The Psychoanalytic Theory of Neuroses*, Fenichel recapitulated the similarities often noted between neurotic symptoms and affects. He wrote (1946, p. 21): 'Thus the causation of emotional spells and of neurotic symptoms is essentially the same: a relative insufficiency of ego control because of either increased influx or blocking of discharge. Both emotional spells and neurotic symptoms are partial substitutes, of a more archaic nature, for the normal ego motility.'

Affects which appear to arise spontaneously always have unconscious stimuli and, in practice, we find affectivity tends to be high where frustration, particularly internal frustration, is marked. Waelder distinguishes neurotics from other mental patients by their hyper-affectivity, which he equates with disorder of instinct (1936, p. 93). Glover thinks that 'the primary obsessional state is essentially an affective state or, rather, a sequence of alternating affects having very simple unconscious ideational content', and that all the complicated obsessional rituals 'have the same object in view, viz. to provide an ever more complicated meshwork of conceptual systems through which affect may pass in a finely divided state. When, for some reason or other, these rituals are interfered with, we observe once more the existence of massive affects' (1935, p. 137). A patient suffering from conversion hysteria realized very early on that she either developed symptoms or 'felt rotten'. Nobody could teach her anything, or change her opinion, about her motives for forming symptoms. In practice, one can often observe not only symptoms but impulsive behaviour which is designed to short-circuit affect development. I had one patient who regularly felt the strongest possible urge to break off analysis at once whenever she was threatened with any considerable dose of transference affect.

The conception of affects as tension-phenomena is, of course, in line with Freud's earliest formulations of the working of the psychic apparatus and the pleasure-pain principle (1932a). On the quantitative side we have, I think, to conceive of some threshold above which instinct-tension becomes appreciable as affect, and of a higher threshold, which may be attained either by the strength of the stimulus itself or by damming due to frustration, above which affect becomes intolerable and necessitates some immediate discharge, either outwards or inwards. Weiss's views on the analogies between bodily and mental pain accord with this (1934). The fact that all affects are either pleasurably or painfully toned and not infrequently mixed, indicates some general relationship between degree of tension and pleasurable or painful toning, but the precise relations are still exceedingly obscure. As Freud noted in regard to erotic tension (1930a, p. 68), it is quite obvious that very high tensions of pleasurable affect can be enjoyed, whereas very low tensions of painful feeling can be intolerable. Qualitative factors have also to be taken into account. Further, if one puts Freud's earlier views on the production of pain (1915a, p. 67) alongside his latest views on the development of anxiety (1933, pp. 122, 123) one feels that one is approaching a situation in which pain and anxiety are the same thing and all instinct-tension threatens to become anxiety-tension. This would do away with what Freud himself has always insisted on, namely, the variety of instinctual impulses existing in human nature. It seems safer to suppose, with McDougall (1922, p. 47), that every primary impulse gives rise to its own qualitatively specific affect and probably also has its own quantitative thresholds. (At a later date Edward Glover wrote (1939, p. 307): 'It is, at any rate, plausible that there are as many primitive affects as there are primitive ego nuclei.') Certainly, the whole situation is greatly simplified if (following Ernest Jones, 1936, p. 278) fear is recognized as a primary emotion which does not have to be derived from libidinal or aggressive instincts, but is easily aroused in connection with them.[1] It accords with Freud's notion of the essence of anxiety as anxiety of helplessness (1936, p. 126) and does not contradict the view of birth as the prototype of human anxiety experience. The first fear situation in life must leave its stamp on the psyche and tend to be reactivated in later situations which involve the same primary affect. In fact, it seems to be a notion which has sound biological and psychological backing. Moreover, the three types of response to fear which one can observe in animals, namely, flight, immobilization, and attack, one can also observe

---

[1] The clinical relations between anxiety and sadism are well established (Klein, 1932, chap. viii). The relation of fear to 'self-preservation' and the position of the latter in the Eros-Death classification are still far from clear.

in infants, and they have their parallels in psychic activities. The difficulty is, of course, to sort out what are primary instincts and emotions. It often appears that the same instinctual impulse may give rise to a variety of feelings and, moreover, we never have to deal with single impulses. But fusion of impulses and variation of affect take place in relation to objects. Clearly, we shall not get any further by considering the relation of affect and instinct without taking into account their ego-connections. Here, the most hopeful approach would appear to be the developmental one.

III. AFFECT AND EGO DEVELOPMENT

Classifications of the contents of consciousness or modes of ego experience are all based on the introspections of self-conscious adult egos. What is the state of affairs at the dawn of consciousness in the infant? Here we can only speculate, but what inferences can we draw from clinical evidence and from our all too scanty records of the behaviour of infants in arms? It becomes more and more apparent that the earliest hypotheses were vitiated by the usual type of fallacy, by the attribution to the baby of an integral ego of the adult type. I am myself convinced that Glover is right in considering 'that the earliest ego tendencies are derived from numerous scattered instincts and converge gradually until, about the age of two, a coherent anal-sadistic organization is established' (1932c, p. 8), and that, in the beginning, there are as many ego-nuclei as there are more or less definitive reaction systems. After all, we know from observation that consciousness is at first intermittent and discontinuous. The new-born baby spends more time asleep than awake, and waking, when spontaneous, is usually due to some need or discomfort. When enforced it is frightening. In either case it is often highly emotional. Infantile reactions are full of feeling and of the all-or-none type. For the time being the baby is psychically living wholly in the immediate present experience, with nothing corresponding to the adult perspective. The point is that each of these sporadic flashes of consciousness is an ego-experience in so far as it is conscious and it leaves a memory-trace which can be re-activated and which may be regarded, from the point of view of ego structure, as an ego element. Any such element stamped in by repeated experience could form an ego-nucleus, and it is not difficult to see how it must come about that an instinctual oral primacy will correspond with an ego-oral-nuclear primacy, nor why it is that early linkages occur between different ego-nuclei, or how varied these linkages can be. Thus the complexity of oral symptomatology, stressed by Melitta Schmideberg (1938), reflects the range of variation which is possible in the character of the initial nuclei and in their early linkages. From analysis one gets the impression that linkages occur very easily through simultaneous or rapidly succeeding activation of different nuclei in relation to a common object. It is not, however, ego-development as such which concerns us here, only the connections with affect. Affect, as inferred from its expression in behaviour, can be aroused by internal conditions or by external happenings. It is influenced both by the internal need and by the nature of the response from the outer world with which this need is met. The affect manifested is, in fact, the index to the fate of the impulse and to the nature of the beginning psychic object-formation. A good external object is one which satisfies instinct and so produces a state of contented feeling. The good or bad nature of the psychic object will be determined by the pleasant or unpleasant feelings experienced in relation to it. Or, as Joan Riviere expressed it (1936b, p. 418), a good feeling creates a good object, a bad feeling a bad object. Nowhere, perhaps, is the constant interplay between external and internal reality more obvious than in the realm of affect.

At the beginning of mental life we are accustomed to posit a phase, prior to object-differentiation and cathexis, that we label primary identification. This initial stage is, by definition, lacking in cognitive discrimination. It is presumed to be a state of feeling-awareness but it can scarcely be devoid of sensory impressions. The very ambiguity of the English word 'feeling' indicates that this state is a fusion of sensory and affect awareness. The child must sense the breast, for instance, before it begins to perceive (*i.e.* recognize) it, and it must feel its sucking sensations before it recognizes its own mouth. It will develop recognition wherever there is a basis for it in sensory experience. Thus, knowledge and cathexis of self and knowledge of the external world and object cathexis will proceed simultaneously. Freud said 'the ego is first and foremost a body-ego' (1927, p. 33), but it would seem that there might be advantages at this stage in saying that the ego is at first a series of sensation-egos, part-body part-object nuclei. Joan Riviere showed the importance of organic sensations in relation to internal object formation in her Vienna paper (1936b).

The child is first concerned with objects only in relation to its own feelings and sensations but, as soon as feelings are firmly linked to objects, the process of instinct-defence becomes a process of defence against objects. The infant then tries to master its feelings by manipulating their object-carriers. The mechanisms of introjection and projection are essentially methods of mastering feeling, phantasied as concrete dealings with objects. In practice, we usually find that wherever a symptom, *e.g.* diarrhoea, occurs that can be interpreted as anxious expulsion of bad internalized objects, it has also to be understood as an attempt to get rid of undesired affects. For example, an obsessional neurotic carried her child to term by the help of recurrent attacks of diarrhoea. She did protect her child by expelling faecal bad objects, but what she was trying to cure in herself by this process was her ambivalent emotional conflict.

The sharp contrast which appears to exist in infancy between good and bad objects is, perhaps, partly the result of the completeness of the alternation of early feelings (the infant in a rage is a different infant psychically to the contented baby) and, perhaps, also due to the fact pointed out by Hardcastle (1935, pp. 9, 10) that the baby, at first, probably cannot distinguish between the real sensation and the hallucinatory image evoked during privation. This unsatisfying image may not only force the child towards reality, as Freud thought, but also form a constant focus for 'bad object' formation.

It is clear that affects must play an important part in the progressive organization of the ego, although we have always to remember the reciprocal action which goes on here, by which affects themselves become modified through their organization in ego systems. The child who urinates happily after sucking to its heart's content will establish a very different type of linkage between its oral and urethral ego systems to that of a child perpetually wetting itself in angry privation. In general, those nuclei will tend to integrate and those feelings to blend which are similar. Freud's 'pure pleasure ego' (1915a, p. 78) may never have actual existence, but we accept ego-synthesis as a function of libido. It is positively toned 'good' objects with their correlated 'good' body-systems which provide a stable core for the slowly growing me-system, the co-ordinated personal ego which seems to emerge about the second year. The appearance of this definitive 'I', with its capacity for self-consciousness as distinct from what is called simple consciousness, corresponds with the transition described by Melanie Klein (1948, p. 284) and Joan Riviere (1936b, p. 413) from part-object relationship to total object appreciation and cathexis, a transition which, in Klein's opinion, regularly ushers in a depressive position due to the accompanying recognition of its ambivalence towards its objects. This primitive ambivalent 'I' may resort to the manic defence (Riviere, 1936a) of denying its own aggression, or, as Edward Glover pointed out (1935), it may begin to employ the wide range of obsessional manœuvres to preserve itself from the melancholic and paranoiac situations which its alternations of feeling tend to produce. It is very doubtful if any human being ever achieves complete object-relationship in the sense of finally discarding part-object relationships, any more than anyone achieves complete ego-integration. It is a question of degree.

It must be in the early definitive 'I' stage that affects begin to become co-ordinated into enduring attitudes of love and hate towards real persons. We should, I think, avoid a good deal of unnecessary confusion if we used different words for different grades of affectivity. It is true we have not yet decided what the primary affects are, though we have seen that there is a good case for recognizing fear as such, but we are justified in supposing that, in so far as they are qualitatively distinct, they are simple, *e.g.* appetitive longings, anxieties, and angers. Ernest Jones' grouping of instincts under the headings 'attraction' and 'repulsion', 'like' and 'dislike' (1924, p. 261), might well be applied to affects. Alexander's vectors (1935, p. 406), incorporation, elimination, and retention, express the logic of impulse rather than of the emotions themselves and are paralleled by the major defence mechanisms. They do not contribute towards qualitative discrimination amongst affects. But one can group affects qualitatively as sympathetic in the literal sense, or antipathetic.

If we keep affect as a generic term, in English the word 'feeling' would seem to me the best to reserve for these earliest waves of relatively undiluted affectivity, which may be object-less in the adult sense but which are invariably associated and closely interwoven with sensations. The first affects connected with objects, affects arising in ego-nuclei in relation to relatively simple part-object systems, might rank as the first emotions.[1] The attitudes, which are not in themselves emotions, but which are dispositions to experience certain emotions about certain objects, we might conveniently call sentiments, the term used by Shand (1914, p. 50). I believe that we could learn a great deal from more detailed study of the vicissitudes of emotions and the genesis of sentiments.

But there is a further complication. We have not to deal only with pre- and post-personal periods of ego and affect development. We also have to cope with ego-differentiation, with super-ego as well as ego integration. Many English psycho-analysts tend to agree with Melanie Klein (1932, chap. viii) as to the early beginning of super-ego formation, but it is still mysterious why some introjections result in super-ego identifications and others in ego-identifications. A clue is perhaps to be found in the tendency of good objects to be assimilated to the developing me-systems. In the adult, the line between ego and good super-ego or ego-ideal is seldom so sharply defined as that between ego and hostile super-ego. The infant wants, above all, to avoid painful feelings, so from the beginning bad systems tend to be isolated, except in so far as they join with one another to form composite bad systems. It has to be emphasized that all presentation systems are ego-object systems, however rudimentary,[2] and all have an origin in sensory experience, however distorted this may become in phantasy elaboration. Many such systems may come into existence which never become integrated with the definitive ego, and in this sense Melanie Klein is right in maintaining that some phantasies revealed in analysis have never been conscious, *i.e.* in the sense that they have never been accessible to the definitive ego or self-consciousness. This is, doubtless, one reason why some affects are so inaccessible and their associated phantasies so difficult to verbalize. They are, genetically, pre-verbal. Affect language is older than speech. The infant uses its voice to convey its feelings long before it has

---

[1] But compare McDougall (1922). Ernest Jones suggests that emotions may be distinguished from simple feelings by their more extensive bodily reverberations.

[2] There is no essential contradiction in the conception of the progressive integration of part-egos (differentiated presentation systems) into a personal ego and the notion that 'oceanic feeling' in the phase of primary identification may be the prototype of mystical experience.

any words. As Ferenczi (1916, pp. 190-191) pointed out, it establishes communication with the external world by such feeling-speech as crying and crowing long before it learns to talk. Regression to feeling-speech is not infrequent during analysis of early infantile situations.

We have here a way out of the dilemma provided by the apparent existence of repressed affects. The repressed is, indeed, cut off from the main ego, but it is, in itself, a primitive ego-fragment. A certain paradox exists here in theory. By definition, the id is an unorganized reservoir of instinctual drives and yet the repressed unconscious, which always exhibits some degree of organization, is also attributed to it. It would seem that we should transfer the repressed unconscious to the primitive ego system. In dealing with affects we are dealing not only with impulse-object tensions but also with inter- and intra-ego tensions.

What happens when a repressed fragment of ego-experience comes into consciousness? The patient feels the emotion he was formerly unable to endure. If we can reconstruct for him by transference interpretation the conditions which originally provoked this feeling, and if we can uncover the infantile reality-bases of his phantasies, the experience will fall into perspective as a part of his personal history. In structural terms, the dissociated ego-fragment can become integrated with the reality-ego. Abreaction does not do away with the liability to feel, though it reduces the pathological intensity of the infantile emotion. Its major function is to open the hitherto barred path from id to personal ego. Working-through is, in part, a drainage of residual affect pockets, but, in essence, it is a stabilizing process of ego-assimilation and re-integration.

Federn (1936) expresses some very similar views, but with differences which I attribute, in the main, to his effort to make his theory of affect fit in with his views on narcissism and on ego-boundaries. Thus, he at first contrasts affects with cathexes. He says, 'bei den Objektinteressen tritt das Ich mit einem libido-besetzen Objekt in Beziehung, bei den Affekten mit einem libido-besetzen Vorgang des Ichs selber' (*op. cit.* p. 13). But he has to admit that affects also arise in relation to cathexes. His definition of affects is 'Affekte entstehen stets zwischen zwei aufeinander wirkenden Ichgrenzen und sind verschieden je nach der Art der Triebbesetzheit des Ichs an diesen Grenzen' (*op. cit.*

p. 14). But he is obliged to go beyond this in the case of some affects, in particular anxiety, which arise inside the ego. On the whole, affects accommodate themselves more readily to nuclear than to boundary conceptions.

IV. SIGNIFICANCE OF AFFECTS FOR PSYCHO-ANALYTIC TECHNIQUE AND THERAPY

Affects are indices of the dynamic and economic conditions obtaining in the psyche. We cannot too often remind ourselves in psycho-analytic practice that, in dealing with affects, we are dealing with manifestations of living energy. Whatever the object with which the analyst may be identified at any given moment, and whatever mechanism or combination of mechanisms may be responsible for the creation of the immediate transference situation, the transference relation is always and throughout an affective relation. I have no intention whatsoever of minimizing the importance of intelligence in psycho-analysts, but it is vital to remember that the process of analysis is not an intellectual process but an affective one. Analysis cannot proceed unless there is established between analyst and patient that mysterious affective contact which we call 'rapport'. We must interpret affects intelligently, but we can only do this in so far as we make direct contact with them by 'empathy'. It is only by empathy that we can be certain what the patient is feeling. To my mind, accurate empathy is indispensable to sound analysis. The wisdom we need is a combination of intelligent insight with emotional understanding. Moreover, we have not only to register and interpret affect in impulse-object terms: we have the further task of analysing the affects themselves. Almost all the affects we meet clinically are highly differentiated end-products. In so far as we are able to unravel the tangled skein of a composite affect, we lay bare a fragment of developmental history. We can not only trace history, we can see history in the making. We can watch the process of affect modification going on under our eyes. We may legitimately express the process of cure in structural terms as permanent modification of the super-ego, but, in fact, we produce this modification only in so far as we enable the patient to re-feel the feelings he originally entertained about the objects he has introjected. The problem of super-ego modification is, in practice, the problem of resolving transference anxiety and transference ambivalence. In the progressive libidinization of transference hate we have the story of super-ego modification. We must have logical theory, but we do not work with theory, we work with living impulses and feelings. Hence, we should do well to check our theory by constant reference to our working experience of affects.

PROBLEMS CONNECTED WITH THE WORK OF MELANIE KLEIN

I. SUMMARY OF KEY VIEWS AND SOME REACTIONS TO THEM

THE work of Melanie Klein is often described as exhibiting two phases, the first of which is embodied in her earlier papers and in *The Psycho-Analysis of Children* (Klein, 1932).

The first phase and some of the issues it raised were summarized in Chapter I (p. 23 *et seq.*) and its main features only will be recapitulated here. These include (*a*) the relation of anxiety to aggression, (*b*) the conception of anxiety as a spur to development, (*c*) the occurrence during the first year of a phase of maximal sadism and of specific anxieties engendered by it, (*d*) the dominance in infancy of introjection and projection as mechanisms of defence, together with (*e*) the early activation of genital (Oedipal) impulses, and (*f*) the early beginning of super-ego formation. Apart from their content, difficulties involved in the wording of the new views accrued from the beginning, *e.g.* about phraseology in which concepts relating to experience occurred alongside concepts belonging to metapsychology, and about ambiguity in the use of terms such as 'super-ego' and 'whole object'. Such ambiguities and difficulties in formulation are an ever-present problem in psycho-analysis, but they are thrown into high relief and acquire special importance in relation to differences of opinion, because they are such a fertile source both of misunderstanding and of muddled thinking.

The new views struck some psycho-analysts with the force of an 'illumination' and probably the majority of British analysts found them stimulating and enlightening in varying degree, though a number of originally friendly critics later became convinced opponents. From the first, however, the dangers

---

[1] Based on 'A Prefatory Note on Internalized Objects' and 'Internal Objects and Theory' (*Int. J. Psycho-Anal.*, 1939, vol. xx, p. 241, and 1942, vol. xxiii, p. 107), and parts of papers included in later chapters.

attendant upon enthusiasm appeared to be present, such as the tendency to premature generalization, selective over-emphasis, lack of perspective, and faulty evaluation of the new in relation to the general pattern of pre-existing theory. Thus, concentration on endo-psychic factors seemed to induce real or apparent under-estimation of the influence of environmental factors, and the conception of development as 'mastery of anxiety' together with the hypothesis that 'anxiety springs from aggression' tended to assign undue priority to aggression over all other instincts (see p. 41). Clinical experience supports the view that aggression readily evokes anxiety but affords no proof that this powerful stimulus is itself also the *fons et origo* of anxiety. In the animal kingdom the rôle of fear appears to be basically self-preservative, and human anxiety is a variant of fear. Hence, it is desirable to recognize aggression as an important stimulus to anxiety, but less justifiable to go beyond this and posit aggression as the source of anxiety. Clinical experience also shows that aggression may be evoked by anxiety, *e.g.* Anna Freud (1937, p. 107 *et seq.*) describes how this can happen via defensive identification with the aggressor. Commenting on this phenomenon, Reik (1941, p. 14) maintains that ego defences are mostly directed against the primary affect of fright and that anxiety is itself a secondary, protective reaction, 'a buffer or safeguard adopted by the ego to ward off fright'.

Among other problems of emphasis, it soon became apparent that Melanie Klein's views on the dominance, in early infancy, of alternating mechanisms of introjection and projection tended to suggest that early development is wholly a matter of reciprocal processes of super-ego differentiation and object-relationship, leaving no room for primitive ego development or larval reality-sense. As already noted (p. 39), it was by way of constructive criticism and in the endeavour to correct this one-sided emphasis that Edward Glover made his most fruitful contribution to theory, his hypothesis of the nuclear origin of the ego. It also became clear that there were striking differences between the object-concerned picture of infancy drawn by Melanie Klein and the auto-erotic and narcissistic objectless picture drawn by Freud, and that much argument could be expected about happenings in the first year of life.

Reconstructions of the course of development during the first year are strictly conjectural, since they can derive only from an observer's interpretation of the behaviour of infants in arms or from inferences drawn from the behaviour of older children. The published case histories (Klein, 1932) show that Melanie Klein often obtained information about the previous behaviour of her young patients, and one may be willing to allow that this information was reasonably accurate, in spite of the wide margin of error which often obtains in parents' accounts of their children. But the ages given for the actual beginning of treatment (two and three-quarter years, three and three-quarters, six, five, etc.) appear to justify the view that the 'clinical evidence' for Melanie Klein's reconstruction of the first year is mainly inference from conditions observed at later ages. Affective interpretation of the observed behaviour of infants may often be accurate; for example, a consensus of opinion among child psychologists (Bowley, 1949, p. 109) that anger, fear, and affection are normally distinguishable during the first month of life accords with the bulk of lay experience and is probably correct. Naturally, more detailed accounts of the whole course of psychological development during the earlier months become increasingly conjectural and diminishingly self-evident. These considerations apply with greater force to reconstruction of early happenings from findings at later dates and are the basis of numerous contentions that Melanie Klein reads back into early development conditions that obtain only in later stages.

In 1934, what has come to be known as the second phase of Melanie Klein's work began with her publication of 'A Contribution to the Psychogenesis of Manic-Depressive States' (Klein, 1935), recently reprinted in her second book, *Contributions to Psycho-Analysis, 1921-1945* (Klein, 1948a, p. 282). In this she posited a genetic connection between paranoia, depression, and mania, and ascribed their differentiation to changes in object-relationship, related to developmental changes in the ego. In paranoia, the relatively unco-ordinated ego is still chiefly concerned with self-protection against persecutory part- or organ-objects, readily identified with faeces. With increasing co-ordination of the ego, identification of the self with 'good' objects becomes possible and, from now on, 'preservation of the good object is regarded as synonymous with the survival of the ego' (Klein, 1948a, p. 284). Co-ordination of the ego is accompanied by the transition from part to whole object-relationship, *i.e.* the object becomes a whole person and no longer an important organ or part of a person. Depressive feelings of loss of the good object as a whole now become possible and a variety of anxieties concerning its preservation or destruction ensue. Phantasies that the good object is in pieces which cannot be put together again are typical of the suggested 'depressive position', as are convictions of dead or dying internalized objects. Dread of the dangers to the self and the good objects anticipated during this phase may lead to 'manic defence', *i.e.* to the omnipotent denial of psychic reality, denial of the importance both of the objects and of the risks to which these are exposed, together with paradoxical hyper-active efforts to master and control all objects.

Depressive anxieties may also initiate restitutive drives; the infant now strives to restore the damaged object and to make reparation for the harm it feels has been done by its hostile and sadistic impulses. More definitely obsessional mechanisms may also be brought into play. Basically, the normal or abnormal outcome of the depressive phase depends on whether or not secure identification of the ego with good internalized objects is effected. The depressive position occurs as early as the fourth or fifth months of life and, in this 1935 paper (Klein, 1948a, p. 282), is held to be the central position in development, a cross-roads from which diverging paths lead to various types of abnormality and to normality. A 1945 modification of this view is quoted later (p. 84). In normal mourning the infantile depressive position is reanimated but is gradually surmounted by identificatory reinstatement of the good parents and the recently lost external object.

No adequate account of Melanie Klein's work can be given in summary form. However, since most of the remainder of this chapter derives from papers read by the author to the British Psycho-Analytical Society, this bald outline has been given for the benefit of any readers less familiar with Melanie Klein's views than the original audience. As already stated in the Introduction, controversy about this work raised both general and specific problems, *i.e.* specific problems concerning the validity of Klein's hypotheses and general problems of the approach to, and handling of, differences of opinion amongst psycho-analysts. In this chapter the two aspects run together. Some of the general discussion is better fitted to a theory seminar than to a book but has been included for the sake of preserving continuity.

II. SUBJECTIVE DIFFICULTIES ATTENDING 'INTERNAL' OR 'INTERNALIZED OBJECTS'

From 1936 onwards, 'internal objects' became increasingly controversial issues. Opinions about them ranged from over-valuation to under-valuation, even to repudiation as 'not analysis'. This, in itself, was ample evidence of the fact that psycho-analysts were not yet able to see Melanie Klein's contributions on this subject in true or stable perspective, and indicated that one of the major tasks before the British Psycho-Analytical Society was the clarification and scientific assessment of these views.

Clear thinking about 'internal objects' is not easily achieved, because of the difficulties besetting our approach to them. Any advance in theory may be accelerated, retarded, or otherwise affected by circumstantial difficulties within the bounds of the analytical circle itself, as distinct from the world at large. They spring from current permutations and combinations of 'personal equations', relationships, questions of prestige, policy, and other sources. They may be serious and hard to deal with, but they are, to a large extent, independent of the actual content of the theory itself, extrinsic rather than intrinsic. In the case of inter-nalized objects, in addition to a variety of extrinsic or circum-stantial difficulties, we are probably all confronted with intrinsic difficulties, subjective reluctances, unconscious resistances, more anxiety-laden than any we have hitherto been called upon to overcome in our pursuit of psycho-analytic knowledge. Our individual reactions will, of course, be specific and will have to be recognized and dealt with individually, but it may be that there are certain general considerations that apply to all of us in some degree.

In the first place, whatever our views on introjection and pro-jection, on the rôle these play in development, and on their relationship to other mechanisms, we have to-day to recognize that all of us make some use of these mechanisms and that fre-quently we have what we might call a character preference for one rather than for the other. It would seem that any decided preference, *i.e.* habitual use of, and reliance upon, one member of the pair, must tend to create its own special effects in the realm of theory we are considering. People who make consider-able use of introjection in maintaining their personal adaptation to life, probably, on the whole, feel more at home with concepts relating to 'internalized objects'. For that very reason they may accept hypotheses concerning them too readily and too uncritically. They are also naturally disposed to feel that the world within really matters much more than any world without. On the other hand, people who habitually make greater use of projection mechanisms seem likely to have far more difficulty in appreciating that 'internalized objects' are in any sense real. It is common knowledge in psycho-analytic practice that dealing with repression and projection defences are very different tasks. While the undoing of repression may be arduous and the immediate release of affect painful, the end-result is usually a phase of relief and easing of tension. The reversal of a projection is not only more difficult to bring about, but may result in a marked increase of tension for some time. Since the reception of hypotheses has much in common with the reception of interpretations, it is no light thing to ask anyone whose peace of mind is facilitated by the successful use of projection to explore the maze of internal object-relations. Nor should it surprise us if people with a character preference for projection lay stress on the relations of the internal world to external reality and are not content to consider it in isolation. The more dependent we are upon the preferential use of introjection or projection respectively, the greater the danger of our becoming extremists in one direction or the other. Although the majority of us are not extremists in either direction, it is nevertheless highly probable that we all start with some degree of natural bias prejudicial to objectivity. Hence, it is urgently necessary in dealing with these topics to pay careful attention to evidence and opinions opposed to our own natural inclinations in order to make sure that we are not cooking our evidence to the recipe we prefer.

A second group of difficulties centres in the fact that recognition of 'internalized objects' as entities contravenes the normal tendency of the ego towards synthesis, and that awareness of them as such in the adult is more or less pathological, though it may be normal in earlier phases of development. The so-called normal person has succeeded in becoming a relative whole. His 'internalized objects' do not ordinarily lead a recognizably distinct existence but are more or less permanently integrated into an organization which he is justified in calling a unitary ego, 'himself'. Even in a conflict with instinct or with conscience the components involved are normally felt to belong to the total personality; they are the individual's own impulses, his own conscience, not foreign bodies. Attempts to dissect ego structure are often reacted to as if they constituted a real danger to stability. The personality 'atom' responds as if the investigation of its structure meant the actual dissolution of its mental electron organization and a regression to psychic chaos. Even Freud himself seems to take for granted in his earlier writings that the primitive ego is a unit. But in 1914 he says definitely: '. . . It is impossible to suppose that a unity comparable to the ego can exist in the individual from the very start; the ego has to develop' (Freud, *C.P.* iv, p. 34). Self-preservative or narcissistic prejudice in favour of a unitary ego may constitute one of the reasons why Edward Glover's conception of the nuclear structure of the primitive ego (Glover, 1932c) and its progressive integration has not yet received the attention it deserves, though it is gradually becoming more widely accepted, *e.g.* by Fenichel (1946, p. 39). It may be noted that this nuclear hypothesis is one that Melanie Klein herself is willing to credit (see Klein, 1948a, p. 283).

In clinical psycho-analytic practice, it seems to be a fact that internalized objects only announce themselves as such in cases in which it is obvious that normal ego-synthesis is defective. Thus they are common in severe neuroses and borderline cases and, in the writer's experience, particularly in cases in which depression is a marked feature of the symptom picture. These foreign bodies vary in badness, but they all belong to the 'devil' group. The patient either laments that there is no health in him or is conscious of potentialities for good that are inhibited, of frustrated capacities. In certain character-types one may come across 'good object' discrimination. In one instance there is a strong urge to pass on and re-create a grandfather ideal in the person of a son. Here the degree of dissociation of the object is nothing like so definite as in the usual run of bad objects. The ideal is felt and thought about, not as a foreign body, but as a part of the self inherited from the grandfather, that must be passed on. This conjunction of imperfect ego-integration, depression, and 'bad objects' is to be expected on theoretical grounds, if ego-synthesis is taken to be a function of libido (Freud, 1927, p. 64). Whatever differences exist, there has been agreement from the beginning with regard to the weakening or inhibition of libido in depressives and the heightened ambivalence of their object-relations (Abraham, trans. 1927, p. 137). In the writer's experience it makes a considerable difference to prognosis whether or not the real prototypes of the internalized 'bad objects' were objectively 'good' or 'bad', but nevertheless it appears that these psychic objects are distorted by projection of infantile sadism ('imagos'). In other words, awareness of 'bad objects' inside connotes imperfect mastery of infantile sadism and the persistence of methods of defence that may be normal in earlier phases, but cannot be regarded as normal in adults. We may differ in our ideas regarding the amount and kind of sadism with which the human infant has to contend, but we shall probably agree that the mastery of infantile hatred is one of the most difficult tasks which the individual has to undertake, and that such mastery is not easy to maintain and is readily impaired. (The present state of world affairs underlines the failure of 'civilization' hitherto to solve this problem socially.) Small wonder, then, if we shrink from full investigation of states of mind that antedate such mastery. Moreover, whether or not we subscribe to Melanie Klein's formula that the survival of the ego is dependent upon the preservation of a good whole object identified with it (Klein, 1948a, p. 284), we should probably all endorse Freud's views on the predominance of identification in early libidinal relations (Freud, 1927, p. 35) and the secondary character of much of the libido cathecting the adult ego (*op. cit.* p. 85). Indeed, if one admits no more than the existence of secondary narcissism, it becomes evident that inquiry into the way it came into being may arouse severe anxieties. The more such exploration is unconsciously registered as a danger to stability, a threat of disintegration, the more likely we are to rush to precipitate conclusions. We may either grasp at any excuse we may be offered to justify rejection and denial of findings brought to our notice, or we may swallow them whole too readily and too uncritically. Either way affords escape from the long-drawn-out toleration of strong anxieties that reservation of judgment in such matters may entail.

Since the realm of 'internal objects' is one in which native or character bias is especially prone to distort the thinker's would-be objectivity, it is the more to be desired that as many psycho-analysts as possible should report any relevant clinical findings. A wide casting of the net and a big haul of evidence would call for ruthless sorting of the catch, but comparative study and pooling of experience offer some hope of the cancelling-out of effects due to individual subjective bias. The production of new theory is always the work of a few minds endowed with creative imagination, but those of us who do not feel ourselves to be gifted in this way still can, and should, regard ourselves as research workers sharing responsibility for testing and verification.

Although it is necessary to recognize the inevitability of subjective bias and to devise methods that aim at reducing or neutralizing its effects, it is just as necessary to ban the public interpretation of any psycho-analyst's suspected bias as an illegitimate method of argument, a nuisance detrimental to discussion. Such methods do not help to elucidate the facts and it is only the facts themselves and their most probable explanations that we need to establish. In discussing theory, unless we are discussing the subjective motivation of hypotheses as a research problem, we have no concern with the subjective reasons why individuals hold certain points of view but only with the degree of objective validity attaching to the points of view themselves.

We have to work on the assumption that we are all biased and all tendentious in one way or another. The kind of tendentiousness that can be most usefully exploited in the interests of science is curiosity about facts. Since we are human beings and not science robots, we all have numbers of interests other than fact-finding. But it is immaterial how many motives we have, or how mixed these motives may be, so long as they do not take precedence over fact-finding in our scientific work and discussions. Indeed, one indispensable condition for health in a scientific society would appear to be the existence, in a large enough majority of its members, of the ability to give fact-finding the necessary priority over other motivations. Organization may favour or it may hinder the maintenance of this priority but it cannot of itself create it.

To summarize these general considerations: clear thinking about 'internal objects' appears to be specially prone to subjective interference. We can try to reduce the effects of such interference: (a) by co-operative effort, comparative study of clinical findings, and intensive and extensive discussion and testing; (b) by individual effort to subordinate all other motives, however legitimate in themselves, to the search for facts, i.e. by maintaining, as steadily as we can, a rigorously scientific attitude.

III. TERMINOLOGICAL DIFFICULTIES AND RELATED PROBLEMS

The next problem is: Are there any features in our technical language or in Melanie Klein's presentation of her work hitherto, that impede or do not aid clear thinking? Ambiguity and confusion are still rife in our terminology, and Melanie Klein's work does suffer from the general lack of precise definition. Melitta Schmideberg considered this source of difficulty in detail. Alix Strachey (1941) pointed out that the word 'internal' is used to mean (1) 'mental', (2) 'imaginary', and (3) 'imagined as being actually inside (the body)'. Hence, we must ask Melanie Klein to which type of 'internal object' she is referring in any given instance. We must be sure that we do understand the exact meaning that Melanie Klein herself intends to convey and not some other meaning.

Confused usage of the word 'internal' is an example of a more general source of ambiguity, our ready tendency to mix our modes of thinking. The bulk of our time is spent in the consulting-room rather than in the study. Hence, we often fail to keep the basic distinction between percepts and concepts constantly present in our minds when we turn from the actual happenings in the consulting-room to their theoretical implications. The work of psycho-analysts is carried on almost entirely in terms of perceptual experience. We recognize the necessity of this when we say that theory and theoretical formulations have little or no place in interpretations given to patients. On the whole, we are less vividly alive to the corresponding conclusion that perceptual terms have little place in theory. Theory is primarily concerned with generalizations from the particulars of the consulting-room. These particulars are, indeed, our data and also to a great extent our ultimate criteria, but theory itself is a body of concepts and should be expressed in the language of abstraction. Terms such as 'ego' and 'object' have no appropriate place in the consulting-room. What happens there happens in terms of 'I', 'you', 'he', 'she', 'it', and 'they', and is dealt with in these specific and personal terms, the terms in which we lead our ordinary lives. But personal terms have no authentic place in general theory. This distinction in our modes of thinking is not an easy one to maintain and we shall do well to help ourselves to maintain it by avoiding the use of perceptual terms in relation to concepts. The choice of words to serve as technical terms is largely arbitrary and new ones constantly come into use. But where a word is already in use as a technical term, it is preferable to use this word in relation to other technical terms rather than a new word with more personal and concrete associations. Thus, it is probably better always to talk about the 'stability of the ego', rather than the 'safety of the ego'. 'Stability' is already in common use as a technical term and can appropriately be used with the technical term 'ego'. 'Safety' is a word which implies that someone is feeling safe, an experience that only a person can have. The phrase 'stability of the ego' is a theoretical translation of the consulting-room experience 'safety of the self'.

The issue involved is more than a matter of words. The phrase 'stability of the ego' is not a mere theoretical translation of the consulting-room experience 'safety of the self'. It is the scientific description of the objective condition obtaining in the mental organization of a person who feels subjectively that his 'self' is 'safe'. Thus James Strachey [1] writes: 'The patient may describe how he feels that he is losing his identity, that his "self" is in danger of falling in pieces or is being attacked by dangerous enemies and that he is worried about its "safety". That's *his* account of what's happening. But what's the *scientific* account? That may very well depend on whether the patient is a hysteric or a schizophrenic. If he is a schizophrenic, the scientific account may be that "the stability of his ego is threatened". But if he is a hysteric, the scientific account may be quite different—for instance, that "the stability of his ego is *not* seriously threatened in spite of his feelings or behaviour". So that a failure to distinguish sharply between the *patient's* language and *scientific* language is not in the least a merely linguistic mistake but may result in capital confusions or errors in our view of the real events.'

This vital distinction between subjective and scientific description of psychological events may also be illustrated by a bodily pain due to a physical stimulus. Thus, if a man with an over-acid stomach eats a sour green apple, he will probably experience pain. He may say about this pain: 'That apple is burning a hole in my stomach'. This, in effect, is a phantasy; the processes set up in his stomach feel like that. The things that are really happening in the stomach will be more accurately inferred and described by the physiologist. Confusion between

[1] In a letter, quoted by permission.

phantasy and objective fact, or, as Alix Strachey (1941) puts it, between *figment* of the mind and *function* of the mind, is every whit as disadvantageous to the psycho-analyst as to the physiologist. The advantage the physiologist enjoys over us is that his inferences about gastric function can be verified by more error-proof methods. But this renders it all the more imperative for us to aim at clear thinking about mental function and accurate expression of our ideas.

Melanie Klein (1948a, p. 282 *et seq.*), in her account of the 'depressive position', is describing what is, to all intent, an animistic phase of development. It is manifestly unfair, as Joan Riviere once said in discussion, to label as an animist anyone engaged in investigating the phenomena of animism. But Melanie Klein's methods of description do sometimes give rise to uneasy doubts as to whether her views are not, in fact, animistic. She is so keenly alive to the child's actual beliefs that she sometimes gives the impression of explaining the theory in terms of these beliefs. Thus, if the term 'ego' is to stand as a concept of a psychic organization it is better to reserve it for this abstract use and not to personify it and use it instead of the child or the self. 'I' and 'self' are the consulting-room equivalents of the study 'ego'. Thus, it is formally correct to say 'the ego has introjected the object', but formally incorrect to say that it can 'feel distressed about it' (Klein, 1948a, p. 289). Again, 'incorporation' is a term which belongs to the child's phantasies of persons and things being literally inside its body, not to an ego mechanism. Phrases like 'the difficulties which the ego experiences when it passes on to the incorporation of whole objects' (*op. cit.* p. 289) do give a misleading impression. It does not in the least follow that Melanie Klein is an animist; it does follow that her presentation of her ideas does not always safeguard her against this conclusion.

The writer became convinced that one of the major difficulties in coming to grips with Melanie Klein's views is that her generalizations tend to be expressed in perceptual rather than in conceptual terms. She seems to mix the language of phantasy with abstract terminology, and it is perhaps her choice of too concrete words that is responsible for some types of confusion in her hearers. Susan Isaacs [1] says: 'It is Melanie Klein's particular genius that she can and does appreciate the fact that the

[1] In a letter, quoted by permission.

child's *experience* is in terms of sensation, feeling, perception; that abstract terms are indispensable, but only when they have a real content; otherwise they can serve as screens to hide psychic reality'. Certainly our generalizations should be in the closest possible accord with experience. They should be derived from living experience and continually be referred back to it. But this does not alter the fact that the detailed sequence of a child's actual experiences is something different in kind from any generalization about experience. To take an illustration from geography, the child's experience is the countryside itself, which he and his analyst explore together; theory is only the map. The better the cartographer knows his countryside the more accurate will be the map he makes for the use of walkers. Susan Isaacs is right in objecting to faulty and obscurantist generalizations; they can be fully as misleading as bad maps. But maps are drawn according to certain necessary rules or conventions. The conventions of theory are those of logical, conceptual thinking. The problem for theory is one, as Freud (1933, p. 107) said, 'of the introduction of the right abstract ideas, and of their application to the raw material of observation so as to bring order and lucidity into it'.

Melanie Klein lays herself open to misunderstanding in her generalizations by a choice of terms too close to her specific source material. Thus, in the expression 'whole object' she uses the word 'whole' to distinguish a person-object from an organ- or part-object. But she also uses the term 'whole' in the sense of undamaged or intact, to distinguish it from the object which a child in a certain state of anxiety feels to be in pieces. Now it is quite possible to imagine a person being dismembered, since persons and things can be dealt with in phantasy in any way human imagination can devise, but it is not possible to conceive of a mental object being literally shattered—one cannot take a hammer to a mental object. But this impasse is largely artificial, a consequence of mixed thinking.[1] If the metapsychological mental object is thought of as a system of mental processes, it can be conceived as being more or less well integrated and as more or less liable to disintegration. Such a system can also be conceived as either integrated with, or excluded from, the major ego-organization.

[1] In referring to this impasse on another occasion, the author herself committed this error, as was noted by the late Susan Isaacs (Isaacs, 1945, p. 60).

The ego system corresponding to the 'whole object' could scarcely be a very simple one, but would itself be a synthesis. As libido is the agent of ego-synthesis, it is easy to assume that the 'whole object' system would be more stably integrated the more the actual relationship between parent and child evoked a preponderance of libidinal attitudes in both. It is also easy to assume that integration might fail if the relationship were too ambivalent, or that disintegration might ensue in a phase of severe sadistic tension. Thus, stable synthesis of a libidinal object-system with the ego-organization would be the theoretical equivalent of secure identification of the self with a loved person. Freud himself suggested '. . . that the character of the ego is a precipitate of abandoned object-cathexes and that it contains a record of past object-choices' (Freud, 1927, p. 36). This implies that the self is a synthesis of identifications. Thus, the organization of the ego will reflect the sequence of the individual's relationships, and its relative stability or instability will be conditioned largely by the quality and intensity of these relationships. Most psychoanalysts would agree that adequate experience of satisfaction in infancy favours stable ego-integration, whereas undue frustration impedes it.

At first Melanie Klein seldom seemed to draw any distinction between realistically good objects, proven so by actual experience of satisfaction in relation to them, and idealized good objects, which may emerge as a reaction to privation. Idealization does not necessarily promote ego-stability, though it is a common result of ambivalent conflict. Susan Isaacs discussed the relations of these two types of object and some of the disadvantages of idealization. She concludes (Isaacs, 1945, p. 62): 'Yet at certain stages of development and under some conditions, idealization *may* contribute something to the stability of the immature ego'. Melanie Klein herself elaborates this theme in her 1945 paper (Klein, 1948a, p. 359).

IV. 'INTERNAL OBJECTS' AND THEORY; EXPERIENCE AND METAPSYCHOLOGY

It would appear, then, that if we are to put ourselves in a position to estimate the value of Melanie Klein's contribution to metapsychology, we must put her hypotheses (as distinct from her observations, her data) into a form in which they can be thought about in correspondingly abstract terms. This will often involve translating statements about subjective experience into terms of mental structure and function. It does not follow that any one of Melanie Klein's views which lends itself to translation into metapsychological terms is therefore true, but perhaps any view which proved completely refractory to such translation should be regarded with suspicion.

Abstract thought scarcely enters into clinical work as such and it certainly does not make its appearance in infantile phantasy. Melanie Klein has a quite exceptional gift for unearthing the ramifications of phantasy, *i.e.* for bringing to light material from which theoretical inferences can be drawn. Phantasy is a sort of ticker-tape that records happenings on the mental stock exchange. But the observer has to infer from the figures themselves whether the market is rising or falling, and this inference is, in effect, a generalization from the specific figures recorded. In dealing with theory we have constantly to work from data to generalization and from generalization back to data. We cannot afford to neglect either aspect. Indeed, advance in some sciences has gone hand in hand with increased facility in abstract thinking. Thus, when the physicists first postulated the atomic structure of matter, they conceived atoms as indivisible, minute lumps which combined together to form larger lumps. These ideas have been superseded, largely in consequence of conceptual thought leading to the devising of experiments which ultimately succeeded in splitting the atom. The theory of the structure of matter became such that matter could be described by Bertrand Russell (1931) as 'a wave of probability undulating in nothingness'. The laboratory methods of the physicists are at present useless to us, but the conceptual mode of thinking is probably as essential to us as to them. We need not refine our mental objects to nothingness, but we cannot have them lumpy. We must distinguish between living experience and our theoretical inferences about it.

It is, of course, imperative to inquire into the evidence for the existence of 'internalized object' phantasies, but, in so doing, one will be inquiring into the existence of a special type of animistic phantasy and not into some new phenomenon which has no precedent in psycho-analysis. Tracing the history of the concept 'internal object' through the literature makes it plain that

Melanie Klein is no more responsible for the introduction of the concept itself, or the related concepts of 'introjection' and 'projection', than she is for the concepts of 'oral sadism' or 'anal sadism'; and she has never made any such claim. What she *is* responsible for is a detailed elaboration of the rôle and inter-relationships of 'internal objects', especially in early infantile development. We have, therefore, to consider the specific features of this detailed elaboration if we are to arrive at any sound conclusions about the relationship of her work to psycho-analysis as a whole. We must ask, for instance, in what respect and to what extent, if any, do Melanie Klein's hypotheses over-step the limits of consonance with such statements of Freud as: 'Identification with an object that is renounced or lost as a sub-stitute for it, introjection of this object into the ego, is indeed no longer a novelty to us. A process of the kind may sometimes be directly observed in small children' (1922b, p. 67). Or, concerning identification with introjected objects: 'At any rate the process, especially in the early phases of development, is a very frequent one, and it points to the conclusion that the character of the ego is a precipitate of abandoned object-cathexes and that it contains a record of past object-choices' (1927, p. 36). Or, again, writing of the consequences of accepting a differentiating grade in the ego: 'Let us reflect that the ego now appears in the relation of an object to the ego ideal which has been developed out of it, and that all the interplay between an outer object and the ego as a whole, with which our study of the neuroses has made us acquainted, may possibly be repeated upon this new scene of action inside the ego' (1922b, p. 103). Phantasies about 'internal objects' no more contravene Freud's memory-trace hypothesis than any other kind of phantasy. Remembering and phantasy-ing are different modes of psychic activity but both depend upon reactivation of past experiences. Artificially simplified, the con-cept of an 'internalized good object' is the concept of an uncon-scious phantasy gratifying the wish for the constant presence of the mother in the form of a belief that she is literally inside the child. Such an unconscious phantasy would help the child to retain conscious memory of its mother during temporary ab-sences, though it might fail to bridge a prolonged absence. A two-year-old child's memory of its mother will not be a simple system but the resultant of two years of life with her. The con-scious memory will be the accessible part of a far more extensive unconscious mother-system having its roots in earliest infancy.

Where differences appear, we need to decide whether these differences are of the nature of contradictions or expansions of pre-existing theory, and whether differences in detail amount to cleavage in basic principles. Any decision arrived at should be based on careful consideration and reconsideration of evidence. Where evidence is insufficient or inconclusive, judgment may have to be reserved, pending the outcome of further research.

In considering where and how new ideas fit, or fail to fit, into pre-existing theory we need to take into account another kind of perspective—what are the relative proportions of the new and old?—are the old pattern and the new drawn to a common scale?—how does the new addition affect the balance of the whole? Freud himself seemed always to be conscious of the un-charted ocean of ignorance surrounding the solid ground of knowledge that he established. Just because we know so little by comparison with all that yet remains to be known, we tend to be enthusiastic over new knowledge. This is harmless, and even helpful, so long as we keep the new knowledge in propor-tion and in relation to established knowledge. But it would be a poor geographer who, in his delight at mapping fresh territory, threw away all his other maps. The new map only develops its full value when it is drawn to the same scale and fitted into its right context. Melanie Klein found a way through the 'dim and misty' regions of the infant mind by pursuing a thread of object-relationships. To change the metaphor completely, she struck a repaying vein in the gold mine of infantile phantasy, the vein of object-relationships. She naturally concentrated on working the vein to the uttermost, and has, in effect, started a gold rush. The yield of ore is rich, though it seems to vary in gold content and to need more thorough processing before it becomes estab-lished currency in theory. But, clearly, there are other veins and other mines. No description of infantile development from one aspect alone can be finally adequate. If every aspect is con-sidered from every possible angle of approach, then we may begin to get a more comprehensive, though never a final, theory. The risks of concentration on a single aspect or field are the usual risks of over-emphasis, leading to lop-sidedness in the theory pattern.

One way of stating the problem before us is to ask the ques-tion: Is a theory of mental development in terms of infantile object-relationships compatible with theory in terms of instinct vicissitudes? W. R. D. Fairbairn,[1] whose views are of Kleinian lineage but, nevertheless, his own, and not to be considered as identical with hers, answers this question in the negative. In his opinion, the line of thought initiated by Melanie Klein is incompatible with the classic libido theory. He thinks her views (and his) involve as complete a re-orientation as the supersession of Ptolemaic by Copernican astronomy. For him, it is a case of one or the other: either the libido is essentially object-seeking or it is essentially pleasure-seeking. To the present writer the question savours of a false antithesis and should, in principle, admit of an affirmative answer whether or not current theories are compatible in their present form. An affirmative answer derives from the consideration of the nature of instinct. By Freud's (1933, p. 125 *et seq.*) own definition: 'An instinct may be described as having a source, an object and an aim. The source is a state of excitation within the body, and its aim is to remove that excitation; in the course of its path from its source to the attainment of its aim the instinct becomes operative mentally. . . . The aim can be attained in the subject's own body, but as a rule an external object is introduced, in which the instinct attains its external aim; its internal aim is always a somatic modification which is experienced as satisfaction.' Thus pleasure-seeking is too narrow a description of the aim of instinct. It is just because attainment of the aim of an instinct in relation to a suitable object is felt as pleasurable that we so often describe the process of discharge as gratification or satisfaction. It is, perhaps, unfortunate that Freud shortened his pleasure-unpleasure principle to the pleasure principle. Avoidance of unpleasure is quite as compelling a motive as search for pleasure. The infant, dominated by the pleasure principle, is intolerant of delay in discharge (*i.e.* unpleasure). Transition to the reality principle implies increase in the capacity for enduring psychic tension (unpleasure) until such time as external (and internal) circumstances permit suitable discharge.

It is, however, indisputable that analysis of the id preceded analysis of the ego. In the first place, more emphasis was laid on impulse and aim than on objects, although Abraham (1924, p. 480 *et seq.*) soon recognized that libidinal development implied parallel development of object-relations. Our current preoccu-

[1] In a letter, quoted by permission.

pation with objects may be healthy inasmuch as it tends to correct the original concentration on impulses. Thus, Freud writes (1933, p. 126 *et seq.*): 'We are ... still in ignorance about many of the characteristics of the instincts and their history. ... A great deal of our perplexity also arises from the fact that we have not devoted any attention to the alterations which the instinctual impulses originally belonging to the id undergo under the influence of the organized ego.' Taken in conjunction with the earlier quoted statement that 'the ego is a precipitate of abandoned object-cathexes' we have grounds in Freud's own work for thinking that the object aspect of instinct calls for close scrutiny. But, though the vicissitudes of instinct and the serial story of objects may well repay separate intensive investigation, surely the results of these investigations should be capable of correlation. If they appear to be incompatible, there may be something amiss with one or the other, or both may need some degree of modification. The complete story must take account of impulse, object, and relevant affects. With this amplification, the writer is of opinion that what she said in 1934 (p. 32) is still true, namely: 'It is evident that we can no longer study development in terms of a theory of impulses alone. We must at every stage be prepared to take into account the type of ego organization through which they operate and the mechanisms by which they are controlled, including the degree of ego differentiation and of reality-sense development which obtains. That is to say the theory of development in terms of libidinal stages has to be expanded into a theory of developmental stages of the whole psyche.'

There is nothing inherently improbable in Melanie Klein's suggestion that infants pass through earlier phases of development which are just as typical as the classical Oedipus stage. The conception of libidinal primacies is itself an assumption of this kind. Critics object for various reasons to Melanie Klein's expansion of a concept of libidinal primacy into a concept of a developmental position of the psyche. However, the time for thinking of development solely in terms of libido is long past. The life story has to be told in terms of the child's experiences as it struggles to adapt its instinctual demands to successive life situations (endo-psychic and environmental). Critical stages in the subjective story correspond in theory to critical stages in the progressive organization of adaptive mental processes. Melanie Klein's attempt to expand the concept of primacies into a concept of developmental phases or positions is, therefore, an effort in the right direction. The real problem is to decide the validity and adequacy of her particular conception of a 'depressive position'.

V. INFANTILE OBJECT-RELATIONSHIPS

Although controversy is not limited to hypotheses concerning early infantile life, differences of opinion on the genesis and development of object-relations are crucial. Melanie Klein's views are held by some critics to attribute undue precocity to the infant. In particular, it appears to them difficult to reconcile Melanie Klein's assumption that the infant very soon begins to love its mother, in the sense of being concerned for her, with Freud's conception that in the earliest months the infant is concerned with its environment only in relation to its own wishes. This view led Freud to term the earliest phases of development auto-erotic and narcissistic and to presume them to be objectless. The types of early object-relation inferred by Melanie Klein are also thought to imply too early endo-psychic co-ordination of instinctual drives. Such early co-ordination seems incompatible with the spontaneous changes of mood and apparently unrelated impulsive actions which can be observed to be characteristic of young children, at least up to the age of two years. But, if we regard development as the gradual and progressive organization of originally unrelated process-systems into more or less integrated systems from which the major ego-organizations finally emerge, the two views may not be so antithetic as they appear to be at first sight.

Adaptive responses are assumed to occur at all ages, but it is also assumed that responses vary in complexity from simple instinctuo-motor or sensori-motor reactions in the tiny infant to the far more intricately organized reactions of adults. The first gleams of consciousness are very intermittent and we think of them as probably simple and undifferentiated by comparison with the conditions revealed by introspection in the adult. The baby appears to be his reactions of the moment. We, as observers, may say that his life is a sensory-affective-impulsive one. We may say, for example, that because the baby reacts to a loud noise he probably hears the noise, and we can posit in this hearing the presentational basis of subsequent awareness of sounds as sounds. For the baby, however, there are presumably just happenings, total situations to which he responds totally as his impulses and feelings dictate. These happenings seem to be felt from the beginning as pleasurable or painful and the types of response dictated are clearly distinguishable. Hence, it is permissible to think of infantile relationships beginning as relationships to total situations but as relationships of sharply contrasted types: definitely affirmative or appetitive relations to gratifying pleasurable situations and unambiguously negative ones to conditions of pain and frustration. Thus, at one moment the baby may appear to be, to all intents and purposes, a smiling contentment, and a few moments later a different baby altogether, a scowling rage. Situations of both types will naturally arise in connection with all the infant's different instinctual urges and all the variety of stimuli impinging on him from without. The second experience of a similar situation will already be modified by the first experience. Hence, we can recognize in 'yes, yes'-situations the germ of 'pleasure-me' systems or nuclei, the forerunners of love-relationships to objects, and in 'no, no'-situations the germ of ego-differentiation and the forerunners of hate-relationships to objects.

The transition from the earliest sporadic reactions to organized ego-object reaction-systems will presumably be effected through various stages of partial organization, motivated by instinct-interest and determined in detail by the specific course of adaptation, that is, by the actual events of the individual infant's life. The classical 'libidinal primacies' represent early stages of organization. There is a considerable amount of clinical and behaviouristic evidence in support of the view that the initial partial organizations constitute relatively autonomous systems and are mutually exclusive in the sense that they compete for control of consciousness and motility. If these assumptions are approximately correct, three consequences should follow. Firstly, early behaviour should show rapid alternations of mood and should appear spontaneous and quickly changeable; it should not show any very obvious signs of internal co-ordination between instinctual urges of markedly different types. Secondly, early object-discrimination would be highly selective and would tend to yield sharply divided types of mental object (wholly 'good' or wholly 'bad') corresponding to the sharp division between pleasurable and painful situations and the all-or-none responses to them. Thirdly, ego-integration, definitive object-relations and ambivalence or multivalence, as distinct from alternations of 'love' and 'hate', should emerge together as the result of processes comparable to those described by Freud (1925) in more purely ideational terms in his paper on 'Negation'.

The issue of precocity can be finally settled only when it becomes possible to estimate more exactly the normal rate of progress of mental organization. There would appear to be scope for great variation in this rate; some time-limits are set by physiological conditions.

The surveys carried out by Dorothy Burlingham and Anna Freud on young children in a residential war nursery are highly relevant here (*e.g.* Burlingham and Freud, 1942). Norms of growth and development during the first year generally accepted by child psychologists are also of interest. Thus, in her recent book, *Modern Child Psychology*, Agatha Bowley notes that jealousy can be detected in infants of three months, and that they pay selective attention to faces and recognize familiar persons (Bowley, 1949, p. 109). Among observational data she lists as 'well-known facts of development' the relative predominance of negative expressional movements over positive ones and of defensive reactions to stimuli over positive responses during the first two months. Also 'The expression of strong emotion in relation to the feeding situation' and 'The frequency with which healthy, normal infants may bite the breast, even before the appearance of teeth, as well as the numerous occasions when he may smile or show signs of pleasure and affection' (*op. cit.* p. 114). The observable differences between the behaviour of newly born babes and infants of six months certainly give the impression that the pace of development during the first six months is very rapid. Recognition of familiar persons at three months could scarcely occur without their having acquired some positive definition as objects.

Exact knowledge about psychological heredity is conspicuous by its absence. It is known that very few patterns of motor behaviour are inborn in the human infant, but nothing is known with certainty about innate predispositions to mental organization or the time at which they take effect. This is still a field of surmise and different inferences are drawn by different workers in accordance with their varying angle of approach.

It is certain, however, that an apparent precocity is often introduced into accounts of early life by the terms in which it is described. Pre-verbal experience must be described in words for purposes of discussion and the use of words and the construction of sentences inevitably imparts a kind and degree of organization to the description which could not have been present in the experience to which it refers. Thus, some of the precocity attributed to the infant as described by Melanie Klein is due to the fact that an adult cannot interpret any infantile experience and make it intelligible to other adults without subjecting the experience itself to some degree of falsification or retrospective sophistication. It seems that sensitive adults may feel a baby's feelings with some degree of accuracy but cannot put these feelings into words without passing them through the modifying medium of their adult organizations. It is likely that this process of retrospective sophistication is not limited to adults, but will tend to occur in every phase of development in connection with conscious revival of experience belonging to preceding phases. Edward Bibring (1947) considers that Melanie Klein 'retrojects' into early phases of development much that belongs to later stages.

Phantasy-systems which emerge from repression in adults contain many elements derived from post-infantile life which, in their turn, succumbed to repression and seem to have become assimilated to systems of earlier origin. The infantile systems may themselves exhibit signs of developmental stratification. Thus, they often reveal a number of different versions of the same theme; for example, a primitive oral theme may appear in an anal-oral version and this may be repeated in a genital version. In other words, the revival of a primitive experience tends to assume novel forms corresponding to the current life situation in which it is revived, unless the ego-systems are pathologically retarded in development, disintegrated, or completely dominated by mentally traumatic revivals. The existence of such conditions in adults suggests that a phantasy which can be demonstrated in a child of two years may have unmistakable reference to suckling or weaning or other very early infantile happenings, and may, in fact, constitute a revival of such experiences. The phantasy in the two-year-old, however, may take a form corresponding to his current development rather than to the age to which its content refers. To stage a primitive phantasy in play is to dramatize it in a way not open to a baby before it can handle toys freely.

The play will show unmistakable subject-object differentiation, but this differentiation may belong to the current production of the phantasy and it should not be taken for granted that it was necessarily present in the original experience.

VI. PROGRESSION, REGRESSION, AND DEPRESSION; THE STATUS OF THE CLASSICAL OEDIPUS COMPLEX

The criticism that Melanie Klein's descriptions of infantile development imply undue precocity of various types is allied to two further criticisms. The first is that her account of development is almost wholly progressive, *i.e.* that she fails to appreciate the rôle of regression in development, above all the part it plays in aetiology and symptomatology, with the result that she tends seriously to underrate the significance of the classical Oedipus phase. In short, the adoption of a 'central depressive position' would appear to oust the Oedipus factors from their finally decisive part in neurosogenesis. Melanie Klein's 1945 paper is in part a response to criticism on these lines (see p. 84). The second criticism is that the Kleinian estimation of infantile phantasies turns them into a kind of 'enclave' totally incompatible with the basic concepts of metapsychology. Thus, Edward Glover recently concluded that the logical outcome of Melanie Klein's work is, in effect, the production of a new metapsychology, a deviation from psycho-analysis resembling the Rank 'Birth Trauma' deviation. His 'Examination of the Klein System of Child Psychology' (Glover, 1945) contains much sound criticism but is so polemical that it amounts to an exposé of the worst that could happen if the majority of psycho-analysts accepted quite uncritically every considered and unconsidered word uttered by Melanie Klein and regarded them as constituting a self-sufficient theory of mental life. Such an outcome would be disastrous, but, to the present writer, the real situation appears far more complicated. In her opinion, the work of Melanie Klein cannot, and should not attempt to, stand alone, but neither should it be dismissed as a deviation without value. The far from easy task before constructive critics is the separation of the corn from the chaff and the utilization of the former as grist to the mills of psycho-analysis. Melanie Klein has focused attention on the formative pre-history of the Oedipus phase and, apart from vexed questions of precise chronology and aetiology, she has in fact greatly enriched our appreciation of the complexity of the interplay of object-relationships (internal and external, identificatory and definitive) which result in the decisive pattern of post-Oedipal ego and super-ego organization, the ground plan of future personal development. One is often tempted to wonder whether, if Freud had recognized the internal economy of melancholia *before* he formulated his theory of narcissism, he and Abraham would not themselves have carried further their exploration of intra-psychic animism. Its exploration is of great importance, since the more irrational aspects of human life and behaviour, *e.g.* the sphere of beliefs and values, not to mention politics, are largely dominated by animistic thinking, and rational thinking is far more influenced by it than is generally recognized. The proportion of rationalization in reasoning is frequently high.

The conception of a closed system of infantile phantasy, or enclave, as a kind of magical entity dominating future development is highly undesirable; it can arise only out of too concrete notions about mental life. Every mental event is a process, or series of processes; memories and phantasies are not stored in a three-dimensional mind, like pictures in a gallery or books in a library; they are modifications of the psychic energy pattern whose permanence is implied in Freud's own hypothesis of memory traces. A current reaction is always the resultant of an immediate stimulus acting on the organism as modified by past experience. It is, therefore, no exaggeration to say that the time-sequence of experience is decisive in the sense that earlier happenings inevitably modify later events. The kind of influence exerted by any particular experience, *e.g.* a given phantasy, on later development will depend upon the economic fate of that experience. An ego-syntonic phantasy will contribute to the pattern of ego-organization and undergo further developmental modification along with the ego, whereas an ego-dystonic phantasy may form the nucleus of a dissociated and, therefore, potentially pathogenic system. Glover (1943) himself accepts the relative autonomy of dissociated systems. Bibring (1947) criticizes any attempt to explain the whole of subsequent development as completely determined by infantile 'residues', and says, very rightly, that a theory of residues is acceptable though its exclusive application is not.

It is in relation to the suggested 'depressive position' and the content of 'depressive phantasies' that under-estimation of regression and its effects is most noticeable. It is a well-established clinical fact that pathological depression involves the re-activation of oral conflicts. Even a transitory depression in a mild anxiety hysteric will yield a crop of oral phantasies and evidence of cannibalistic anxiety. The form of such phantasies is usually more or less adult, *i.e.* the primary impulses and feelings, revived by regression, appear in modern dress. Nevertheless, if cannibalistic anxiety can be revived by regression, it must have existed, though in more primitive guise, in the infantile period. Depression in the adult, however, involves much more than purely oral revivals. In adults with acute 'separation' anxieties, the physical presence of the mother-substitute is not only reassurance that she has not been destroyed but is also positive assurance that she is not consorting with father or wasting her substance on other people. Evacuation anxieties often seem to be as strong as biting ones. The content of depressive phantasies in adults does not suggest an exclusively oral aetiology; it rather suggests far-reaching regression from unmanageable Oedipal conflicts. It is a generally accepted proposition, however, that happenings at the late or classical Oedipus stage are necessarily much influenced by pre-Oedipal history. It is, therefore, quite probable that primary 'oral' difficulties complicate primary 'anal' development and, together, predispose to regressive solutions of Oedipal conflict.

Behaviourist observations suggest that ego and super-ego systems attain an appreciable degree of coherence by the time that what Ferenczi called 'sphincter morality' is established. The effort to acquire sphincter control provides a life-situation that seems peculiarly well adapted to induce preoccupation with 'internalized objects' and to bring the infant up against problems of ambivalence as such. It seems likely that many earlier anxiety crises now revive and can be given more definite content, though they may be further crystallized during the ensuing Oedipus phase. Learning to speak and learning to walk involve their own particular anxieties and problems of control, but it seems to be 'lavatory life' which is especially prone to become overcharged with mixed feelings. Few psycho-analysts would doubt that in this life-situation the faecal stool becomes a very definite object, though it may be questioned how far the primitive nipple-object and its penis-heir antedate it as clearly discriminated objects and how far they acquire retrospective definition. There is one source of grief and dismay in becoming clean which was noted by Freud, Ferenczi, and others, which we rather tend to lose sight of when stressing the aggressive significance of evacuation. Making water and passing stool can express quite other than angry feelings, and often, in the beginning, seem to be of the nature of libidinal activities, spontaneous outpourings of responsive appreciation or proto-gratitude, rather than despite. The enforced recognition of the fact that these infantile libations are not acceptable may be acutely depressing. Some people never recover from this painful discovery, and they retain throughout life the hopeless conviction that anything they have to give is without value, or is even 'bad'.

Mystical literature (see p. 217 *et seq*.) abounds in illustrations of the kind of thinking and feeling which Melanie Klein regards as typical of 'depressive phantasies'. It thus affords ample corroboration of the existence of such phantasies in persons living centuries before the advent of psycho-analysis, and contradicts any suggestion that such phantasies are artificial products of technique or fabrications of modern minds. On the other hand, the 'manic-depressive' conceptions and experiences of the mystics usually exhibit clear signs of Oedipal preoccupations and post-Oedipal regression. The evidence of mysticism, therefore, supports the view that Melanie Klein has not so far paid enough attention to the rôle of regression in the retrospective crystallization of depressive phantasies or in the aetiology of manic-depressive states. The intra-psychic reality asserted by the mystics and by adult manic-depressives often seems to function as a defence against the recognition of an unbearable historical reality, a painful actual relation between parent and parent, or parent and child. A related type of 'denial' defence is illustrated by the theological doctrine of the Trinity. This is a doctrine of the indivisible unity of a spiritualized and masculinized Holy Father, Three Persons but One God; it is an affirmation of libidinal and personal solidarity between parents and child which constitutes an absolute denial of all tensions between them. Mystical literature thus tends to confirm the point of view arrived at by Ella Sharpe in her paper 'From *King Lear* to *The Tempest*', in which she said (1946, p. 28): 'If this had been a theoretical paper instead of an essay in interpretation, its title would have been "The Rôle of Regression in Manic-Depression"'.

VII. MELANIE KLEIN, 1945; HER OWN
SUMMARY AND COMPARISONS

In her (1945) paper, 'The Oedipus Complex in the Light of Early Anxieties' (Klein, 1948a, p. 339), Melanie Klein herself devotes more attention than hitherto both to regression and to idealization, and also modifies her views on the 'depressive position'. She writes (1948a, p. 380): 'In the two preceding papers I have repeatedly referred to the infantile depressive position as the central position in early development. I would now rather suggest the following formulation: the core of infantile depressive feelings, *i.e.* the child's fear of the loss of his loved objects, as a consequence of his hatred and aggression, enters into his object relations and Oedipus complex from the beginning.' The term 'core' is still open to the charge of constituting an enclave, but, clearly, depressive feelings may be experienced long before they can be formulated in definitive object-relational phantasies such as come to light in the analysis of older children and adults. This revision, therefore, goes some way towards diminishing the apparent precocity suggested by earlier statements, though it may not seem to every psycho-analyst to go far enough. It remains desirable to insist that the earliest subjective animistic experiences almost certainly lack the detailed definition and the emotional refinement which are imparted to them when they are reanimated by regression from a later phase of development in which self-object relationships have been more highly elaborated.

At the end of the same paper (Klein, 1948a, p. 377 *et seq.*), Melanie Klein herself summarizes and compares her own views with the classical conception of the Oedipus complex. Among the points of major importance are the following:

(*a*) 'According to Freud, genital desires emerge and a definite object choice takes place during the phallic phase, which extends from about three to five years of age, and is contemporaneous with the Oedipus complex.' 'As I see it, the boy's and girl's sexual and emotional development *from early infancy onwards* includes genital sensations and trends, which constitute the first stages of the inverted and positive Oedipus complex. . . . It is during the stage of genital primacy that the positive Oedipus situation reaches its climax' (*op. cit.* pp. 386, 387).

(*b*) Freud thought the vagina remained unknown to both

sexes and that the infantile genital primacy was exclusively phallic, whereas 'in my view, infants of both sexes experience genital desires directed towards their mother and father, and they have an unconscious knowledge of the vagina as well as of the penis' (*op. cit.* p. 387). Melanie Klein is not alone in differing from Freud on this particular point. Karen Horney (1933) asserted infantile denial of the vagina, and, in this country, Ernest Jones (1927), Sylvia Payne (1935), and the present author (1936) incline to regard this organ as more important in infancy than Freud assumed. On the other hand, Helene Deutsch (1946, p. 181-3) agrees with Freud, and it is, indeed, essential to her conception of the nature of the feminine 'genital trauma' that the vagina should be functionless in infancy. According to Deutsch, supposedly vaginal phantasies are misinterpreted anal phantasies. More evidence is needed on this problem, but precise information is hard to obtain.

(*c*) Freud (1924b, p. 271) thought that in the boy 'the phallic stage of the genital organization succumbs to the threat of castration'. In Melanie Klein's opinion, 'The closer development approaches genital primacy, the more does castration fear come to the fore. While I thus fully agree with Freud that *castration fear is the leading anxiety situation* in the male, I cannot agree with his description of it as the *single factor* which determines the repression of the Oedipus complex. Early anxieties from various sources contribute all along to the central part which castration fear comes to play in the climax of the Oedipus situation. . . . In my experience the Oedipus situation loses in power not only because the boy is afraid of the destruction of his genital by a revengeful father, but also because he is driven by feelings of love and guilt to preserve his father as an internal and external figure' (Klein, 1948a, p. 389).

(*d*) Freud (1932b, p. 286) thought that feminine development began with a long 'phase of exclusive attachment to the mother, which may be called the *pre-Oedipal phase*'. The girl's desire and failure to receive a penis from her mother usher in her castration complex and ultimately cause her to turn to her father, so initiating her Oedipus complex. According to Melanie Klein, 'The phase in which, according to Freud, the girl is exclusively attached to her mother already includes, in my view, desires directed towards her father and covers the early stages of the inverted and positive Oedipus complex.

85

While, therefore, I consider this phase as a period of fluctuation between desires directed toward mother and father in all libidinal positions, there is no doubt in my mind as to the far-reaching and lasting importance of every facet of the relation to the mother upon the relation to the father. Penis envy and castration complex are always inherent features in the girl's development. But they are very much reinforced by frustration of her positive Oedipus desires. . . . The feminine desire to internalize the penis and to receive a child from her father invariably precedes the wish to possess a penis of her own. While I agree with Freud about the prominence of the fear of loss of love and of the death of the mother among the girl's anxieties, I hold that the fear of having her body attacked and her loved inner objects destroyed essentially contributes to her main anxiety situation' (Klein, 1948a, pp. 389, 340). Helene Deutsch's theory of feminine development is quite different from Melanie Klein's but both agree in emphasizing the importance of the mother-relation and the secondary nature of 'penis envy'. It is fairly commonly recognized among psycho-analysts that Freud's conception of feminine development is the weakest part of his work.

(e) According to Freud the super-ego is formed by the introjection of the parental objects which concludes the Oedipus phase. Hence feelings of guilt (tension between ego and super-ego) are post-Oedipal phenomena. In Melanie Klein's view, 'The first introjected object, the mother's breast, forms the basis of the super-ego. . . . The earliest feelings of guilt in both sexes derive from the oral-sadistic desires to devour the mother. . . . Guilt does not emerge when the Oedipus complex comes to an end, but is rather one of the factors which, from the beginning, mould its course and affect its outcome' (Klein, 1948a, p. 388). The chronology of guilt is mentioned again in Chapter VI (see p. 274 *et seq.*).

A doubt still remains whether typical depressive phantasies are not, strictly speaking, typical manic-depressive phantasies. There is a very evident difference between recognizing the liability of all infants to depressive feelings and to phases of preoccupation with internalized object-relationships and asserting that such feelings and preoccupations are of equal developmental significance in all infants. This question of relative importance needs more elucidation if the impression is to be successfully corrected that Melanie Klein and her closest adherents tend to think of all human beings as conforming to a single manic-depressive type. The emphasis on 'depressive feelings', like the emphasis on oral interests, needs counterbalancing if it is to free itself from seeming to approximate to a mono-phasic or mono-instinctual theory of development (cf. Glover, 1945, p. 90).

Their preoccupation with 'internalized objects' has also raised doubts as to whether Melanie Klein and her followers are not themselves mystics and have not developed a magical technique which deals with these objects on their own terms. But recognition of the fact that human beings entertain mystical and magical beliefs is itself realistic, and psycho-analysts should find it possible to investigate such beliefs without themselves becoming mystics. If the analysis of hysteria does not usually convert a non-hysterical analyst into an hysteric, there is no reason why the analysis of manic-depression should turn him into a mystic. There is, naturally, always the danger that unsuspected defences in the analyst may lead him to concur in similar defence systems in his analysands. This is one of the main reasons for requiring candidates (student analysts) to undergo a comprehensive training-analysis and for subsequently diversifying their training controls (*i.e.* the supervision of their initial clinical work). The problem of training-transference (*e.g.* the tendency of trainees to accept their analyst's opinions uncritically and to imitate their technique too rigidly) is very real, but surely it is not insoluble, provided that the aim of training remains the development of a responsible analyst, and that it does not degenerate into the mere transmission of the trainer's own views and personal technique. Clearly a responsible psycho-analyst must be able to use his own judgment and learn from his own clinical experience.

VIII. THE SCIENTIFIC POSITION

It is possible to make a creed of any theory, but the scientific position is that the work of Melanie Klein is a series of hypotheses which call for long-term critical evaluation in relation to theory as a whole and to personal experience in psycho-analytic practice over a period of years. Such hypotheses call neither for belief nor disbelief, for immediate acceptance or immediate rejection *in toto*, but for detailed examination and testing on both the intellectual and the practical planes. Any psycho-analyst who can adopt this 'scientific attitude' is adequately realistic and can investigate and make practical trial of Melanie Klein's work without fear of succumbing to mystical beliefs.

The assessment of Melanie Klein's views is only a special instance of the more general problem, the attitude of psycho-analysts towards any changes in theory, other than the numerous modifications effected by Freud himself. Most scientific societies welcome deep and far-reaching differences of opinion amongst their members, because the occurrence of such differences is regarded as a sign of vitality and growth: indeed, uniformity of opinion and progress in science rarely coincide. New ideas meet with varying degrees of opposition, but, however severely they may be criticized, if they prove to be substantiated they are eventually absorbed, in whole or in part, into general theory. The barrage of criticism then moves forward to the next oncoming set of new ideas. Psycho-analysts have two main reasons for attaching what may be unduly great importance to relative uniformity in theory. These reasons spring from the circumstance that we have three functions to perform: research, therapy, and training of intending practitioners. It is in relation to the two latter functions that we hanker after uniformity and standardization, and find ourselves in a dilemma if we think current differences may amount to incompatibility. It is, however, very necessary for us to recognize that uniformity easily conduces to stasis and that a static science is dead.

Scientific truth can never be absolute, because hypotheses are formulated in the light of contemporary knowledge. In consequence, as knowledge grows, older hypotheses become inadequate and have to be revised, expanded or reformulated to contain newer facts. Freud did this himself, time after time, and if psycho-analysis is to continue to develop as a living science this process of recasting hypotheses and expanding theory must also continue. A parallel is often drawn between Freud and Darwin: the status of both in science is unassailable. But many more facts have come to light since Darwin enunciated his theory of natural selection, and the theory of evolution has been adapted accordingly. We should be prepared, and indeed hope, for similar growth and development in analysis. To expect to conserve the letter of all Freud's statements, as a kind of 'Bible of Psycho-

Analysis' is to condemn psycho-analytic inquiry to stasis and, therefore, psycho-analysis as a science to death. The growth of a science is a process of continuous adaptation of theory to continually expanding awareness of facts. But the main principles established by Freud will survive in so far as they do correspond with facts. The name of Freud will endure with the principles, but they will survive not because Freud established them, but because they are rooted in psychological facts.

The criteria of a new hypothesis are: is the hypothesis necessary?—is it a fuller or a better explanation of a certain range of facts?—does it cover more facts?—and so on; *not*—who is the author? New theories are a matter of proof, not partisanship. If we cannot be bound by an Old Testament according to Freud neither can we profit by a Gospel of the Good Object. Our therapeutic and training responsibilities are, indeed, heavy, but they call for courage rather than for timidity in our approach to new ideas and differences of opinion. Above all, they demand that our handling of all differences shall be as strictly scientific as our subjective limitations permit; complete objectivity, like final truth, is an unattainable ideal for human beings. We shall only safeguard therapy and training, and do honour to Freud by continuing his work, in so far as we succeed in putting first our common task and mutual responsibility, the furtherance of the *science* of psycho-analysis.

CHAPTER IV

PSYCHO - ANALYTICAL THEORY: ITS NATURE AND BEARING ON RESEARCH AND PUBLIC RELATIONS[1]

I. THEORY, THERAPY, AND RESEARCH

THE formulation of psycho-analytical theory and the practice of therapy began together. A reciprocal relationship continues to exist between them because the consulting-room remains our principal laboratory. This close association has many advantages, but also disadvantages, and it is not by any means easy to keep the partners on a footing of equality.

Most of us earn our living by practice and this fact of itself tends to overweight our interest in problems of technique and therapy. This tendency is furthered by the constant pressure of therapeutic responsibility. The result is that we too often think of theory chiefly as a necessary background and adjuvant to practice. The number of psycho-analysts spontaneously attracted to theory is limited by comparison with those primarily concerned with matters of practice. These differences in interest arise in personal variations in temperament and mental equipment. Clinical and theoretical ability do not always co-exist and, when they do, they are not always present in equal measure. But psycho-analytical societies are, by constitution, scientific associations and not merely trade unions of clinical practitioners. If we wish to further the science of psycho-analysis, to increase knowledge of mental life so as continually to widen the range of its potential application, we have to recognize that the development and advance of sound theory is as important as the maintenance and extension of sound practice. We cannot afford to give one aim priority but must pursue both concurrently. In the present chapter, however, attention will be concentrated on theory and the vital questions of the influence of theory on technique and practice will not be broached. Among recent discussions of these

[1] Revised version of 'Theory, Practice and Public Relations' and 'Notes on Metapsychology as Process Theory', *Int. J. Psycho-Anal.*, 1943, vol. xxiv, p. 119, and 1944, vol. xxv, p. 97.

latter problems are papers by Sylvia Payne (1946) and Sandor Lorand (1948) respectively.

Although, owing to native differences in interest and ability, there will inevitably continue to be divisions of labour among psycho-analysts, there is one sphere, namely, that of clinical verification, in which all practitioners should accept at least minimal research responsibility. Up to the present, the consulting-room has been the psycho-analyst's principal laboratory and, in spite of the current rapid extension of experimental and other methods of inquiry, it is still the only one in which the majority of practitioners have opportunity to work. With all its limitations this laboratory evidently has compensating advantages, because out of it have come results that have done much to revolutionize modern psychology and psychiatry. But, in the consulting-room, the chief means of verification employed in other sciences are not available; we cannot perform controlled experiments or repeat them precisely, and the psycho-analytic situation can be standardized only to a degree far short of uniformity. It is said, not without justice, that in psycho-analytic research intensity of examination replaces extensity of sampling (Isaacs, 1939, p. 159), but intensity of examination is no safeguard against error due to subjective bias in the examiner. This may be corrected to some extent by comparing the results obtained by a number of different workers; pooling of clinical experience is an obvious and practicable, if incomplete, safeguard against errors due to individual bias. Hence every psycho-analyst should regard it as part of his professional duties to do what he can in the matter of verifying accepted hypotheses and testing new ones in the light of his experiences in his daily work.

It is admittedly not easy to combine research and therapy, and it may take years for an individual analyst to come to a definite conclusion on a given issue. But this does not alter the fact that individual testing is a communal responsibility to which, as a group, we are not yet sufficiently alive and which we do not stress enough in our training of candidates for qualification, *i.e.* student analysts or intending practitioners. We shoulder our therapeutic responsibilities as a matter of course but sometimes ignore our research obligations, individual responsibility for research not being generally recognized. Moreover, our ideas about the nature and functions of theory are often confused and inaccurate.

What then is theory? How do research and therapy differ and how are they related? Theory is, in essence, simply intelligent explanation. A scientific theory is an explanation based upon adequate evidence which indicates the relationships existing among the data it covers. A science is an organization of knowledge covering a particular range of facts with their most probable explanations, so far as these have been arrived at. Scientific research is the orderly pursuit of knowledge. Scientific methods are simply rigorous procedures of reality-testing, designed to ensure the maximum of probability and the minimum of error.

In our own case, technique began as a method of therapy and has proved to be an instrument of psychological research. Theory began as psychopathology—strictly speaking, as a psychopathology of hysteria. Apart from its ramifications into other special fields, psycho-analytic theory has become a general psychology, a theory of mental life and of personality as a whole.

Although our sphere of interest is mental life and our methods are adapted to this sphere, the thinking which issues in psychoanalytical knowledge is the same kind of mental activity as the thinking about chemical data which issues in knowledge of chemistry. Archaic modes of thinking may creep into would-be objective reasoning and introduce various sources of error, but the principles of cognition work in the same way and achieve comparable ends whatever the data to which they are applied. The result of their efficient working is the mental construction we call knowledge.

For the thinker, the activity of thinking is a mode of living: the conclusions he reaches form part of his experience and modify his future thinking. But, objectively considered, knowledge is not life, it is only a system of information about something, e g. about mental life. Theorizing is intellectual creation, but a theory is a work of science in the same sense that a picture is a work of art. Knowledge is as much a mental tool as the array of physical tools man has been so prolific in devising to further his human ends.

The subjective and objective functions of knowledge are apparent in clinical practice. The process of analysis is not primarily a process of instruction; it is a process of mental reorganization. Interpretations are not voiced with the aim of teaching but of enabling the patient to become aware of his own subjective problems and to deal with them in such a way that he becomes capable of more tolerable and more effective living. The acquisition of insight is a part of the total process of reorganization, and such objective knowledge about himself as the patient gains he can, thereafter, use to greater or lesser advantage. The analyst's theoretical preconceptions will help to determine the way in which he apprehends his patient's situation. He will, also, deliberately use his knowledge in assessing his impressions and in formulating his interpretations.

The ultimate aim of analysis as a therapeutic process is to enable the patient to live more satisfactorily. As a process of research, the ultimate aim of analysis is different. It is simply the acquisition of knowledge about mental life, the fashioning and improvement of a tool which can then be used to promote living.

Therapy and research have in common the proximate aim of understanding the patient. The term understanding can be used in a purely intellectual sense, as of understanding a problem in mathematics. When we talk of understanding a patient, however, we generally mean something more than intellectual apprehension of what he is saying. We imply that we are capable not only of thinking about the patient but of thinking and feeling with him enough to enter, at least partially, into his emotional attitudes. This situation we describe as empathy and we think it comes about when our own unconscious and that of the patient are *en rapport*.

We have, as yet, little exact knowledge about empathy or *rapport*, but it is evident that feeling *with* the patient implies a type of relationship more akin to identification than to object-relationship. Thinking *about* the patient is clearly object-relationship. I imagine that we vary greatly in the degree to which we individually combine identification and object-relationship in our work, but I do not see how any of us can avoid sustaining both these relationships in some proportion. It is this combination or alternation of relationship to our patients that is all too often reflected in confused thinking about theory.

The two kinds of relationship underlie the distinction I recently ventured to draw between subjective and objective theory (described less ambiguously in Chapter V as personology and metapsychology). Both alike are formulated from the data of experience. Subjective theory deals with the data from the standpoint of the living person and should, therefore, express itself in terms belonging to experience. For subjective theory 'I' is appropriately rendered 'self'. It is, in short, a psychology of meaning in the widest sense of that word. On the other hand, objective theory deals with the same data from the standpoint of a temporarily detached observer. Since its approach is essentially impersonal, it should express itself in impersonal language. For objective theory 'I' is the 'ego'. It is, in effect, a psychology of mental function. What is experienced as meaning can be objectively described as a functional integration of mental processes. There may be only one event, the psychological event, but there are very definitely two distinct methods of approaching and describing it. This dichotomy affects not only psycho-analysis but psychology in general. As T. H. Pear says (1948, p. 160): 'Psychologists, both here and in America, are often distinguished by the emphasis, theoretical and practical, which they place upon one of two aims: the discovery of general laws of mind, or the description and understanding of the unique undivided personality'. The results of both approaches have to be correlated, and can be used to correct each other. At our present stage of thinking development, the distinction between them is readily lost and we should gain by choosing words which help to keep the difference clear.

Subjective theory is of particular importance not only in therapy but in all forms of work that involve direct contact with individuals or groups. In these fields what is required is not primarily objective knowledge of the mental apparatus but understanding of the individual's personal situation. To be of real service in human affairs, knowledge must be applied with personal understanding, and it would seem that this is a feature of that elusive characteristic we call wisdom.

If understanding is so important and generalization about personal experience so helpful in dealing with problems of everyday living, why should we trouble about pursuing objective knowledge with a view to establishing highly abstract general laws of mental function? Has the conception of mind as an apparatus for the regulation of instinct tension, or that of mental structure as organization, any practical as distinct from intellectual value? Is abstract thinking a luxury for those who like it, a flight into depersonalized phantasy, or is it a practical necessity and useful work?

In my opinion, abstract thinking is just as necessary in psychology as in any other branch of science. It could ultimately be just as fruitful in improving the psychological conditions as it has been in improving the physical conditions of human life. As we all know, the improvement in human living conditions that is now physically possible is jeopardized by psychological factors.

Advance in the natural sciences has come about in divers ways, sometimes almost by accident. It is a fact, however, that the application of science, *e.g.* in industry, has extended further and faster since the more fundamental laws of physics, chemistry, and biology were recognized. Until general laws are established, suitable applications cannot be predicted but must wait upon trial and error, a method which may be successful but is always wasteful. When fundamental laws are known, some probable applications can be deduced from these laws and others can be eliminated as impossible. The need for wasteful trial and error is at least diminished.

Let us take a simple example from our own practice. We do not advise an hysterical woman to marry in order to see if this may cure her. We know in advance that it cannot cure her, because we have learned that hysteria is a psychological disorder, and that she can only profit fully by marriage as and when she becomes at least convalescent. This knowledge about hysteria derives in the first instance from Freud's discovery of the mental mechanism of repression. This he inferred, partly, from the nature of the patient's associations but, mainly, from observed alteration in behaviour, the retardation or cessation of associations, the first phenomena of resistance which he encountered. Phenomena connected with resistance are experienced and the results of repression can be felt in various ways. It is also true that the operation of repression can be indicated by means of what we usually term functional symbolism. A patient of mine who could hardly force herself to speak at all, dreamed about a door locked on the inside. But repression itself is never a part of experience; it is silent. I do not doubt that the locked door also had historical meaning; other evidence suggested that a 'primal scene' took place in a room locked from inside. But we should never have understood the dynamic effects of repressed memories if Freud had not first provided us with the objective concept of repression as an explanation of the phenomena of resistance.

If I may summarize this portion of the chapters I submit that, whether we like it or not, we all have research responsibilities. We evade these unless we pay due attention to the theoretical implications of our own clinical data. We are ill-advised, as scientists, if we concentrate exclusively on the treatment of our patients. I submit, also, that there is nothing intrinsically mysterious or alarming about theory which is only the system of probable explanations. Theory aims at stating the general laws which can be deduced from the specific clinical data. Correct observation of data is the first step. We have reason to think that, in our own case, accurate observation is not a purely intellectual process but also a matter of correct empathy. Once our observations are registered, objective or abstract thinking about their general implications has an indispensable rôle to play both in advancing knowledge itself and in facilitating its application.

II. ABSTRACT THINKING

Before considering in more detail the nature of metapsychology and its bearing on our public relations, particularly with other sciences, I should like to try to make our notions of abstract thinking rather more precise by indicating something of what we surmise about its genesis. This will involve reference to the vexed question of psychological reality.

Abstract thinking is no less subjectively determined than perception and the risk that it will be dominated by unconscious preconceptions is, perhaps, even greater than in perceptual thinking. For this reason alone, constant reference to and checking of hypotheses by data is imperative. The form of any hypothesis is always influenced by unconscious determinants, since we can only apprehend things in ways permitted by the specific structure of our individual minds. The fact remains, however, that the objective truth of any hypothesis does not depend upon its subjective conditioning but upon its fitness to explain the facts it covers. Naturally, the more we become aware of the unconscious determinants of our own thinking the better chance we have of estimating how far our preferred conceptions are likely to correspond to the facts. We all have some coefficient of personal error which we cannot eliminate, and it is much safer to assume that one's own coefficient of error is high rather than low, and positively dangerous to forget that it exists.

We consider abstract thinking to be among the most recently evolved functions of the human mind. We assume that it has a long history behind it and that it is still far from fully matured.

It is true, as Susan Isaacs reminded us, that all words are concepts inasmuch as they are all generalizations. But concepts vary in degree of abstraction, in much the same way as displacements of instinct vary in remoteness from its primary aims. The statement that apples fall to the ground is a true generalization, but it is a long way from this generalization of perceptual experience to Newton's concept of gravitation.

If we consider the development of human intelligence, in the individual or in the race, we think of an ascent from sensation through perception to imaginary and verbal thinking and all the various grades of generalization.

Cognition, however, does not develop independently: its growth is an integral part of mental development as a whole. We may disagree about subsequent chronology, but we agree, I think, in assuming that the infant's mental life is at first purely sensory-affective and that any discrimination it evinces is dictated solely by pleasure and pain. We also agree that primitive 'me-ness' is bound up with pleasure identification and primitive 'not-me-ness' with pain repudiation. Broadly speaking, functional phases in the mental development of the individual may represent stages in the evolution of mind. The transition described by Freud from the pleasure-pain to the reality principle is easier to understand if one thinks of it as perhaps representing a transition from an archaic to a more modern type of mental adaptation. The transition appears to involve the advance from identification to object-relationship and from affective to cognitive discrimination.

Such a point of view indicates a genetic link between object-relationship and cognition. It emphasizes the primary rôle of cognition, i.e. the provision of more detailed information about the external world than is afforded by pleasure-pain discrimination. Most of this information is mediated to the adult by his long-distance receptors and, in consequence perhaps, we are inclined to overlook the part played by the other senses in the development of cognition. This genetic link forces the way of knowledge to be a way of detachment. When we bring our intelligence to bear on ourselves and our mental life, we are constrained to treat them as if they were temporarily external objects.

The transition to the reality principle is never complete and it is not only the sexual instinct which tends to remain under the sway of the pleasure principle. Cognition undoubtedly plays a highly significant part in ego development through the establishment of manifold relations with the outer world which are, in their turn, reflected in ego structure. The dynamics of ego organization nevertheless appear to be fundamentally the dynamics of pleasure-synthesis and pain-dissociation. Ego modification is, therefore, a consequence of feeling rather than of knowing. Repressed memories are recovered when the resistance to feeling their unpleasant affects is overcome.

The difference between knowing and being is the difference between intellectual knowledge and character structure. Ernest Jones (1942) lately reminded us how often our behaviour is superstitious. Outgrown habits of thought that formerly had emotional value for the individual may continue to influence his conduct indefinitely, and the adult sceptic frequently behaves like a believer.

The direction of cognition to the scientific study of mental life is the newest and probably the most difficult use to which we have put our intelligence. It has become a truism that our own conscious experience is the only reality of which we have direct, first-hand awareness. This truism is accepted by us because our minds have attained the stage of development which allows us to appreciate that our perceptions are not identical with the sources which stimulate them through our sense organs. We can now recognize that perceptions are reports on the environment; they supply the kind of information about the external world we need to have in order to survive. This was not a truism to primitive man nor is it to the human infant. For primitive man it was presumably very much more important to distinguish correctly between friend and foe than to differentiate between his perception and the person of whose presence it informed him.

The distinction between perception and its external object has come to have potential survival value for civilized man. Perception, as experienced, retains its pristine subjective conviction that what we see is there as we see it. This self-evident character persists in spite of the fact that we know that information supplied by perception is highly selective and can, on occasion, be positively incorrect. By refusing to take perception at its face value and by devising means of correcting and supplementing the evidence of their senses the natural scientists have acquired an impressive amount of knowledge about the physical universe. To achieve an equivalent knowledge of mind we must take a critical attitude towards all the phenomena of subjective experience. Freud soon found that consciousness was as inadequate a guide to the structure of mind as perception is to the structure of matter. Clearly we must detach ourselves from experience and think objectively if we are to penetrate beyond its face value and form adequate conceptions about mind. When we try to think, we find that emotional attachment constantly impedes intellectual detachment: in other words, we discover the limitations imposed on us by the structure of our minds.

III. PSYCHOLOGICAL REALITIES AND THEIR CRITERIA

What are the phenomena to which we attribute psychological reality? Instinct and perception are both borderline concepts. We do not accord psychological reality to either the instinct stimulus or to the sensory stimulus; we accord it to all the mental responses activated by these stimuli and to all the endopsychic determinants of these responses. We find, moreover, that the psyche is not chaotic but is an ordered cosmos whose structure and laws we endeavour to infer from the data of subjective experience.

Our criterion of psychological reality, as such, is both dynamic and experiential. We understand, for instance, that we must accord equal subjective reality to hallucinations and to perceptions. As far as their psychological reality is concerned, they differ only in their *provenance*: hallucination is a response to current instinct and endopsychic stimuli, whereas perception is a response to a current sensory stimulus.

So far no difficulty arises. We tend to become confused when we realize that, in the face of these strictly psychological considerations, we remain convinced that there is a sense in which perception is more real than hallucination. We judge rightly that perception is more consonant with the actual situation of the individual in his immediate environment. What we accord to perception is the higher survival value of correct orientation towards the outer world. We can only avoid mental confusion if we remember that the criterion by which we judge perception to be more valid than hallucination is a criterion, not of psychological dynamism, but of biological or psycho-biological adaptation.

In grading psychological realities by psycho-biological criteria we see mind in functional perspective. We agree that psychological theory should be expressed in strictly psychological terms, because, apart from all other considerations, this rule works. Nevertheless, as scientists, our approach to psychology is fundamentally biological. We consider mind to be a product of evolution and the human being to be a unity, a psycho-physical organism whose mental functions have come to be his chief instrument of adaptation. We regard mind as the mediator between instinct and environment. This rôle of mediation has led not merely to a vast increase in the range and plasticity of human motor responses, including the mental motility we call thinking, but to the progressive development of ways and means of endopsychic adaptation. The complexity of our mental organization is now so great that we may say that human beings have definite psychological, in addition to basic organic, needs. Man cannot live without bread but he can no longer live fully by bread alone. It seems not improbable that all those human needs frequently called spiritual will, in course of time, be generally recognized as psychological needs.

It was not too difficult for the rationalists to show that many religious beliefs and dogmas were not corroborated by the findings of natural science. In the first flush of pride in the achievements of human reason it never occurred to them that they were dealing only with the superficial manifestations of profound needs which religion had at least appeased. We know more now about the intricate organization of the psyche. Although the argument from design does not convince us of the objective existence of God, it does induce in us a more becoming intellectual humility. We can appreciate that those who ascribe the modern chaos of human values to the breakdown of religion are not without some justification. The remedy they suggest, however, a return to obsolete dogma and ritual, seems to us on a level with recommending a return to hand industry as a cure for the social evils of industrial civilization. We need to discover how to live without the comfort of illusion and how to create new systems of value based on more realistic conceptions of our psychological necessities.

The inquiring mind runs special risks in exploring the bases of animism and religion. This is the region in which the desire to know is at all times liable to be squeezed out by pressure from both id and super-ego directions, and to be replaced by quite other drives. After all, our psychological reality sense is larval by comparison with our more efficient but still highly imperfect sense of external realities.

We can use our psycho-biological criteria of adaptation or survival value as a measure of consonance not only with external reality but with instinctual and endopsychic demands. We can say, for instance, that endopsychic adaptation is the more biologically realistic, the more adequately it evaluates the relation of instinct to its object. By this standard, also, hallucination is unrealistic because it reports instinct satisfaction, although what actually exists is instinct deprivation. The method of resolving ambivalence by idealization and denigration is also biologically unrealistic, because the idealized object is held to be far more satisfactory than it is in fact, and the denigrated object far more dangerous and frustrating. This method is employed by all of us to some extent but is none the less archaic. It is a commonplace that a major source of difficulty in adaptation is the persistence of methods of defence which have outgrown their utility and ceased to have current survival value.

At the present day it is an open question whether the human race has not now lost more than it may originally have gained by super-ego differentiation. We cannot suddenly undo the consequences of numberless years of evolution, but we may hope to learn how to supplement the deficiencies in what we may call our psychological reality sense. The life value of any given endopsychic adaptation can only be determined by psycho-biological criteria. Happiness is a psychological aim which can be attained in pathological euphoria, but it can only be reached and maintained with any degree of security when psycho-biological adaptation is effective, *i.e.* when instinct is achieving adequate direct or indirect satisfaction in relation to the outer world.

These topics are something of a digression here and will be more fully discussed in later chapters. It will be better to return now to the main subject of this chapter, the nature of metapsychology.

IV. METAPSYCHOLOGY AS 'PROCESS' THEORY

Concerning the description of psychic processes, Freud (1922a, p. 1) wrote that '. . . a presentation which seeks to estimate, not only the *topographical* and *dynamic*, but also the *economic* element is the most complete that we can at present imagine, and deserves to be distinguished by the term *metapsychological*'.

The topographical method of description was used by Freud in his initial formulations regarding the relation of the unconscious to consciousness and also in his later explanations of id, ego, and super-ego inter-relationships. Topographical description is, however, more relevant to brain anatomy and physiology than to psychology. Dynamic and economic terms seem intrinsically more appropriate to the strictly psychological description of mental processes.

The dynamic aspect of a process is its drive; description of this aspect usually involves reference to the intensity and quality of the drive. The economic aspect is the tension-regulating function; that is to say, the changes effected by the process in the endopsychic energy distribution. To describe a process as originating in a heightening of tension and as issuing in a resolution or relaxation of this tension is to describe it from the economic point of view. To-day, the term economic is more frequently used in reference to the distribution of energy between process-systems, the mental organizations, than in reference to individual processes. Since the distribution of energy between systems appears to be effected through the agency of so-called mental mechanisms, these mechanisms may be regarded as processes having specialized economic functions. Such processes regularly issue in endopsychic disposal of excitation and not in motor discharge.

Although the dynamic and economic aspects of a process are distinguishable and can be separately considered, they remain interdependent aspects of one process. The economic effect of any given process is intimately connected with the impetus and direction of its drive. It will be evident that metapsychology is not personal history but general theory; it is objective description in impersonal terms of mental processes and their organization, inferred from the study of personal experience and behaviour.

The argument of this chapter-section is that metapsychology is a process theory of mind. There is nothing original in this argument; it neither adds to, nor subtracts from, the present content of metapsychology; it is no more than an explicit statement of a point of view, a dynamic and economic 'Psycheanschauung' that has been implicit in theory since the publication of *The Ego and the Id* (Freud, 1927). The general theory of psycho-analysis, in its most abstract definition, is a psychology of mental processes and their organization. For such a psychology, mind has ceased to be a static structure or a substantial thing and has become a dynamic entity, a nexus of activities and a sequence of adaptive responses. Recognition that metapsychology belongs to the category of process thinking alters nothing in theory itself, but it at once relates psycho-analysis to the whole movement of modern scientific thought which is described by Waddington (1944, p. 48) as a '. . . movement away from analysing into things and towards analysing into processes'. To stress the advantage of recognizing process and organization as key concepts is not to imply any denigration of more specific hypotheses. The theory of the unconscious, for example, is enhanced rather than diminished in value by inclusion in the process theory of organization; the theory of organization, however, includes all mental processes, conscious and unconscious.

It is true that Freud himself does not appear to have drawn this conclusion in so many words. It is, nevertheless, implicit in his work and has been accepted more or less tacitly by analysts for some time. It is most clearly indicated by comparison and combination of his earlier with his later work. For instance, in 1899, he uses topographical description and mechanical analogy in elaborating what he calls the 'fiction' (Freud, 1932a, *Revised Trans.*, p. 550) of the psyche as an apparatus for the regulation of instinct tension. At the same time he leaves no doubt as to the dynamism or the continuity of psychic processes. He writes: 'All our psychic activities proceed from (inner or outer) stimuli and terminate in innervations' (*op. cit.* p. 495). In another passage he writes of a wish as a 'current in the apparatus' (*op. cit.* p. 550). Freud's earlier thinking was impeded in some ways by the mental climate of the period, which was mechanistic and associationist. In spite of this, it is difficult to read his chapter on 'The Psychology of the Dream-Processes' (*op. cit.* pp. 470-570) without coming to the conclusion that, for him, the theoretical unit of psychic life was always a complete, dynamic process.

In 1923, in *The Ego and the Id*, Freud recognized the so-called structure of mind as dependent on organization. He now defines the ego as a 'coherent organization of mental processes' (1927, p. 15). He attributes the differentiating grade in the ego, thenceforward called the super-ego, to post-Oedipal parental identifications 'in some way combined together' (*op. cit.* p. 44). He contrasts the unorganized id with the organized ego and super-ego. Freud often personified the ego, but this habit does not detract from the impersonal objectivity of its definition.

Thus Freud's work provides the key concepts of process and organization. Quotations such as the foregoing point to the conclusion that metapsychology is process theory, a conclusion that can readily be tested by a study of his books. We saw in Chapter I (p. 39) that as early as 1914 Freud wrote: 'It is impossible to suppose that a unity comparable to the ego can exist in the individual from the very start; the ego has to develop' (1914, *C.P.* iv, p. 34). But, even after 1923, it remained most natural to him to stress the coherence of the ego, and he continued to envisage its development mainly as the growth of a unitary ego from weakness to strength. We also noted that Edward Glover (1932c) was the first person to appreciate the developmental significance of the new definition. He suggested that a coherent ego-organization is reached by the progressive integration of more primitive and relatively independent ego-systems, which he termed 'ego-nuclei'. In a more recent paper (1943, p. 12) he concludes that 'structurally, the strength of the ego depends on the degree of integration of various early nuclear components. . . . The weakness of the ego depends on the degree to which early nuclei retain energy and are capable of a degree of autonomic function—in this way preventing mental energies from being distributed amongst more integrated layers.'

The process view of mind is the objective equivalent of the complex interplay of subjective urgencies that analysts glimpse from time to time in moments of insight into the directives of personal life. It is in terms of process-concepts that we may hope gradually to systematize metapsychology. Freud did not formulate a complete and finished theory; what he provided was the groundwork of a scientific psychology, a beginning and not an end. The numerous gaps in psycho-analytic knowledge, the confusions in terminology, and the inconsistencies in theory, including those in Freud's own writings, make it clear that formidable tasks lie ahead. Indeed, it becomes increasingly evident that every aspect of analytic theory calls for re-examination in the light of process-concepts. As scientists, analysts must not use Freud's own formulations as immutable standards by which to measure the validity of new hypotheses: Freud's work cannot be both a 'Bed of Procrustes' and a 'Pierian Spring' (cf. Jones, 1946,

p. 11). But in his dynamic and economic conceptions of mental life Freud opened to us a theoretical approach, a view of mind, sufficiently inclusive in its scope and sufficiently plastic in detail to allow for any modification of subsidiary hypotheses that may now be found necessary.

Progress in metapsychology is essential to the furtherance of psycho-analysis as a science. Constant revision of theory is not all that is necessary, nor is it an end in itself; it is no more than a means to understanding and thus to control of the psychological conditions of human living. Human beings do not live theoretically, they live personally; '. . . the psychologist has not to deal with ideas but with persons acting' (Wolters, 1943, p. 183). Abstract thinking, however, has its own contributions to make to the service of persons.

The conclusion that metapsychology is process theory seems to the writer inescapable. The more detailed considerations that follow concerning the nature of mental processes and mental organization do not constitute a systematic review of theory nor do they propose final conclusions. They are comments on selected points, and any suggestions made are tentative in character.

V. MENTAL PROCESSES

In metapsychology it is assumed that the mental process is the hypothetical unit of psychic life. It is tempting, though undoubtedly rash, to borrow terms from physical science and to say that, dynamically, a process may be conceived as a wave of activity and, economically, as a quantum of energy. It is safer, perhaps, only to distinguish the dynamic aspect, the drive, from the economic aspect, the quantity of excitation or mental energy involved. The right of psychologists to use the term energy is not universally conceded, but analysts find it useful, as some quantitative term is needed to make clear the distinction between the impetus and the direction of mental activity. In Fenichel's opinion (1946, p. 14), 'The concept of a "quantity" of mental energy is exactly as justifiable or unjustifiable as the introduction of other scientific working concepts that have proved practical'.

Processes are initiated by inner and outer stimuli. Analysts, however, regard instinct as the prime mover, the continuous stimulus to psychic activity. They do not under-estimate the part played by external stimuli in evoking and modifying responses and in canalizing the paths of instinct-expression in the outer world but they regard these responses to external stimuli as motivated and sustained by instinctual drives. We respond to the external stimuli to which we are predisposed to respond; our sensory sampling of the outer world picks out stimuli that are of instinctual interest. We live in a Universe common to all but we also live in individual worlds carved out for us by our specific personal interest-systems. Instinct shapes the individual world but environment exercises a selective influence upon instinct. The relationship between organism and environment is neatly expressed by the use of genetical terms, which Hollitscher (1943) recently employed in a different connection. The phenotype (the individual organism as it appears) is the resultant of the interaction of the genotype (the innate potentialities) and the environment (which favours the development of some potentialities and impedes the development of others). The analyst can safely regard his phenotype, the human being, as a psycho-physical organism whose personality results from the interaction of his instinctual endowment with his psycho-physical environment. The analyst must constantly remember, however, that in the human being interaction is effected mainly through the agency of mental processes, and that these are conditioned by their mental organization as well as by instinct and environment. Human adaptation may be said to be multi-polar rather than bi-polar interaction, since the evolution of mental mediation has developed a variety of endopsychic conditions that have to be satisfied in addition to those imposed by instinct and environment.

Instinct is another term open to criticism, but its analytic use is unambiguous. It refers to the innate needs of the organism which stimulate mental drives and has no reference to unlearned motor behaviour. Instinct is described as a borderline concept because the organic need is distinguished from the mental drives to which it gives rise; thus, for example, the sexual instinct is regarded as stimulating libidinal mental drives. Libido is a group name for the total of libidinal drives generated in the psyche by sexual stimuli. The exact relation between physiological instinct-tension and mental energy need not be considered here. It is enough to recognize instinct as the stimulus to psychic activity and to assume that psychic activity will continue as long as its stimuli are operative.

The mental process-response to the instinct-stimulus reaches its goal either with the innervation of the musculature or with the activation of further mental processes. The latter, in their turn, may issue in the mental motility called thinking, or in the unconscious behaviour called mental defence. Dynamically, a mental defence-mechanism is an endopsychic vicissitude of instinct. All those other vicissitudes of instinct variously called symptom - formations, sublimation, etc., not excluding ego-differentiation, result from the continued operation of instinct-stimuli on a psyche modified by the activation of defence-mechanisms. Where the primary path of discharge is blocked, energy is diverted by circuitous routes to secondary outlets and instinct thus acquires new avenues of expression. It is more accurate to speak of the organization of the ways of instinct-discharge, which is the sequel to the endopsychic organization of mental process-responses, than of the organization of instinct itself. It is not the instinct-stimuli which become organized but the adaptive responses and the channels of discharge. The distinction between free-flowing primary processes and secondary processes may be theoretically desirable, but it is of evolutionary rather than practical importance, since both grati-fication and frustration occur from birth onwards, if not before and during birth. If the economic law of the psyche is that frustration of a primary process activates secondary processes, then, hypothetically, the infant's first hallucination is the result of secondary processes activated by the first experience of frustra-tion severe enough to fulfil whatever quantitative conditions may be necessary to provoke hallucination.

All processes are alike in that they are waves or currents of activity, but they differ among themselves both in impetus (in-tensity of drive, energy) and in direction (trend or quality of drive). Impetus seems to be correlated with the intensity and frequency of instinct-stimuli and trend with their specific character. For convenience, processes may be said to differ quantitatively and qualitatively, but trend or direction are probably better process-terminology than quality. Whichever term is used, it is evident that, for example, the process-equivalent of an erotic wish differs in direction or quality from the process-equivalent of a murderous wish and both of these differ from the trends activated during a moment of intense concentration on a mathematical problem.

The hypothetical unit of experience corresponding to the hypothetical unit-process is not an atomic impulse, affect, or presentation, but a relationship of impulse, affect, and presentation. This is true whether these aspects of experience are recognizable, as in the adult, or undifferentiated, as we presume them to be in the new-born infant. Hypothetical units are convenient figments to illustrate the parallelism between subjective reaction and objective wave of activity, but, in fact, the simplest conscious experience is probably the equivalent of a whole series of processes. The point it is sought to emphasize is that, whether viewed subjectively as experience, or objectively as process-activation, mental life is a sequence of adaptive responses. This conception seems indispensable and is frequently implied in Freud's use of the term 'wish', though, on occasion, 'wish' is used in a more limited sense as the equivalent of instinctual impulse ('conative tendency'). Analysts can agree with Wolters that thinking is adaptive behaviour and should join him in abandoning the 'mythology of ideal entities' (Wolters, 1943, p. 181), but they do no violence to process-thinking in retaining the differentiation between the conative, affective and cognitive aspects of subjective experience.

To psycho-analysts it is the difference between conscious and unconscious processes that appears to be of major dynamic and economic importance. They regard consciousness as pertaining to processes belonging to the so-called reality-ego organization, and unconscious processes as either naturally unconscious or actively prevented from becoming conscious by mental mechanisms. The organization of the ego is not itself regarded as conscious. Consciousness, at any one moment, is the functional synthesis resulting from the current activation of the ego organization. Wilhelm Dilthey, recently introduced to English readers by H. A. Hodges (1944), stressed the 'functional unity' of mental life but failed to grasp the full complexity and lability of mental organization. Conscious processes are always accompanied and partially determined by unconscious processes, but the latter may be activated without giving rise to conscious processes. The continuity of mental life is not affected by interruptions of consciousness, since it is dependent on the uninterrupted activation of unconscious processes.

The progressive patterning of systems of response, that is, process-organization, depends upon retention and modification which appear to be twin characteristics of mental life as fundamental as excitability itself. It is sometimes argued that retention is manifested only through modification, that is, that all that is really retained of an experience is the modification effected by it which influences future experience. Clinical data support the view that modification is an invariable effect of retention, that it is independent of conscious recall, and that it occurs whether or not the modifying experience is accessible to consciousness. Clinical data, on the other hand, do not support the view that retention only operates through modification. Happenings like the re-emergence of long repressed memories of early childhood into adult consciousness give the analyst grounds for assuming that, if certain economic conditions be fulfilled, any past experience can be revived in something closely approximating to its original form. In metapsychological terms, it seems probable to analysts that any process-system that has once been activated can be re-activated and, further, that it can be re-activated either as an independent system (in which case the subjective experience is revived in memory if it is accessible to consciousness) or as a component of another process-system which it modifies. Psycho-analysts can, therefore, express the facts of retention by saying that experience registers in the psyche in such a way that it can be revived as experience or memory, and also in such a way that subsequent experience is invariably modified by preceding experience. Freud's 'law of psychological determinism' is a mechanistic rendering of the operation of retention and modification.

Under the influence of associationist terminology, Freud (1932a, p. 495) called the registrations of experience in the psyche memory-traces and assumed that they are themselves unconscious but that their re-activation gives rise to images. Image-formation certainly appears to depend upon retention. It is agreed that sensory-affective experience must precede either hallucination or imagination. But images are not revived in isolation, they are revived in relation to their original impulsive and affective concomitants. Federn (1938) attributed his ultimate recognition of a vaguely familiar face to the reawakening of the ego-states previously connected with this face; *i.e.* the memory (name and circumstances) resulted from the revival of the past ego-situation. Hence, memory-traces are probably better thought of as experience-traces rather than as sensory-traces. To describe the mental organizations as systems of memory-traces is inadequate unless the memory-trace is regarded, objectively, as a response- or process-trace. Traces need not be thought of as literal imprints stamped in the mind but as functional predispositions. The so-called structure imparted to the psyche by organization is a predisposing pattern of response. Edward Glover (1947b, p. 1) includes the 'memory-trace' in his basic concepts, which thus form a triad: 'In the dynamic sense, the concept of instinctual *energy*; in the structural sense, the concept of a *memory trace*, and in the economic sense, the *mobility of quantities* of instinctual energy'.

It may be that retention and 'repetition-compulsion' (Freud, 1922a, p. 24) are two ways of describing one characteristic of mental life. Perhaps we should assume that, once a given process has been activated by a specific stimulus, it will be re-activated by every succeeding stimulus of the same type. Such an assumption makes it far easier to understand modification and the genetic continuity of mental life. It becomes natural rather than surprising that even an old man of ninety should continue to be actively influenced by events which occurred during the first six months of his life. The simplest explanation is not necessarily the most adequate, particularly in psychology. It may be noted, however, that Freud's conception of a repetition-compulsion 'beyond' the pleasure principle is a conception that the primordial tendency of processes is to repeat themselves. This tendency can, on occasion, overcome the tendency to avoid pain although the normal relation to pleasure and pain is that the tendency to repetition is reinforced by adaptive success (pleasure) and inhibited by adaptive failure (pain). Such a conception agrees with biological and physiological thought concerning the development and functions of the nervous system and makes reflex action the prototype of repetition-compulsion; it is consistent, so far as I can judge, with many of the results of experimental inquiry into memory and habit-formation, and is borne out by the ordinary experience of everyday life. For instance, if one forms a habit of spelling a word wrongly and this mistake is pointed out, one may, with more or less difficulty, correct the habit, or rather, form a new habit of spelling the word correctly. But every time that one is fatigued, or preoccupied with the content rather than with the form of what is being written, the faulty spelling will tend to recur. The obvious inference is that the mental energy required to inhibit the old habit in favour of the new is either not available or is otherwise engaged.

Psycho-analysts are probably on firm ground in regarding

instinct as the constant stimulus to psychic activity, but Freud's remark (1933, p. 124) that 'the theory of the instincts is, as it were, our mythology' still holds good. To my mind, the field of instinct enumeration and classification is very debatable ground. The existence of numerous polarities in mental life is indisputable, as is also the fact that the interplay between what psychoanalysts call libido and aggression is a cardinal feature of mental economy. I do not propose to enter here into the arguments for and against the assumption of a 'death instinct' or into the reasons for this seemingly unfortunate choice of term. I will limit myself to the suggestion that the conception of classes of instinct may prove more satisfactory than the conception of unitary instincts. Instincts manifest themselves in a succession of specific drives and it is open to argument that more than two classes of instinct are required. Up to the present, psycho-analysts seem reluctant to accord full instinct status to self-preservation, though they safeguard themselves by admitting that the group of life instincts is not necessarily limited to the sex instincts. It may be that a number of different instincts are comprised in the death class, some of which belong elsewhere. Loewenstein (1940), sharing Hartmann's view that the self-preservative instincts were unduly neglected and objecting for various reasons to the conception of a 'death instinct', or of an instinct of aggression, as such, proposed a return to Freud's original dual classification of love and hunger, libido and ego-instincts, in the form of sexual and 'vital instincts of self-preservation' or 'somatic instincts'. He would regard aggression as belonging to the somatic group. Simmel (1945) regards destructive energies as manifestations of self-preservation and the latter as essentially libidinal in nature although it can be object-destructive. The main point to note is that in the present state of knowledge, the theory of instinct ought not to be regarded as a closed chapter. On the contrary, many conceptions of instinct are still 'superb in their indefiniteness' (Freud, *op. cit.* p. 124).

VI. ORGANIZATION, INTEGRATION, DISSOCIATION

Turning from process to organization, there is a great deal yet to be learned about the exact ways and means by which relatively stable ego and super-ego organizations develop and maintain themselves, and also about the temporary changes of pattern which continually occur within these major organizations. One difficulty arising in Freud's formulation of the threefold constitution of mind must be faced at the outset. It is contradictory to regard the id as an unorganized reservoir of instinct and, at the same time, to regard the repressed as part of the id. Clinical experience insists that the repressed is organized and that its organization continues during life. Freud himself (1927, p. 29) indicated a solution, because he not only defined the ego as a coherent organization of mental processes but as 'that part of the id which has been modified by the direct influence of the external world'. The repressed may be regarded as a reject from the ego and there are other reasons for considering repressed systems to be dissociated primitive ego-systems. Whether any reservoir of instinct can be said to exist apart from the constantly recurring stimuli of organic need is debatable. The endopsychic economy itself constitutes a reserve of mental energy, inasmuch as the operation of mental mechanisms binds energy which is released for other purposes if defence breaks down or some less expensive mechanism of control becomes available.

Clinical justification for the concept of the id is supplied by observations of adults in whom dread of uncontrollable impulse and overwhelming emotion is marked. This is often associated both with conscious and unconscious dread of revival of painful past experiences and with a variety of animistic anxieties, amongst which fear of being at the mercy of some brand of 'devil inside' is perhaps the most common. In reference to a psyche in which definitive ego and super-ego organizations have established themselves, the concept of the id would seem to cover all those process-systems which do not appear to belong to the current ego or super-ego. In this relatively late stage of development, the id-systems may be said to represent the infant's own primitive wishes (or such of them as are ego-dystonic) and the super-ego the parental counter-wishes. It seems most probable that ego-synthesis and ego-differentiation begin, proceed, and culminate together in the emergence of definitive ego and super-ego organizations, leaving systems dystonic to both to constitute id-'nuclei'. It is, however, extremely difficult to decide whether the ego-differentiations which occur in intermediary stages, such as those mirrored in animistic phantasies, would be more accurately described as id- or super-ego-nuclei. This is one among the many obscure problems of development that await further clarification.

Certain other points regarding the development of organization will be discussed later, but, before considering these, a brief reference must be made to the general nature of organization. Mental life is paradoxical in that it is both conservative and progressive, repetitive and creative, and it is well not to overlook this paradox. The effects of past experience are preserved in the mental organization through which they influence current experience. Relatively stable organization implies the canalization of responses into habitual patterns and carries with it differing degrees of loss of plasticity in response. Organization thus tends to limit the range of reactions possible to any given individual. The mental organization, in detail, will be as specific as the individual's personal experience. Characteristic types of organization are, however, recognizable and are implied in all classifications of libidinal, character or clinical types. But this conservative and predetermining rôle of organization should not lead us to think of organization as permanently fixed; mental organization is not static shape but constant renewal of functional pattern. It is accepted that repression is not a single act but a course of action that has to be maintained, and it should also be accepted that organization is perpetual reorganization even where plasticity is reduced to such an extent that the successive reorganizations become almost stereotyped repetitions.

Psycho-analysts rightly emphasize the continuity of mental life, which is, for them, one of the best established facts. Hence, they cannot agree with the view expressed by H. G. Wells (1944) that personality is an illusion. His opinions are, however, very useful reminders that mental life is not only continuous but also continually new. We are the same people to-day that we were yesterday in so far as there has been no interruption in our mental lives, and what we are to-day is largely determined by what we were yesterday. But we are also new people to-day in so far as we encounter a new series of stimuli, and are re-synthesized from moment to moment in response to these stimuli. When we feel that we are 'not ourselves' or 'surprise ourselves', the reorganization of the moment is following an unaccustomed pattern. Mental life is progressive or emergent because the re-synthesis of the moment is not only conditioned by what has happened in the past but by what actually is happening in the present. The current synthesis is always the resultant of what we are when we meet the new situation and what the new situation brings to us.

Integration is not mere summation. For instance, the reality-ego as a whole is more than the sum of its component systems. Integration is always relative, never absolute, and organization varies both in stability and in adaptive efficiency. Integration of the personality as a whole is not to be confused with integration of the reality-ego alone since this is only one of the major systems. Integration of the personality implies a degree of harmonization between super-ego-, ego-, and id-drives which amounts to some degree of integration of the total psyche. Experience leads to the assumption that a sufficient number of closely knit process-systems are so regularly integrated with the major ego-organizations in the same functional pattern that they enable the ordinary person to retain his identity. Even in the normal person, however, it is assumed that there are frequent changes in the subsidiary component-systems of the ego and super-ego. The functional integration of the psycho-analyst at work with a patient in his consulting-room is not the same as it is when he is reading the newspaper by his own fireside. In the consulting-room his reality-ego, for instance, is temporarily dominated by component-systems which are no longer in control when he is relaxed at leisure. We assume temporary changes in ego-pattern of this type in the same way that we assume temporary changes in range and scope by way of synthesis and dissociation. The clue to multiple personality may lie in switching from one major pattern to another, in kaleidoscopic changes of process-pattern more thoroughgoing than those which accompany normal changes of mood or occupation.

Any system functionally integrated with the ego-organization operates for the time being through that organization and does not exert independent influence. Its energy is at the disposal of the ego. A system dissociated from the ego regains its independence except in so far as it may link up with other ego-dissociated systems (*i.e.* with super-ego- or id-systems). Its energy is not at the disposal of the ego. Permanently dissociated systems can be thought of either as primitive ego-systems which have never formed part of the definitive ego-organization, or as systems dissociated at a later stage. In either event, a dissociated system operates in competition with the ego and is potentially pathogenic. If the group of processes corresponding to the clinical

'Oedipus complex' is dissociated as a whole, it can operate as a pathological *enclave*, with all the familiar neurotic consequences. What Freud (1924b) called the 'passing of the Oedipus complex' can most readily be understood as a distribution of its component systems between the ego- and super-ego-organizations. When this happens, the Oedipal systems play their part thenceforward through the ego and super-ego and cease to operate independently, whereas, in neurosis, they constitute relatively independent centres of activity. It was said in Chapter III (p. 80) that some psycho-analysts consider that Melanie Klein's views on the genetic importance of infantile phantasy introduce false notions of an unchangeable *enclave* in the unconscious. This impression may be chiefly due to the fact that she stresses the enduring influence of infantile experience and does not clearly emphasize the difference between two different economic situations. In one an early phantasy-system is functionally integrated with the ego-system and operates through it, as in the case of successful sublimation; in another situation a phantasy-system retains or regains its autonomy and operates independently, as in the case of compulsive action.

The difference between temporary ego-synthesis and temporary ego-dissociation can be illustrated by reference to conscious memory. For example, when we meet an old friend our greeting will be determined by our past experience of this friend, but, at the moment of meeting, we may recognize and welcome such a friend without recalling any single incident from the past. The mental systems connected with the friend here act as component-systems functionally synthesized with the ego-organization. In the course of conversation it may happen that an incident from our common past may be recalled, but the re-activation which yields the conscious memory temporarily dissociates the corresponding systems from the remembering ego-system. Though readily accessible to consciousness, such memories, while being recalled, have a temporary 'not me' quality which we may express by saying, 'Do you remember that we did such and such a thing?' Memories have the quality of full 'me-ness' only if they are so vivid and gripping that one temporarily ceases to be a 'remembering me' and re-lives the past for the moment as if it were present.

These comments on the nature of mental organization are far from exhaustive. They seek to emphasize only two points of cardinal importance: first, that mental organization involves continual reorganization and, second, that although mental life is conditioned by organization, it is also emergent or new from moment to moment. It is adaptive activity, and the living being is always becoming.

VII. THE BEARING OF METAPSYCHOLOGY (PROCESS THEORY) ON THE INTERNAL DEVELOPMENT OF PSYCHO-ANALYSIS AND ON PUBLIC RELATIONS

It was emphasized in Section IV of this chapter that recognition of the fact that metapsychology belongs to 'process' categories of thought does not modify the content of theory in any respect; it simply 'places' metapsychology in the scientific universe of discourse. But this recognition is not without significance for the internal development of psycho-analysis. For instance, it has a bearing on the problem of defining psycho-analysis as a whole since it is clearly more consonant with liberal definitions (provided these remain true to fundamental principles) than with elaborate and detailed 'strait-jacket' definitions. Again, a grasp of the unitary nature of psychic processes and their inevitable flow from initiation to resolution and of the complicated interplay between instinctual, endo-psychic, and environmental factors at work in 'organization', is a useful aid in assessing new contributions for balance or extremism; it favours a sense of proportion and is incompatible with developments in theory which emphasize one factor or aspect of mental life to the undue exclusion of others. Thus metapsychology confirms the importance of cultural factors in the patterning of the ego-organization but it contradicts any purely or predominantly cultural theory of personality development and personality disturbance, such as that now sponsored by Karen Horney (*e.g.* Horney, 1946).

Psycho-analysis is so young that its findings, as distinct from its basic principles, are necessarily incomplete, and it is inevitable that, in the course of its growth, switches of interest should occur from one aspect of mental life to another, which tend to focus attention and produce temporary over- and under-emphases in one or another direction. It seems to be the general opinion, in the United States (see Zilboorg *et al.*, 1945) as in this country, that psycho-analysis is passing through a period of internal crisis. It is just in stormy weather that metapsychology can aid in keeping the ship on an even keel. Psycho-analysis must preserve its own balance if it is to render any aid to the wider world crisis (Bion, 1948). The trend to fission, *i.e.* the tendency of authors of new ideas and critics of older views to dissociate themselves from the parent movement and initiate fractional or derivative schools of their own, may have been unavoidable in the past, but is not a very healthy trend. For wholesome and balanced growth, psycho-analysis requires continuous self-criticism and tentative modification from within. There is both need and ample scope for active minds within its limits. A sense of perspective inspired by metapsychology would certainly hinder, rather than foster, the development of personal idiosyncrasies into full-blown alternative theories of mental life.

It is perhaps in the sphere of public relations that more general recognition of the 'process' nature of metapsychology could have most immediate and potential significance. The implications of psycho-analysis are so wide that these public relations are many-sided and far-reaching. Hitherto psycho-analysts have concerned themselves mainly with relations with the lay public and with other 'applied' professional groups, *e.g.* psychiatry, medical psychology in general, education, and such mixed groups as child guidance and delinquency. In the past there has been cause for dissatisfaction with these relations but they seem at present to be definitely improving. An aspect of public relations that has been comparatively neglected is that with other 'pure' sciences, although this is a sphere that will become increasingly important. The institution of the 'Ernest Jones Lectures', the first two of which were delivered to the British Psycho-Analytical Society by Professor Adrian (1946) and Professor Waddington (1947), is a decisive step in this direction. Relations with sociology have developed more rapidly in the United States than in this country, but there is now in being in London the Tavistock Institute of Human Relations, to which a number of psycho-analysts belong and which publishes, in collaboration with the Ann Arbor (Mich. U.S.A.) Research Centre for Group Dynamics, *Human Relations*, a quarterly journal of studies towards the integration of the social sciences. The need for more adequate co-operation among all sciences bearing directly on human life problems is urgent; isolationism can only render them, individually and collectively, less effective than the older established so-called natural sciences that have so profoundly altered our environmental conditions.

In regard to the lay public we are in a similar position to any other specialists. We can disseminate knowledge of psycho-analysis in as simple a form as possible; we can also discuss the bearing of psycho-analytic findings on matters of current interest and indicate potential applications. One practical hint which works is probably more convincing to the layman than volumes of simplified theory. In many fields we do not yet possess the detailed knowledge which would enable us to give practical advice.

Relations with the lay public and with other professional groups involve a certain amount of general theory but, on the whole, they involve a much higher proportion of 'applied' as distinct from 'pure' science. Psychopathology is a kind of half-way house between 'applied' and 'pure' science, although our psychopathology is even more closely interwoven with our general theory than medical pathology is with physiology. It is our 'pure' psychology, our general theory of mind, which is most likely to serve as a bridge between psycho-analysis and the 'pure' sciences and which has most to offer towards the eventual unification of scientific psychology.

To speak of the unification of psychology at this date may seem ironical and futile: nowhere is the infinite variety of the human mind better illustrated than in the multiplicity of current psychologies. But let us look for a moment at conditions in sciences such as physics or biology which have achieved some degree of coherence. How, and in what respect, are they unified? As a rule we find general agreement about data. We also find agreement at the point farthest from the initial data, *i.e.* in the general principles which provide the most comprehensive cover for the data. In between the data and the general principles there are often differences of opinion and rival hypotheses. For instance, all physicists subscribe to that fundamental view of the universe which they call the energy concept. But there are two theories regarding the nature of light, the quantum and the wave theory. Each was deduced from experimental data and each provides an adequate explanation of its own data. It is only quite recently that theories have been formulated (by Dirac, Heisenberg, and others) which combine these initially irreconcilable hypotheses. All biologists subscribe to the theory of evolution, but there are many and diverse views as to the mechanism of the process.

Such differences do not disturb the unity of the sciences as a whole, partly because there is agreement about data and general principles, but mainly because the differences resolve themselves as knowledge progresses. A striking example of the reconciliation of previously rival concepts occurred a few years ago in neurophysiology (Fulton and Nachmansohn, 1943). Previously the transmission of impulses across synapses was held to be either a chemical or an electro-motive phenomenon. In 1943 it was discovered that acetylcholine metabolism is intrinsically connected with the electrical changes occurring everywhere at the neuronal surface.

In Freud's dynamic and economic theories of mental life and in his view of mental 'structure' as organization, we already have concepts as general and as comprehensive as the energy concept in physics or the concept of evolution in biology. The importance of this to our public relations lies in the fact that notions of this kind are not limited to psycho-analysis. Fundamentally comparable ideas are present in brain physiology and in some other schools of psychology. To give only one or two examples. Progressive organization and integration are the key to all Sherrington's thinking about brain and mind. The concept of organization is central to the Gestalt school. One original psycho-analyst has effected a personal revision of psycho-analysis, largely under the influence of Gestalt conceptions (Perls, 1947). Head's concept of a 'postural schema' has had a stimulant effect on English psychologists (see Oldfield and Zangwill, 1942, p. 43), particularly on the thought of Bartlett and Wolters (*e.g.* Wolters, 1943). M. D. Vernon has carried out a series of inquiries into the influence of schemata on perception, etc. (*e.g.* Vernon, 1947, p. 48). Current views about mental schemata are, in some respects, very close indeed to psycho-analytical ideas about component mental systems.

It is clear that dynamic and economic conceptions of mental life are becoming ever more prevalent among psychologists and human scientists in general. It may be that the basic principles which could lead to a kind of federal union amongst a number of autonomous disciplines are already in being, though not yet recognized as such. What seems less open to doubt is the use that we could make of those aspects of our theory that are not limited to psycho-analysis. It is in our general notions of mental processes and their organization and the correlated ideas of integration and differentiation, synthesis, and dissociation, that we may find our most likely and convenient means of improving our relations with other sciences. Metapsychology is general theory but it is psychology; it is derived by inference from the detailed study of living persons. It is, however, no longer subjective but objective psychology, and, because it is objective and impersonal, it may prove more adaptable than subjective theory to some forms of experiment and mathematical expression. An interesting attempt was made by the late W. Baggally (1947) to give mathematical formulation to ego-theory.

Process thinking is a kind of thinking familiar to modern biologists, physiologists, and experimental psychologists, and the language of our general theory is therefore better known to other scientists than the more private clinical jargon that serves us very well but is often abhorrent and meaningless to them. The better they understand and appreciate the quality of our general theory, the more respect they are likely to acquire for our more detailed hypotheses and for the hitherto suspect research technique by which we have arrived at them. It is surprising how often the significance of modern psycho-analytic theory fails to be appreciated by non-analysts, however well informed they may be of Freud's earlier work. Even Sherrington, who is so up to date in other respects and who recognizes Freud's work as a great advance in the study of mind, writes of 'the unconscious of Freud which is only temporarily unconscious and has been conscious once and may be again' (1940, p. 307).

On the other hand, many sociologists and other experimentalists are fully alive to the relevance of psycho-analytic conceptions to their own spheres of research and are utilizing them in their work, *e.g.* the team investigation into the relation between frustration and aggression carried out at the Yale Institute of Human Relations (Dollard *et al.* 1944) and the 'field theory' work initiated by Lewin. In his last book, Kimball Young summarizes and discusses (1947, p. 230) the various methods of studying personality now in use and says of psycho-analytic theory (*op. cit.* p. 283): 'Actually, psychologists and psychiatrists and social scientists are constantly engaged in testing, more or less adequately, various features of the theory. No doubt, in time, this theory will merge with others to form one which we hope will be more adequate than any we now have.' Many of these undertakings are listed in his Bibliography. Hartmann and Kris (1945) and Kris (1947) have commented on these favourable trends to experimental validation, but have pointed out, particularly in their critical discussion of 'field work', that not all psycho-analytic propositions are equally amenable to experimental investigation. 'Dynamic propositions', involving only present-day situations, are easier to test than 'genetic propositions' which involve developmental history. So far the greater portion of this type of work has been carried out in the United States.

VIII. THE PROBLEM OF RESEARCH TRAINING

In view of all these 'experimental' developments, the question arises as to what special training may be desirable for psycho-analysts with a bent for research, who may not wish to limit themselves to the minimal responsibility for clinical verification mentioned at the beginning of this chapter. It is obviously desirable that such intending or fully fledged psycho-analysts should familiarize themselves with all that is going on in the experimental field and should understand the principles underlying current techniques and statistical methods. Advances in psychoanalytic theory itself, and, perhaps more likely, advances in application, may well emerge from experimental work, but it should never be forgotten and may, therefore, be repeated here, that the consulting-room has been, and still remains, the principal laboratory of psycho-analysis. Clinical practice can degenerate into a more or less sterile routine, equally fatal to therapy and to research, but provided the psycho-analyst retains his capacity to adapt himself to, and to learn from, his patients, ten years' practice will teach him more essential facts about human nature than ten years' work in an experimental laboratory. It is true that all the factors which enter into the psycho-analytic situation are by no means fully understood as yet, and it is rich in sources of error, but the psycho-analyst's daily work offers him a series of informative relationships with living persons. It offers this under conditions in which, despite or, perhaps, because of the lack of strict control and standardization, far more of the intimate pattern and developmental story of personal life comes to light than is ever revealed in ordinary social intercourse or under such experimental conditions as have hitherto been devised. Hence, it is to be expected that decisive advances in psycho-analytic theory will continue to derive from the consulting-room. Collaboration between clinician and experimentalist is greatly to be desired, but the psycho-analyst who wishes to contribute the fullest value in any such partnership should be well grounded in clinical experience.

Apart from native ability and personal interest, which are here taken for granted, clinical experience is the basic equipment for psycho-analytic research. Whatever the main aim of practice, whether therapy, research, or a combination of both, the indispensable training for clinical work is personal analysis. It is only possible to understand other people's feelings and impulses in so far as one is able to recognize and tolerate one's own. Being must here precede knowing; one must become self-aware and develop some degree of subjective reality-sense before one can hope to grow in knowledge of other personalities and of mental life in general. It is far more difficult to maintain a 'scientific attitude' in psychology than in the less intimately personal sciences, like physics. This is more true of psycho-analysis than of other branches of psychology, for the simple reason that the farther we penetrate into the maze of unconscious life, the more likely we are to lose a strictly realistic approach. For example, it is easy to understand that one can scarcely recognize or assess, in another person, a specific type of anxiety of which one cannot tolerate awareness in oneself. It is perhaps less easy to appreciate the persuasive influence that one's personal way of dealing with a specific anxiety may exert upon one's apprehension and evaluation of it. Inability to tolerate one or other aspect of subjective reality is one of the more important factors responsible for secessions and the formation of derivative movements. Persuasion by the structure of one's own mind can be a strong incentive to turn a personal solution into a new school Hence the chief safeguard against fissiparous trends lies in the hope of strengthening subjective reality sense in one generation of psycho-analysts after another and in a consequent improvement of 'scientific' spirit. Hence the importance of personal analysis, followed by a period of clinical work, in training for psycho-analytic research. If the time eventually comes, as it may, when therapy becomes relatively less important than theory and its more general social and prophylactic applications, ample provision for this indispensable basic training will still have to be made if a healthy growth of knowledge is to be ensured.

The human sciences as a group are still in their infancy. Every branch of science has to devise its own most appropriate methods of reality-testing and there will, doubtless, be much argument as well as trial and error in procedure before satisfactory techniques of psychological research are generally accepted and practised. It should be remembered, however, that a basis of agreement already exists among scientists in the attitude of mind with which they approach their work. In so far as the scientist desires to establish the facts as they are, rather than as he wishes them to be, or thinks they ought to be, he is at one with all other scientists. In psychology, the subjective hindrances to progress in knowledge are probably more formidable than any technical difficulties, and the limits of research for any individual are set by the degree of his ability to tolerate psychological realism.

CHAPTER V

METAPSYCHOLOGY AND PERSONOLOGY [1]

I. DEFINITIONS AND ORIENTATIONS

THE word 'personology' is borrowed from Smuts as a convenient term to distinguish the science of personality from metapsychology. Referring to academic psychology, Smuts writes: '. . . The procedure of psychology is largely and necessarily analytical and cannot therefore do justice to Personality in its unique wholeness. For this a new discipline is required, which we have called Personology, and whose task it would be to study Personality as a whole and to trace the laws and phases of its development in the individual life. . . . Personology would study the Personality not as an abstraction or bundle of psychological abstractions, but rather as a vital organism, as the organic psychic whole which *par excellence* it is; and such a study should lead to the formulation of the laws of the growth of this unique whole, which would not only be of profound theoretical importance, but also of the greatest practical value' (Smuts, 1926, p. 293). Although Smuts does not himself recognize psycho-analysis as a pioneer scientific personology, this passage gives a fairly accurate description of one of the major aims of psycho-analytic research.

It is advisable for psycho-analysts to emphasize that they study people not as abstract problems but as more or less well integrated living persons. The term 'psycho-analysis' is misleading when, as happens too often, it is understood to imply that psycho-analysts have no interest in synthesis. While they are trying to disentangle and trace the history of the various components of the total personality pattern, they are inevitably confronted with all the phenomena of synthesis and dissociation which have determined that pattern. Therapeutic success is proportionate to the degree and kind of re-integration initiated by the psycho-analytic process.

[1] Reprinted, slightly revised, from 'Further Notes on the Implications of Psycho-Analysis: Metapsychology and Personology', *Int. J. Psycho-Anal.*, 1945, vol. xxvi, p. 89.

Psycho-analytic personology is a psychology, not an anatomy or physiology, of personality; it is concerned with subjective experience and the motivation of behaviour. There is little objection to describing psycho-analysis as a science of human behaviour, *provided behaviour is understood to include mental, or endopsychic, as well as motor activity.* The biological integrity of man is not in question. The human being is accepted as a biological unity, a psycho-physical organism living in reciprocal relationship with a psycho-physical (or socio-physical) environment. Mental life is regarded as man's chief instrument of adaptation or of mediation between individual necessity and environmental possibility. It is the greater development of his mental life that distinguishes man from other animals: the psycho-analyst, like the biologist, sees this distinctive mental development as the result of natural evolution. Where psycho-analysts differ from many biologists and also from many psychologists, is in their clearer apprehension of the intricate mental organization which has arisen *pari passu* with the increasing differentiation of human behaviour and social organization. Like all other animals, man is subject to biological conditions of survival and dies if these are not fulfilled. Unlike other animals, his mental organization has developed in such a way that he finds his life worth living only if certain psychological conditions are also fulfilled. He may even die under circumstances that are not biologically lethal, *e.g.* the savage who pines away after discovering that he has unwittingly broken a strict taboo, or the physically viable melancholic who commits suicide. It has to be recognized that psychological needs can be as urgent and compelling as primary survival needs, and that, to use a current phrase, a human being requires not only a living but a life: bread, even with the addition of circuses, cannot supply all that is necessary for a full personal life. Most of the needs often distinguished from animal as 'spiritual' needs can be regarded as psychological needs which have emerged in the course of mental evolution; the mystical antinomy between 'spirit' and 'nature' is not necessary to account for their existence.

In psycho-analysis there is implicit a positive and very practical recognition of the fact that human beings live their ordinary lives at a psycho-social rather than at a biological level, and that the outlook for human survival depends upon the adequate solution of psycho-social problems. It is a commonplace that man's control of his physical environment exceeds his ability to create a stable and humane civilization. In his ignorance of his own nature, his over-estimation of his conscious intelligence, and his blind concentration on mastering his outer world, Western man has created a régime like Frankenstein's monster which may crush him altogether if he does not attain a saner attitude towards himself and his fellow human beings within a relatively short time. The atomic bomb may have done more than any other single invention to remove the promotion of world peace from the sphere of humanitarian idealism to that of common-sense necessity. People everywhere are beginning to understand that unless they learn how to live together with all their fellows they run a considerable risk of perishing together. It is equally clear that political and economic arrangements for living together will succeed only in so far as they tend, whether deliberately or inadvertently, towards the solution of the relevant psycho-social problems. To give one simple but striking example of the dependence of economics on psychology: how can the standard of animal husbandry in India be raised effectively so long as the Hindu peasant believes that the cow is a sacred animal? Human dilemmas are seldom so clearly cut as this, but the psycho-social factor is always operative and always decisive for success or failure.

The organized body of attested psycho-social knowledge which would be most useful at this juncture in world history does not yet exist, but the need for such knowledge is ever more widely recognized. If the coming century is to be the 'century of the common man' there are grounds for hoping that it may also prove to be a century of psycho-social research. It may usher in a development of 'the proper study of mankind' comparable to the expansion of the natural sciences in the last hundred years. For the present, trial and error will continue to be the main rule in human affairs, but this is all the more reason why psycho-analysts should seek to further the development and co-ordination of all the human sciences while continuing the exploration of their own field.

Psycho-analysis is fundamentally an individual or personal psychology. Its primary inquiry is into the mental life of real existents, persons living in various complicated relationships with other persons in an environment that is at once common to all and specific for each individual. Whilst positing a reciprocal relation between the one and the many, the individual and the various groups to which he belongs, the accent of interest is on the influence of the many on the one rather than of the one on the many. Psycho-analysis is a psychology, not a sociology. Whatever it may have to contribute to sociology, or to learn from it, its primary work is the study of individual mental organization and personality pattern, not of social organization and cultural pattern. However much the dissemination of psycho-analytical knowledge may expedite the progress of other human sciences it can never render them superfluous; *e.g.* individual psychology cannot replace sociology nor sociology dispense with individual psychology.

II. METAPSYCHOLOGY AND PERSONOLOGY

The kind of thinking which creates scientific knowledge is definitively object-relational, and it proceeds, in the first instance, from particular observations to general conceptions: in the first instance, because deduction, especially in the form of prediction, plays an increasing rôle in modern science. The natural trend of science is therefore towards objectivity and abstract thinking. Since the real existents are particulars, whereas universals are ideal existents, this trend is also towards de-personalization. There is no 'actual entity' (Whitehead, 1929, p. viii) corresponding to the concept 'man' or 'human being'; the real existents are numbers of men or millions of individual human beings. The concept 'man' covers this plurality, whose members, in spite of individual differences, have sufficient characters in common to warrant the over-all classification 'man' as distinct from 'wolf' or 'worm'. Even so, this concept is ambiguous; it can be used by biologists with reference to objective man, the human organism, or it can be used by humanists with reference to personal man with his characteristic mental life and social activity. Human intelligence permits a finer degree of external reality-testing than affective discrimination could supply. Scientific methodology is a refinement of cognitive reality-testing.

The scientific passion for de-personalization is not, however, wholly explicable in terms of a natural trend of thought. The everyday reality-testing of ordinary people involves constant recognition of other people and of their subjective preoccupations. If early object-discrimination is favoured, as there is reason to think, by recurrent alternations of gratification and frustration, and if intense curiosity is often stimulated by anxiety, it is tempting to see in the trend of science to de-personalization an intellectual solution of ambivalence, a tendentious regression from person to part object-relationships which successfully dismembers the offenders who provoked the original conflict. Similarly, the employment of analytic to the exclusion of synthetic methodology suggests a predominance of destructive interests. The impulse to mastery and control, though an advance on primary destructive impulse, is genetically anxious and aggressive and tends to be very imperfectly libidinized. Though we are not yet in a position to give an adequate account of the subjective motivation of scientific thinking, it is, perhaps, justifiable to see in the dangers and defects of scientific method and in the fertile marriage of science and war an over-implementation of destructive drives. It is clear that the potential benefits of science will become actual only in so far as the destructive potentialities are brought under more adequate control.

The hitherto unbalanced trend of science towards de-personalization has not been useless. On the contrary, the age of reason, notwithstanding its nihilistic effects, has done much to free man from age-long bonds of superstitious and animistic thinking about himself and his relation to the universe. In the human sciences impersonal thinking still has a fruitful rôle to play if it is used in conjunction with more synthetic study of individuals as persons. The methods which helped to release man at least partially from animism can be used to carry him forward to a more balanced understanding of human personality and human inter-relationships.

The trend of scientific thinking towards objectivity and de-personalization is represented in psycho-analysis by the development of metapsychology. Metapsychology is the 'pure science' aspect of psycho-analysis and the metapsychologist's approach to the study of mental organization is essentially the same as the physicist's approach to the study of the atom. Apart from its value as a sublimation, the human value of 'pure science' is potential rather than actual; it becomes useful chiefly through its applications. Psycho-analysis, however, was conceived in practice and came to birth as an applied science of psychopathology, although it very soon became apparent that it was more than a pathology—it was, in fact, an infant psychology. Psycho-analysts, like their critics, are aware that the almost exclusive conduct of research through therapeutic practice has obvious disadvantages. But it has one outstanding advantage—it has ensured that psycho-analysis remains an empirical science, a practical personology, dealing with people as individual persons. If it is, in course of time, to render the full service to the daily conduct of human life of which it is potentially capable, psycho-analysis must continue to pay as much attention to the proper development of personology as to the development of meta-psychology. The progress of psycho-analysis as a whole depends upon the correlated development of both its aspects and upon their mutual aid. Metapsychology can yield indispensable in-formation regarding the general laws of mental life, but the understanding of how to use this knowledge in order to raise the psychological standard of life will have to be supplied by personology.

If the progress of psycho-analysis depends upon the further-ance of both aspects of theory, and these aspects are interdepend-ent, why is it necessary to distinguish between them? The answer is that the difference is more than the distinction between the earlier and later members of an ascending scale of generaliza-tion; it is not merely the difference between perceptual and con-ceptual thinking. I do not question the genetic continuity of perceptual and conceptual thinking. I should be content to regard a percept as a sensory concept. Geometrical forms seem to me to be visual concepts of a high degree of abstraction. The more abstract the thinking, the greater is the probability that it may be dominated by unconscious preconceptions. Cosmology is an especially happy hunting ground for unconsciously deter-mined rationalizations. The difference between perceptual and conceptual thinking is relevant because personal experience is largely perceptual and is usually described in perceptual terms, whereas metapsychology is entirely a product of conceptual thinking. It is clear, however, that generalization about experi-ence at once introduces concepts, and that personology itself could not progress without making use of concepts. Both kinds of concept are, indeed, derived from the same data, but the con-cepts of personology refer to experience, whereas the concepts of metapsychology refer to objective mental processes, although they are also inferred from experience. The significant difference is in the attitude and relation of the thinker to his data. In prac-tice, the psycho-analyst alternates to a varying extent between empathetic feeling and thinking *with* his analysand and definitive object-relational feeling and thinking *about* him. Thinking about subjective experience is as much definitive object-relationship as thinking about mental processes, but identification is more fully retained in personology, whereas it is minimized in metapsychology.

Grammatically, metapsychology and personology use the same third person plural 'they'. But, for metapsychology, 'they' refers to neutral 'its', processes or systems; for personology, 'they' refer either to other people or to aspects of experience or behaviour, feelings, wishes, or actions. 'They' here retains the identificatory basis 'those other selves' or 'feelings, wishes, actions such as mine'. The difference is most simply stated by calling metapsychology 'objective theory' and personology 'subjective theory', because reference to a first person singular 'I' is implicit in all generalization referring to experience. Another way of stating the difference is to say that personology is individual psychology, whereas metapsychology is a general theory of mental processes and their organization. In its concentration on endopsychic events, metapsychology isolates mental life more artificially than does personology which studies the mental and motor behaviour of persons accepted as living in an actual world among other people.

If phenomena of para-normal perception or telepathy become substantiated beyond reasonable doubt, psycho-analysis will also have to take into account direct inter-psychic relationships. This would involve some modifications of theory, but would not invalidate either metapsychology or personology. The psyche would deal with incoming telepathic communications in much the same way as it deals with verbal communications, with the probable difference that only ego-syntonic communications would reach consciousness. A telepathic dream would be one in which the sender's message expressed a wish common to both sender and receiver. (Jessie Blundun has interested herself in the psychological conditioning of some apparently 'telepathic' dreams but has not yet published her conclusions.) In daily life we often unwittingly use a happy phrase coined by someone else to express our own views: *per contra* we never adopt phrases that are useless to us or antipathetic in content. Psycho-analysts have, as yet, no complete explanation of the phenomena they are familiar with as 'empathy', 'rapport', etc. They will do well, however, to be cautious in the matter of telepathy, although they have nothing to fear from the establishment of any psychological fact (see p. 241).

It is very easy to pass insensibly from the subjective to the objective approach. The transition is made easier by the fact that many terms are common to both subjective and objective theory; *e.g.* 'mental object' is one among many such terms. It is precisely the distinction between the personal or subjective object and the metapsychological object-system which is readily blurred by the employment of the term 'mental object' for both. 'Object-system' is preferable in many ways to 'object' for metapsychological use. There are also advantages in using the term 'imago' in reference to personal mental objects. It is singularly easy to fall into what A. N. Whitehead described as 'the fallacy of misplaced concreteness' and even easier to give an impression, whether true or false, of reifying abstractions.

The term 'good object' is a legitimate concept, but it is one which appears to me to have more relevance and utility in personology than in metapsychology for reasons that Susan Isaacs herself gives (1945, p. 61): ' "Good" is a general description of the qualities of those objects in the child's mind which call out positive feelings, themselves based upon experiences of pleasure and satisfaction in the past'. To my mind, a concept more free from direct subjective valuation and having less immediate reference to experience would be preferable for metapsychological use, possibly 'libidinal object-system'. But, in thinking of object-systems, it is imperative to remember that, whatever the developmental phase of ego-integration and object-differentiation, any system that can be described metapsychologically as an object-system is an ego-object-system. What is for metapsychology an ego-object-system is, for personology, a dynamic self-object-relationship.

III. NATURE AND SCOPE OF PSYCHO-ANALYTIC PERSONOLOGY

(1) MOTIVATION AND ORGANIZATION

The greater part of the literature of psycho-analysis contributes to the study of personality and no attempt will be made to survey this work in detail, since the aim of these 'Notes' is general rather than particular. Historically, the development of personology exhibits two main phases, namely, character study, chiefly in terms of motivation, and structural study, chiefly in terms of mental organization.

The initial equation of the unconscious with the repressed and the corresponding emphasis on infantile sexual drives meant that character-study began as inquiry into the vicissitudes or transformations of instinct. It is impossible to refer to all the work done by Freud, Ferenczi, Abraham, Jones, Glover, and many others in this field, culminating in Freud's distinction of three main libidinal types (Freud, 1932c). It is perhaps desirable to emphasize that the value of this earlier work is by no means exhausted. Some of it now seems to be incomplete, since description of character in terms of instinct vicissitude alone is no longer adequate; but it remains true that a character-trait is a transformation of instinct. Similarly, the early distinction between reaction-formation and sublimation remains valid though we have not even yet succeeded in expressing clearly their differential economics. Motivation is always ultimately instinctual, and psychological needs differ from primary needs only in degree of instinct transformation. Abraham (1924) very soon realized that libidinal development and the development of object-relations were parallel processes, and his major conclusions are still valid within their own limits. Melanie Klein's work, although the focus of so much current controversy, is, in part, of the nature of an expansion of Abraham's views.

It is chiefly to the second line of inquiry, the structural studies linked with problems of diagnosis and aetiology, that we owe the modern conception of the threefold constitution of mind that has so enriched but also so complicated our knowledge of personality. It is, in effect, to metapsychology that we owe the realization that such familiar conscious experiences as struggle with 'temptation', issuing in the victory or defeat of conscience or in compromise, are true intimations of mental organization. The early study of dreams and neuroses yielded the libido theory, the 'fiction' of the psychic apparatus and the conception of defencemechanisms, particularly repression and regression. The later study of the psychoses, the recognition of an instinct of aggression, the addition of projection and introjection to the growing quota of defence-mechanisms, and the attribution of unconscious components to the ego itself, produced a switch of interest not only from libidinal development to ego-analysis, but also to the intricate relationships between the constituent systems of the mind. In the latter connection, the phenomena attributed to unconscious guilt and need for punishment were among the first to engage attention. In 1937 Anna Freud showed how largely the character of the ego is moulded by the nature of its defensive operations. Stressing the adaptive rôle of the ego to balance its 'defensive' aspects, Hartmann (1939a, p. 62) suggested that the 'primary functions' of the ego constitute a 'conflict-free sphere'. His views are by no means lacking in logical justification, but they approximate to a modern re-statement of the earlier antithesis between libido and ego and, in spite of all his careful reservations, they tend to obscure the cardinal fact that all ego operations are motivated by instinct even when they are evoked by external stimuli and are obvious responses to environment. Self-preservative adaptation to the outer world is not an independent function but a complex resultant of multi-polar adaptation. Hendrick, also thinking that the 'executant functions' of the ego were relatively neglected in psycho-analysis, proposed to add to Freud's pleasure and reality principles a third 'work principle' (1945, p. 95), 'the principle that primary pleasure is sought by efficient use of the central nervous system for the performance of well-integrated functions which enable the individual to control or alter his environment'. The infantile precursors of the 'executant functions' ('partial ego functions') and their developmental integration, are said to be motivated by a specific 'instinct to master' or 'mastery instinct'. While it is true that there are many obvious gaps in psycho-analytic knowledge and much ground still to be covered, it is by no means so certain that the problems of 'work' and of the 'executant functions' of the ego require new principles and instincts for their solution, nor that their solution is so easy. Hendrick's suggestions are too simplistic to carry conviction. Flugel's approach (1948) to the related problems of 'self-sustaining activities', in which *l'appétit vient en mangeant* is more attuned to their complexity. The development of psycho-analytic ego-psychology has recently been summarized by Franz Alexander (1948).

The illumination of the clinical field through metapsychological conceptions has tended to foster the indiscriminate use of terms. In the well-known passage about the relations of the ego Freud wrote (1933, p. 103): 'The proverb tells us that one cannot serve two masters at once. The poor ego has a still harder time of it; it has to serve three harsh masters, and has to do its best to reconcile the claims and demands of all three. These demands are always divergent and often seem quite incompatible; no wonder that the ego frequently gives way under its task. The three tyrants are the external world, the super-ego, and the id. When one watches the efforts of the ego to satisfy them all, or rather, to obey them all simultaneously, one cannot regret having personified the ego, and established it as a separate being.' This is indeed a vivid and arresting picture, and the difficulties beset-ting the reality-self could hardly be more clearly depicted, but it is, nevertheless, a matter for regret that psycho-analysts should be so much impressed by it as habitually to personify the major mental systems. The use of the terms 'the id', 'the ego', and 'the super-ego', is, however, so constant and so widespread in per-sonology that the only feasible way out of the confusion would seem to be to adopt more exact terms, like 'ego-organization' and 'super-ego-organization' in metapsychology. The conscious self often feels like a separate being but it is none the less deluded in this impression. The ego-organization cannot be usefully con-ceived as having independent existence but only as a differentiated nexus of mental systems variously and variably related to other systems, but never unrelated. The term 'person', like the term 'character', is often restricted to the conscious self (also spoken of as the operative self because of its control of voluntary motility) but the only living entity is the whole self, the total personality.

(2) The Total Personality

The publication of *The Ego and the Id* in 1923 (Freud, 1927) marked the transition to modern theory and made inevitable what Alexander (1930) first termed 'the psycho-analysis of the total personality'.[1] Federn's conceptions (1943) of the shifting cathexes of the ego-boundaries appear to be consistent with the theory of mental systems and their organization. The term 'boundary' is a topographical term, a visual or spatial analogy but one that accords with neuro-physiological conceptions of peripheral reactions and synaptic phenomena. Freud himself often used visual imagery; *e.g.* in describing the inter-relationship

[1] Alexander actually introduced the phrase first in a paper at the Homburg Congress in 1925 (*Int. J. Psycho-Anal.*, vol. vii, p. 340).

of the mental organizations he wrote (1932, p. 105): 'When you think of this dividing up of the personality into ego, super-ego and id, you must not imagine sharp dividing lines such as are artificially drawn in the field of political geography. We cannot do justice to the characteristics of the mind by means of linear contours, such as occur in a drawing or in a primitive painting, but we need rather the areas of colour shading off into one another that are to be found in modern pictures. After we have made our separations, we must allow what we have separated to merge again. Do not judge too harshly of a first attempt at picturing a thing so elusive as the human mind.' Process conceptions seem more likely to derive from kinetic and fluid experience of various types rather than from vision. The kind of description that will convey most to any given person will naturally depend upon the latter's own predilections. The choice of imagery will not influence the fact that psycho-analysis offers a dynamic and economic theory of mental life.

The mental structure which is the direct concern of personology is the design or pattern of personality corresponding to the metapsychological type of mental organization. This pattern can be correctly described behaviouristically as an organization of reaction patterns (akin to the schemata of experimental psychologists) created by the habitual modes of mental and motor response acquired during life. But, since life is subjectively a sequence of meaningful dynamic experiences, it is perhaps most suitable to think of personality pattern as the organization of experience which emerges as the result of continuing experience. It is a living pattern in which the past continuously influences the present, directly or indirectly, and in which, to a considerable extent, the future is predetermined by the present. But, although it is true that present experience is modified by past experience, and that, from the dawn of life onwards, there can be no experience absolutely new in the sense of being unmodified by what has preceded it, it is also true that experience is new from moment to moment because the conditions in the present are never in all respects the same as in the past. Plasticity and modifiability vary greatly, but the fate-neurotic, who is most adept at re-creating stereotyped situations, can never succeed in reproducing situations that are identical. Living is always becoming, even when it only means becoming more and more fixed and rigid in personality pattern.

The functional significance of organization should not, however, blind us to the continuing importance of motivation. Better
understanding of organization is inseparable from better understanding of the ways in which primary instinctual drives become
transformed into the bewildering variety of human purposes. In
the series of dynamic relationships that constitute experience the
ultimate drives are instinctual, whether the immediately compelling motives are primary or transformed. There is the further
complication that human purposes tend to be multi-deter-
mined and to derive impetus from a variety of instinctual sources.
Since instinct is the prime mover of psychic activity, research
into problems of instinct can never become unimportant. Indeed, there are many unsolved riddles of instinct (cf. p. 111),
e.g. the status of self-preservation. We may yet come round to
the opinion that the intimate clinical association of anxiety with
aggression is due, in the first instance, to the personal risks of
aggression. We may need to recognize that fear, with all its
derivative normal and pathological anxieties, is the true primary
self-preservative affect, and that anxiety about the fate of indispensable or good objects, readily identified with the self, comes
about by a natural extension of self-preservation. The argument
here is not that this is the case; self-preservation is adduced as an
illustration of an unsolved problem of instinct, to support the
argument that we cannot afford to neglect any aspect of experience and should be ill-advised to concentrate on organization (or
on object-relations) to the exclusion of motives. We should not
rule out the possibility that we may get help in this field from
the comparative study of instincts advocated by the late C. S.
Myers (1945). The expression 'determining tendency' which he
favoured can be used as a synonym for instinctual drive.

(3) Experience as Relationship (Identificatory and Definitive Object-Relationship)

In the preceding paragraph experience was equated with
the sequence of dynamic relationships. If mental life is mediation between instinct and environment, experience is experience
of purposive relationship, whether apprehended as such or not.
The present interest in objects and object-relations is, in some
ways, a healthy corrective to the earlier concentration on impulse, but the series of experiences that constitute the life story

and shape the personality pattern are not objects but dynamic self-object-relationships. However much it may focus attention, the object is only a constituent of a whole experience. An experience is a complete reaction whether the constituent aspects are differentiated to consciousness, or undifferentiated as we suppose them to be in primary identification. It would be wrong, however, to describe experience as relationship unless object-relations are defined in the broadest possible sense as including identification and all the grades of differentiation which emerge from primary identification and issue in classical or definitive object-relations in all their variety. The adjective 'definitive' is used here because it conveys the subjective crux of the situation, namely, that the object is experienced as something or someone distinct from the self, having more or less well-defined characteristics of its own.

In a situation in which dissociated reactions are projected on to an object in the outer world or inside the body and identified with it, the reality-self attains definitive object-relations with another aspect of the total self, which is felt to belong to the object and not to the self. Definitive object-relations are established temporarily within the conscious self in every act of introspection and they occur, both temporarily and in more permanent forms, between the major systems, *e.g.* between reality-self and infantile-self and between reality-self and conscience-self. The exact chronology of the development of definitive object-relations is in dispute but the factor which distinguishes them from identification is perhaps less contentious. As soon as subjective definition, however vague, is acquired and as long as some degree of it is retained, the object will be felt to be distinct from the self. Perhaps all defined objects, whether perceived or imagined, tended originally to carry the same conviction of material reality that they regain in dreams. This is only another way of surmising, with Freud, that mental activity is at first hallucinatory and that the infant, like primitive man, has to learn by painful experience the difference between imaginary objects and objects of perception. Definitive relations between ego and super-ego tend to carry strong conviction of objective reality; mystical belief in the existential reality of God is absolute.

Disregarding the vexed question of the time at which it is legitimate to suppose that objects acquire subjective definition, the broad use of the term 'object-relations' is desirable because the texture of experience is woven of both identificatory and definitive self-object-relationships, whenever and however the latter appear. The economy of the personality is one of total experience, and its pattern is determined by the ratio and distribution of identificatory and definitive relationships. In *The Ego and the Id*, Freud (1927, pp. 65, 36, 44) revised his conception of narcissism and introduced the term 'secondary narcissism' to convey the result of libidinal identification; he also described the ego as a precipitate of abandoned object-cathexes and the super-ego as a combination of parental identifications. Whether they regard the post-Oedipal identifications as instituting super-ego formation or whether they regard them as completing an organization already in course of development, it would seem that all psycho-analysts agree on the general nature of the mental systems. They agree, namely, that these systems consist of identifications or, as I should personally prefer to say, identificatory relationships, more or less stably integrated among themselves. Passages in *The Ego and the Id* (*e.g.* pp. 38, 39) show that Freud understood the strain on ego-stability that may result from incompatible identifications. We are all familiar with the difference between personality types in which the relative stability of the operative self is maintained by a sufficiency of benign identificatory relationships (in Melanie Klein's phraseology—identification with good objects) and the contrasting highly unstable types in which such libidinal integration is defective even to a point where the individual feels he can survive only by maintaining a dependent relationship to another person. We are also familiar with the advantage to the personality of a mainly identificatory relation between reality-self and benign conscience and with the misfortunes of selves which are the victims of conscience aggression.

(4) The Variety of Identificatory Relationships and their Genesis: the Need for Perspective

It should not be supposed that identificatory relationships are any more completely understood than definitive object-relationships. The term 'identification', like many others, is an omnibus term covering a variety of differing economic situations. Apart from the three types, original, regressive, and partial, described by Freud (1922b, p. 65), it is evident that there will be considerable differences in the personality pattern and social behaviour of people prone to what may be called an introjective type of libidinal identification and of people who tend to a projective type. In the introjective type the object is identified with the operative self or with the ego-ideal, and in either case the relation subserves the interests of the person himself. In the projective type, some aspect of the personality is identified with the object, and it is the object whom the person seeks to serve, even to his own detriment. Similarly, de Saussure (1939, p. 465) distinguishes 'between identifying oneself with another person (centrifugal) and identifying another person with oneself (centripetal)'. He would prefer to use the term 'substitution' for 'identification which aims at neutralizing aggressiveness'. The 'genital identification' which Michael Balint (1948, p. 37) regards as characteristic of genital love, is evidently projective or centrifugal in nature. Freud's formula (1922b, p. 75) for the blind devotion of the lover runs: 'The object has taken the place of the ego ideal'. Projective identification of ego-ideal with outer object, human or abstract, would appear to be a feature of the economy of all fanatics. Living together in harmony, whether in small or large groups, clearly depends in part upon an adequate capacity to put oneself in other people's shoes. Genuine altruism, the pedestrian everyday charity that begins at home, as distinct from fanatical devotion to ultra-personal interests, may depend upon projective identification with a fairly well-libidinized operative self. It is a fact verifiable by anyone that people tend to love their neighbours as much or as little as they love themselves. The pattern of social relationships reflects the pattern of the internal economy. To revert to the older terminology, altruism in the sense of willingness to consider other people as other selves and to deal with them as fellow human beings may be implemented by a benign form of narcissism that, by contrast with a variety of actively malignant or passively anti-social forms, may be accounted a positive incentive to civilization.

There is much to learn regarding the genesis of identificatory relationships as well as their economics. Granting that assumptions about the dawn of mental life are, and will probably always remain, extremely hypothetical, the concept of primary identification (oceanic experience) has as yet no serious rivals. Oceanic experience fades into primal unconsciousness but, at the time it begins to be interrupted by flashes of sensory-affective consciousness, it may have the character of undifferentiated awareness similar to that momentarily experienced by some adults in 'coming to' after fainting. There may be a brief but subsequently recognizable interval between becoming conscious and becoming fully conscious of oneself and one's surroundings. It is a moment of 'pure being' without differentiation of self or objects and its pleasure-tone is characteristically high, sometimes so high that the word 'blissful' has been used to describe it in retrospect. Both internal evidence from psycho-analysis and observations of behaviour indicate that, apart from sleep, satisfactory suckling is the condition most likely to re-establish primary identification for the infant. It may be this association which links identification with oral incorporation.

In a paper dealing with oral factors in frigidity, Gregory Zilboorg (1938a, p. 5) writes of conditions among American psycho-analysts that 'there would seem to be something disproportionate in the emphasis of our study of anal as compared with our study of oral reactions. It is difficult, of course, to detect fully the reasons for our unquestionable resistance to a deeper study of oral drives—perhaps the trouble lies not so much in our resistance to the recognition of them as in our predilection for the study of anal drives.' In the British Psycho-Analytical Society the situation is reversed. As a result of the work of Melanie Klein we are no longer in any danger of under-emphasizing oral factors: on the contrary, we are in the opposite danger of concentrating too exclusively upon them. In our study it is the emphasis on oral as compared with all other types of reaction that tends to be disproportionate. This applies also to the emphasis on the mechanisms of introjection and projection to the relative neglect of repression and regression which, however, continue to function whether we attend to them or not. Nevertheless, the conception of a phase of development corresponding to an early oral primacy remains highly probable, although we should think of it as a phase in which oral interests tend to be dominant but are never the only interests at work. Food is, after all, the first necessity for survival and the capacity to distinguish between edible and inedible substances appears very early in the evolutionary scale. It is hardly surprising that the infant should be much swayed by oral interests, especially in view of the fact that he is quite incapable of feeding himself. But the danger now is not that we may under-estimate the importance of early oral interests, both libidinal and aggressive, and their related anxieties, but that we may assign too little importance to the other interests which co-exist with them from the beginning of life. The course and outcome of the initial oral phases are bound to be much influenced by co-existing conditions. They will be determined by the total life-situation, which includes the whole specific congenital endowment of the infant and the particular environmental influences affecting him. To give a very simple example: the oral phase and subsequent history of an infant with a good digestion will clearly be very different from that of an early martyr to colic. In short, however much oral interests may tend to dominate the earliest weeks of life, they presumably never exist alone, and it is as important to appreciate their co-existents and their early inter-connections as it is to emphasize their intrinsic importance. Oral primacy is never oral monopoly.

There are avenues of incorporation other than the mouth just as there are channels of evacuation other than the bladder and bowel. In some people it may appear that breathing is the rhythmic prototype of taking in and giving out; oral interpretations are not likely to have much effect on a patient in mortal dread of asphyxiation due to an actual experience of being over-lain. In such cases, air may have an importance exceeding that of milk. Freud's statement (1927, p. 33) that the ego is first and foremost a body ego is ever more emphatically confirmed. Just as early differentiation of the outer world is sensory-affective so dawning conviction of 'things inside' is based upon endosomatic comfort and discomfort, although the accurate distinction between inside and outside the body is presumably something the infant only learns in the course of time. The experiential basis of all belief and phantasy has often been emphasized. Up to date, it has not been equally emphasized that beliefs and phantasies do not arise from experience and then lead an independent existence, but that they remain intimately dependent upon continuing experience and tend to be reinforced by each repetition of a similar situation. This is the reason why it is therapeutically important, not merely to discover the belief or phantasy as such, but to relate it as circumstantially as possible to the total situation which gave it birth.

Melanie Klein has made it impossible for us to ignore the existence of animistic phases in individual development, roughly corresponding to the hitherto more familiar animistic phases in cultural development. Dispute centres less on the existence of animistic phantasies than on their chronology, developmental significance, and provenance. Our difficulties are increased by the fact that, since the ego is first and foremost a body-ego, we tend to think about mental life first of all by analogy with bodily life. We tend, therefore, to think of minds as concrete entities like bodies and to speak of things happening in the mind as if it were three-dimensional. Thoughts tend to become materialized things and we speak of a storehouse of memories as we might speak of a squirrel's hoard of nuts. It is true that the most highly abstract thinking is developmentally a refinement of perceptual thinking but we are no more justified in regarding images as miniature replicas of the external object of perception than the physiologist would be in equating the neural activity in a sense organ with the stimulus that initiates it. Thinking may be motivated by oral and many other impulses, but thinking is not eating any more than cerebration is digestion. Thinking about thinking is a much more sophisticated occupation than thinking about eating; our primary preoccupations constantly colour our secondary interests and lead us to conceive of them by analogy with more familiar elementary concerns.

The risk of equating mental function with content of experience is particularly great in relation to mechanisms of defence. Although the latter have been inferred from conscious experience and behaviour, it is, as a general rule, their effects which are experienced. Thus, though we may consciously divert our attention in the effort to suppress unwanted thoughts and feelings, we do not consciously experience forgetting. We experience that we have forgotten something, *e.g.* a name, and we may or we may not subsequently experience successful or unsuccessful effort to recall the name; the active forgetting is silent. The operation of a mechanism can be signalized in experience, *e.g.* a dream in which a door locked from inside indicated strong repression. In so far as an operative mechanism appears in experience I think it is true to say that it can only appear as imaginary behaviour, just as I think it is legitimate, in terms of motivation, to describe mechanisms as endopsychic vicissitudes of instinct. I am not sure that it is justifiable to assert that the reverse is true, namely, that the operation of mental mechanisms is invariably reflected in conscious or unconscious experience as imaginary behaviour, or that the occurrence of a particular phantasy of incorporation is proof that a process of introjection is taking or has taken place.

The possibility of simple wishful or anxious forbidden fulfilment by means of incorporative phantasies cannot be excluded, certainly not in adults. Concomitant evidence has to decide the precise economic status of such phantasies in every instance.

Introjection and projection are presumably never the only mechanisms in operation. There is reason to suppose that a primitive type of repression can function very early indeed if infantile experience is too intolerable. This quantitative type of repression may be suspected even in adults if, as sometimes happens, a state of acute mental distress gives way quite suddenly and unexpectedly to comparative calm. It may well be that primacies of interest carry with them primacies of mechanism, but here again, mechanisms never achieve monopoly, only dominance or preponderance, hyper- or hypo-activity. The normal and abnormal relations between different mechanisms have not yet been adequately explored. As Anna Freud writes (1937, p. 57): '. . . The chronology of psychic processes is still one of the most obscure fields of analytical theory'.

Caution needs to be observed in regard to the rôle of progression and regression in development, particularly in regard to fixation. Critical phases in development may be surmounted with more or less success or failure. Even success probably means that a considerable amount of mental energy is locked up in the endopsychic operations which maintain successful adaptation, and failure usually means that a far higher proportion remains indefinitely engaged in a losing battle to resolve an insoluble problem. In addition to providing foci for regression, such arrests or fixations diminish the energy available for subsequent development, but they seldom or never arrest the course of development altogether. Whether it is held that Oedipal trends show themselves early or comparatively late in infancy, there is a considerable measure of agreement (a) that antecedent development inevitably affects the character of the classical Oedipus phase, and (b) that every infant ultimately reaches a stage that can only be legitimately described as some variation of a classical Oedipus phase.. It follows that, however much the issue may be predetermined, the final shaping of the ground pattern of personality, the typing of the mental organization as relatively normal, neurotic, or psychotic, is decided by the nature and outcome of the Oedipus phase. The psychology of adult psychotics and borderline cases cannot be understood solely in terms of arrested progression or of regression but only in terms giving due weight to both. The late Ella Sharpe (1946) drew attention to the part played by regression in manic depression and the significance of 're-instatement of the ideal'.

(5) THE SUBJECTIVITY OF OBJECTS

We cannot leave the description of experience as a sequence of purposive relationships without briefly discussing a point which is not only of importance in itself but which also has a particular bearing on our conception of such mechanisms as introjection and projection. This point is that, even in the case of the most sharply defined object-relationship, the objective constituent of experience is as subjective as an object identified with the self. The naïve conviction attaches to ordinary perception that anything we see is what it appears to be: reason and experience have combined to inform us that this is not necessarily the case. The conviction that something is there is normally well founded, but all that we see of that something is what our present state and past experience enable us to see. We may know all there is to know about the physiological conditions which enable us to see and the physical conditions of light, distance, etc., which influence visual appearances, but nothing of this will alter the fact that vision, in the sense of apprehension of things seen, is a psychological event and that the meaning registered is a synthesis of past and present experience. It is correct to express this by the tautology that mental objects are invariably mental and that the objects of experience, as constituents of experience, are subjective. There is thus no difference in subjectivity between the object identified with the conscious self and the object distinguished from this self, wherever the latter may be localized; the difference is not one of subjectivity but of endopsychic economy, *i.e.* of mode of relationship. From this point of view, introjection and projection appear as methods of changing the mode of relationship.

It is hardly surprising that interest in objects and concern about their fate is prominent in experience since the function of mental life is the establishment of viable relations between the person and his environment and the provision of adequate channels of instinctual expression. Man's highly social nature renders other people the most numerous and important of his instinctual targets. In a distressing situation we may try actively to change the position into something more tolerable, which usually means direct dealings with other people. If practical measures are impossible, we may find a safety-valve in imagining the changes we should like to bring about. But defence mechanisms are not amenable to conscious control; they are involuntary mental, *not* voluntary motor, activities which aim at the reduction of intolerable tensions by endopsychic discharge. Voluntary motor discharge can be used for instinct defence as soon as objects become sufficiently defined to be identified with trouble-causing aspects of the self. It is favoured by the primitive tendency to disown painful experience and feel it to be 'not me'. If this primitive tendency is called 'primary projection', the subjective character of experience may be called 'primary introjection'. Instinct defence may become defence against objects but it remains essentially instinct defence.

In a given conscious experience our attention may be focused on someone else and we may attribute the nature of our experience to that person: *e.g.* if, in response to a smile from a friend, we think 'How nice you are'. The fact remains that what is nice for us is the complete experience of the moment of friendly relationship. It is the character of the operative relationship that determines the niceness or nastiness of the object for the subject. Experience is subjective and therefore selective; we cannot escape the inference that we apprehend other people and things only in so far as they affect us, their meaning for us is the result of our experience of them, and we value them ultimately according to their relevance to our needs. Hence, however much further our intelligence may develop and however expert we may become in technique of research and proof, etc., human knowledge can never become anything other than human knowledge. It has been said that man is the measure of all things; it might be truer to say that man's ultimate measure of all things is himself.

Recognition of the subjective nature of personal objects does not imply solipsism. On the contrary, it is implicit in psychoanalytical theory and practice that object-relationship is interrelationship. Our relationship to other people is constantly modified by their attitude and behaviour towards us and vice versa. For example, the most inveterate dog-lover will behave very differently towards a mad dog and towards a playful puppy. In the case of the mad dog, his habitually friendly attitude will be suspended in favour of self-preservation and he may even kill the dog, whereas, in the case of the puppy, he will probably enter into the spirit of the game. The difference in these reactions depends upon the ability acquired by experience to discriminate between mad dogs and playful puppies. The learning is done by the self but what is learned is a contribution from the external object. We may describe this inter-relationship by saying that the intrinsic nature of the external object influences our experience of it but it is our experience of it that defines its nature for us. Our subjective object is what we apprehend the external object to be. Our impressions vary in reliability as guides to action but, whether our impression is adequately realistic or wholly phantastic, we react to the object as if it were what we think it to be. The degree to which any given relationship is influenced by the intrinsic nature of the external object varies with the strength of the unconscious determinants in the subject. In the extreme case of a sufferer from persecution mania, the true nature of any external object may be totally eclipsed.

(6) REALITY-TESTING

As a result of experience, the developing conscious or operative self normally learns to estimate the nature of persons and things with some degree of accuracy, as the old saw 'a burnt child dreads the fire' attests. It is common knowledge, however, that the degree, range, and reliability of reality-testing varies widely from person to person and in the same person in different situations. Scientific research is reality-testing of a high order, but scientists are often highly unrealistic in regard to matters outside their own special field. The subjective sources of distortion are manifold. We can distinguish in the first instance intensity of motivation. The pressing need that things should be what we want them to be or think they ought to be, to affirm that they are one thing or deny that they are another in order to make them consonant with our desires, can cloud and falsify our appreciation of circumstances to almost any extent. A very common source of distortion is projection resulting in over- or under-estimation of the object according to the aspect of the self identified with it. Projection is such a confirmed mental habit that it is usually recognized only where people suffer from individual delusions, not shared by the majority of their fellows: the delusions active in politics are usually shared by too many people to be diagnosed for what they are.

This reference to projection illustrates the general difficulty accruing to reality-testing from the fact that the conscious self is in more immediate contact with the outer world than with its own instinctual impulses. The division of labour which allots instinct-testing to conscience may free intelligence to attend to the environment but it does this at the cost of depriving it of first-hand knowledge of its own motives. Relatively few people know either what they themselves are or what they really want, *i.e.* what conditions would offer them a worth-while life. The most widespread human delusion, favoured by dense ignorance of our mental constitution, is identification of ourselves with our re-stricted conscious selves, an essentially stultifying conviction. It is a vice in religion that it tends to be other-worldly, but a virtue that it is ultra-egoistic. Every religion regards man as something more than his conscious self.

The conscious self, however, is the locus of intelligence and, if human intelligence directed itself to the study of persons with the same assiduity that it has devoted to the study of the physical universe, it could enable us to know ourselves better and also help us to overcome our present mental disabilities and transform modern mal-adaptation into the beginnings of a more fully humane re-adaptation. The application of intelligence to mental life is both terrifying and humbling to the conscious self. Intelli-gence can be most untrustworthy, but an intelligence informed of its own nature and content to be an agent of life is probably the only trustworthy guide to which humanity can look. That unconscious appreciation of situations that we call 'intuition' may outstrip reason, may sometimes be a saner guide than logic, and may often pass the pragmatic test. But intuition is notoriously variable in its reliability, and its recommendations and conclu-sions must eventually be judged by intelligence. In his most pessi-mistic book, the late H. G. Wells (1945, p. 19) states a cardinal truth: 'Adapt or perish, now as ever, is Nature's inexorable imperative'. The immediate imperative is a psycho-social re-adaptation which gives due weight to the subjective nature and needs of man.

The scope of psycho-analytic personology thus includes the whole of mental life, the dynamics and economics of the total personality. The classification of personality types will be con-sidered in Chapter VI (p. 182 *et seq.*). The inter-relationship of the mental organizations and the problem of personal integration will be discussed in assessing the kind of humanism implicit in psycho-analysis.

IV. THE RELATIONS OF PSYCHO-ANALYSIS

(1) LEVELS OF INTEGRATION

It was said earlier that psycho-analysts study personality at the psycho-social level. This statement tacitly endorses the point of view now current among biologists that evolution has resulted in the establishment of 'levels of organization in the universe, successive forms of order in a scale of complexity and organization' (Needham, 1943, p. 234). Although human beings are psycho-physical organisms, we regard them as living their personal lives at a psycho-social level. In view of our knowledge of the constant interplay and reciprocal influence of endopsychic and environmental factors, psycho-analysts cannot agree either that 'manners maketh man' or that 'people get the government they deserve'. The relation between the individual and society is one of mutual interaction, although the balance of influence in any given person may vary from relative dominance of nature to relative dominance of nurture. In conceding the biological functions of mental life but studying it by a direct psychological approach psycho-analysts assume that people live at a psycho-social level of integration whose laws do not contravene but rather subsume biological laws in the same way that biological laws subsume physical and chemical principles.

Much current distress is due to the fact that recent human behaviour has tended to contravene rather than to conform to biological and psycho-social necessities. Modern psycho-social adaptation has been defective and disintegrative rather than integrative, but the present critical situation of humanity is an opportunity for re-integration which may or may not be successfully utilized. Diagnosis, prognosis, and prescription naturally vary with the individual's angle of approach, but there is considerable agreement in principle among socially minded thinkers as to the kind of situation in which we find ourselves to-day. Thus, Needham sees the next step in human evolution as a level of social integration in which conscious co-operation will supersede competitive struggle. He emphasizes (1943, p. 265) that 'our present civilization is manifestly not a state of stable equilibrium'. He is of opinion (p. 272) that 'the higher stage of integration and organization towards which we look have all the authority of evolution behind them'. This long-range optimism is, however, qualified by the statement (p. 269) that 'to speak of the inevitability of our higher integrative level is to say nothing of when it will come'.

Karl Mannheim (1943, p. 1) writes: 'If I had to summarize the situation in a single sentence I would say: "we are living in an age of transition from laissez-faire to a planned society. The planned society that will come may take one of two shapes, it will be ruled either by a minority in terms of a dictatorship or by a new form of government which, in spite of its increased power, will still be democratically controlled." ' The desideratum is 'Planning for Freedom' (p. 11). The crisis in human valuation is related by Mannheim to the weakening of the directives issuing from basic religious or 'paradigmatic experience'. Evidently influenced by Jung, he writes (p. 135) of the 'despiritualization' of modern life: 'It mainly consists in the evaporation of primordial images or archetypes which have directed the life-experience of mankind through the ages'.

Lewis Mumford (1944) describes the present crisis as having two aspects, external and internal, and summarizes the former by saying (1944, p. 398): 'An age of expansion is giving place to an age of equilibrium. The achievement of this equilibrium is the task of the next few centuries.' The internal crisis grew out of (p. 413) 'the failure of utilitarian man to fulfil the ends of life'. Mumford is of opinion (p. 421) that: 'Only in one place can an immediate renewal begin: that is, within the person; and a remolding of the self and the super-ego is an inescapable preliminary to the great changes that must be made throughout every community, in every part of the world'. And, finally (p. 423): 'Our first need is not for organization but for orientation: a change in direction and attitude. We must bring to every activity and every plan a new criterion of judgement: we must ask how far it seeks to further the processes of life fulfilment and how much respect it pays to the needs of the whole personality.'

How long we may have to wait for the growth and establishment of a more co-operative world system, how much more trouble we may have to endure in the meantime, and what form the emerging social integration will take, will clearly depend to a considerable extent upon the psychological potential of individuals. The 'Four Freedoms' can avail only in proportion to the number of people who attain some degree of psychological freedom and personal integrity. Personal and social integration are indissolubly connected and their interdependence is a limiting factor in both personal and social development.

The conception of levels of integration helps to clarify the relation of psycho-analysis to other branches of human knowledge. If we group all the studies of man, the sciences and the humanities, under one heading we may call this comprehensive group 'humanology', the term 'anthropology' being already pre-empted. Using the term 'humanology' in this total sense, and bearing in mind the conception of levels, it would appear that the most appropriate studies for psycho-social man are the twin disciplines of individual psychology and sociology. It will also be apparent that the rôle played for sociology by such studies as history and cultural anthropology is played for individual psychology by psycho-analysis. The latter supplies, and may hope to supply ever more adequately, the genetic history of persons, whilst history and its related disciplines supply the developmental story of groups and their social organization. It is now accepted that modern world conditions and the present state of nations can be fully understood only in the light of their past history. It should also be recognized that the personality of an individual is only to be comprehended in the light of his specific life story.

It is interesting that one philosopher-historian, R. G. Collingwood, arrived at a conception of the relation of historical past and present very similar to the psycho-analytical conception of the relation of mental past and present. Collingwood (1944, p 67) writes: 'By about 1920 this was my first principle of a philosophy of history: that the past which an historian studies is not a dead past, but a past which in some sense is still living in the present'. Also (p. 69): 'So long as the past and present are outside one another, knowledge of the past is not of much use in the problems of the present. But suppose the past lives on in the present; suppose, though incapsulated in it, and at first sight hidden beneath the present's contradictory and more prominent features, it is still alive and active: then the historian may very well be related to the non-historian as the trained woodsman is to the ignorant traveller.'

The word 'incapsulated' will not be altogether satisfactory to psycho-analysts because it will at once suggest that the past is a pathological enclave. However, it may be as true of history as of personal life stories that aspects of the past can function either as dissociated pathogenic agencies or as integral components of present trends, *i.e.* in the same way that infantile components operate in sublimations. Presumably, any given aspect of the past may be present-syntonic at one period of history and present-dystonic at another. History may repeat itself in the same way that individuals tend to repeat and re-live under fresh circumstances some personally typical life situation. Collingwood had a low opinion of psychology as a science, though he conceded a limited use to psycho-analysis in pathological cases. This, however, makes no difference to the significant parallel between his conception of history and the psycho-analytical conception of personal development. He was alive to the necessity for what we should call 'empathy' in the interpretation of historical events. Thus, he writes (p. 43): 'History did not mean knowing what events followed what. It meant getting inside other people's heads, looking at their situation through their eyes, and thinking for yourself whether the way in which they tackled it was the right way.' History then, like psycho-analysis, has its subjective aspect, the personal interpretation of past events, and its objective aspect, the reconstruction of their sequence. Dilthey maintained that '. . . the human studies cannot reach full efficiency without a thorough discipline in psychology' (Hodges, 1944, p. 17). He emphasized the significance of interpretation to all such studies and stated that (p. 28): 'Interpretation rests on understanding, which rests on a projection of the self into the other, and this is not an intellectual but an imaginative act'.

Sociologists now hope much from their new science of behaviour (not to be confused with Watsonian 'Behaviourism'). A publication (Dollard *et al.* 1939) from the Yale Institute of Human Relations puts to the test of extended observation and experiment a modified version of Freud's earlier theory of aggression as reaction to frustration. The result brings out clearly the limitations of the study of external behaviour divorced from inquiry into the corresponding mental activities. A comprehensive science of human behaviour will entail the correlation of mental and motor behaviour. Julian Blackburn's *Psychology and the Social Pattern* (1945) is described on the cover as 'a first attempt to form a link between General Psychology and Social Psychology on the one hand, and General Psychology and Psychopathology on the other'. Ralph Linton's *The Cultural Background of Personality* (1947) is concerned with the 'new science' emerging from the collaboration of psychologists, sociologists, and anthropologists, 'the systematic study of the interrelations of the individual, society and culture'. Sociology, like psychology and history, indeed like all disciplines which deal with human beings, can work and express its results either objectively, *e.g.* statistically, or subjectively in terms of human purposes and relationships. Both psychology and sociology, in their turn, draw upon and subsume the results of all the other specialist disciplines. Thus, as objective sciences, they must ultimately correlate with biology and physiology and, through them, with biochemistry and natural science in general. On the subjective side they draw upon, and must equally be correlated with, cultural anthropology, history, language, and all the expressive works of man which are storehouses of evidence as to his nature, *i.e.* with the whole realm of art and the humanities, including religion and philosophy. The relation of psycho-analysis to medicine and education will be self-evident.

The contribution which psycho-analysis has to offer to the gestating, rather than nascent, science of psycho-sociology is already considerable. To the objective aspect it offers a dynamic and economic *Psycheanschauung*; to the subjective aspect, an incomplete but in its way equally comprehensive and plastic personology. In addition, it offers a number of more or less direct contributions to sociology, beginning with Freud's own suggestions and continuing down to Flugel's *Man, Morals and Society* (1945) and the present day, one of the more recent publications in this field being Hartmann's *Psychoanalysis and Sociology* (1948). To repeat, perhaps the most characteristic contribution of psychoanalysis is that it supplies for the understanding of personality the story of individual life which is supplied for society by history and cultural anthropology. If the present condition of man and his civilization is to be fully grasped only in the light of past history, how much more is it true that the personality of an adult is to be understood only in terms of the life story which has made him what he is. It is true that the exact course of subjective development, particularly in the earliest months, is a matter of acute controversy among psycho-analysts themselves. But it is a firmly established fact that 'the child is father to the man' and psycho-analysis as a whole already has more to say about this genetic relationship than has any other discipline. It would appear that the course of individual development is, to some extent, parallel to that of racial development and that the evolution of civilization is reflected, however abbreviated and otherwise modified, in the personal history of every individual.

The main argument of the foregoing section is that since human beings live their personal lives on a level of integration that may be called psycho-social, the pre-requisite for intelligent individual and social re-adaptation at this level is the development of the correlative sciences of psychology and sociology. The potential contribution of psycho-analysis to psycho-sociology is already considerable. How far and how soon this potential contribution becomes actual will depend very largely on the degree to which psycho-analysts can learn to co-operate in spite of differences of opinion and to use these differences as stimuli to thought and research both among themselves and in relation to workers in other fields. In brief, it will depend on how quickly they can outgrow disabling tendencies to fission and isolation.

(2) LEBENSANSCHAUUNG

A genuinely realistic and fully humane *Lebensanschauung* would be the natural outcome of a well developed psycho-sociology. Psycho-analysis would certainly share in such a *Lebensanschauung* but it could also help to create it. Since Freud stated his opinion (1933, p. 232), that the young science of psycho-analysis was in no state to formulate *Weltanschauungen* but must share the common *Weltanschauung* of science, which he thought hardly merited such a high-sounding name, two things have become more evident than they were even ten years ago. Firstly the *Weltanschauung* of science is not static; in recent years it has undergone quite revolutionary changes. It is not something imposed from without but something which develops from within as the contributary sciences themselves develop. Up to the present, critics tend to blame psycho-analysis for its share in the scientific 'debunking' of traditional human values and the corresponding failure of science to produce a satisfactory alternative synthesis of necessary values. It must in fairness be said that much of this criticism is based upon popular misconceptions rather than upon authentic psycho-analysis, but it is none the less desirable to stress the positive, constructive implications of psycho-analysis in so far as they are already discernible.

Secondly, though Freud himself was undoubtedly influenced by the mechanistic *Anschauung* dominant in his earlier years, he had ample evidence that his work was revolutionary. He himself admitted this, but he does not appear to have fully realized quite what a challenge his work as a whole was to the older *Weltanschauung*. But clearly, his conceptions of psychological reality and mental dynamism are absolutely incompatible with any of the older conceptions of mechanistic materialism. It will be easier to appreciate that the relationship of psycho-analysis to the world outlook now developing is far closer than to that now outmoded, if some of the recent trends in scientific thought are briefly considered. The two which most concern us here are (*a*) the conviction of social responsibility which is becoming apparent among workers in many different branches of science, and (*b*) self-criticism, leading to revision and expansion of the concept of science itself, together with realization of the dangers of specialization and of purely analytic inquiry, and of the corresponding need for correlation and synthesis.

The awakening of social consciousness finds expression in different ways. It leads some scientists directly into the political field. It leads many who do not themselves enter politics to adopt definite political creeds. It leads a considerable number, irrespective of politics, to concern themselves actively with the relations between science and the state, in the endeavour to secure better provision for research and more adequate utilization of its results for the common benefit. Human welfare is still too readily equated with physical well-being and environmental amenities but recognition is growing that there is a psychological as well as a material standard of living, and that 'mechanized barbarism' is not civilization. The relation of science to industry holds the foreground of attention in this country but, while the economic aspect of the relation is stressed, the psycho-social factors involved are no longer ignored. Much is being said and done in regard to the humanization of industry.

Other scientists are less interested in the direct application of science than in the application of scientific method to all the social and political aspects of human life. They demand government by the empirical facts in place of government by fiction and prejudice, traditional or otherwise. This view is stated by

Waddington (1941), who sees in the adoption of the scientific attitude towards all human problems the best hope for modern man and, in passionate devotion to science, a possible alternative to religion. Such people are alive to the psychological importance of values and standards of conduct and to the need for finding a scientific basis for these to replace the authority of revealed religion. Whereas T. H. Huxley, regarding life as purely a struggle for survival, conceived it to be the moral aim of man to combat the 'horrid' order of nature (Tennyson's 'Nature, red in tooth and claw'), modern biologists like Julian Huxley and Waddington look to the natural course of human evolution to find a guiding line for conduct.

This demand for scientific living is closely related to the second trend mentioned, the self-criticism leading to the expansion of the concept of science and the recognition of the need for correlation and synthesis. Science is ceasing to be identified with the natural sciences and their experimental technique, and is tending to become equated with organized knowledge. The essence of science is its realistic mode of approach to the object of study. Any subject can therefore be studied scientifically and any technique can claim to be regarded as scientific which devises adequate checks and standards of probability suited to its individual field. The realism with which science is equated is no longer mechanistic materialism.

It is also becoming clear that, although the immediate aim of any particular science must be the advance of knowledge in its own field, its long-term aim should be the correlation of its specialized information with the general body of knowledge and its application to human welfare. The departments even of the natural sciences are no longer sharply demarcated; they overlap in many directions. With the increasing emphasis on synthesis, the focus of interest is tending to shift from the outer universe to the study of man and from biology to psychology and sociology. The lag in the development of the human sciences is beginning to be recognized as catastrophic and their furtherance as imperative. There is an efflorescence of psychologies and sociologies and new border disciplines are making their appearance, *e.g.* human biology, social medicine, mass-observation, and centres of research are being instituted such as the Nuffield Foundation at Oxford and the Yale Institute of Human Relations. The human sciences are still far from mature, and their development is impeded by their present lack of agreed common principles and techniques. It is hard to outgrow the conviction that measuring is knowing and that the only real knowledge is knowledge tested by controlled experiment and expressed in mathematical terminology.

These trends are not, of course, the only major changes now taking place in science, nor should it be thought that the views mentioned are shared by all scientists. There are as many re-actionaries in science as in any other walk of life, and there are many scientists still indifferent to anything except the adding of brick to brick in the building of their own speciality. There is as yet little tolerance of psychological reality among many psychologists and sociologists, and, for that matter, still too little among psycho-analysts themselves. But it is a fact that mechanistic materialism is now outmoded, partly as the result of modern work in physics and, neglecting for the moment the mass allegiance of Russian scientists to dialectical materialism, the *Weltanschauung* of Western science is in a state of flux: it is a welter of different viewpoints rather than an integrated outlook. But those trends, which for the sake of brevity may be called neo-realistic and humanist, exist, and they are dynamic because they are exhibited by the progressive minority in science, a minority which includes recognized leaders and pioneers in their own fields. If the development of the human sciences proceeds favourably these trends may eventually become dominant and lead to the emergence of an integrative *Lebensanschauung* and a humanology which is an organized group of co-ordinated disciplines instead of a random collection of more or less isolated, if not competitive, spheres of research.

If any science has a right to describe its essential outlook as realist and humanist, that science is psycho-analysis. At present this is not sufficiently clear to many psycho-analysts and it is certainly not the impression of psycho-analysis current among non-analysts. The remarkable thing about Freud's work is not that it should have been influenced by the intellectual climate of his time or should occasionally express personal preferences, but that its principles and implications should be so far in advance of his time. Hitherto, the progressive and constructive significance of psycho-analysis has seldom been appreciated even by people who accord Freud very considerable esteem. Thus Julian Huxley can write (1944, p. 46): 'Scientific method to-day has reached about as far in its understanding of human mind as it had in the understanding of electricity by the time of Galvani and Ampère. The Faradays and Clerk-Maxwells of psychology are still to come.' This seems to me a definite under-estimate of the significance of Freud's work. It is true that Freud's penetrative genius was impatient of philosophical pretensions, but this personal attitude in no way affects the wider implications of his work. Impatience with the human desire for integrative correlation is, however, a luxury which psycho-analysis can no longer afford.

If it is argued that discussion of *Lebensanschauungen* is a waste of time and unpractical, it may be said that every human being has a personal way of living which might, in the broadest sense of the term, be called his religion, and a specific mental attitude towards life which constitutes his philosophy; he has unconscious preconceptions about his own nature and about the universe and his relation to it, whether or not he has any conscious theories about these matters. Professional philosophy appears to aim at the elaboration and synthesis of defined intellectual conceptions. There is at present much discussion among philosophers themselves regarding the nature and aim of philosophy, what its human values are, etc. It is perhaps true that it is the desire of every voluntary philosopher to 'see life steadily and see it whole', but, as Dorothy Emmet writes (1945, p. 224): 'A metaphysical thinker may try to see life steadily; he cannot see it as a whole. He can only express what he grasps in the perspective of his experience. But the right word, giving articulation to the living relations out of which this perspective is constituted, can enlarge and not straiten further possibilities of responsive awareness.' Some philosophic wholes savour of wish-fulfilment pure and simple, of a personal rebuilding of the universe nearer to the heart's desire and of a self-expressive creation of works of intellectual art. Indeed, John Oulton Wisdom (1947, p. 177) has adduced much evidence in support of his thesis that 'The statements of a speculative philosopher do not directly express facts about the universe but symptomatically express facts about himself—they form his unconscious autobiography'. However, all thinking has subjective determinants and some philosophers are less intent on the formulation of closed 'systems' than on the synthesis and evaluation of trends of thought and advances in knowledge. The late A. N. Whitehead's philosophy of organism is an outstanding example of original and imaginative but, at the same time, correlative synthesis. The following sentence (Whitehead, 1929, p. x) shows how clearly he appreciated the relativity of philosophical truths: 'In philosophical discussion, the merest hint of dogmatic certainty as to finality of statement is an exhibition of folly'.

Within philosophy itself there has lately been a revolution, initiated by mathematicians, against speculative systems and metaphysics, which has come to be known as 'mathematical philosophy' or 'logical analysis'. So far this critical method has been used chiefly as a method of (sometimes necessary) destruction but it should certainly help in promoting greater precision in thinking and verbal expression, and has recalled British philosophy from idealism to empiricism. In its concentration on words and sentences and in its insistence that everything Non-Sense is nonsense, logical analysis appears as an objectivist extremism, to which existentialism is the modern subjectivist counterpart. Bertrand Russell, the Doyen of logical analysis in this country, himself continually transcends its limitations, even in his recent book, *Human Knowledge: Its Scope and Limits* (1948). Quite apart from questions of its validity, human knowledge has now become so detailed and so highly specialized in many departments, that single minds can no longer hope to grasp it in its entirety. However, tentative synthesis of the more general conclusions issuing from the various specialist fields and critical discussion of their implications for life are still possible. In such ways as this it would seem that philosophers could play a useful part in aiding the development of more adequate *Lebensanschauungen* and of more realistic norms of human behaviour. This kind of rôle has frequently been adopted by Bertrand Russell, most recently in his 1948-9 Reith Lectures, *Authority and the Individual* (1949). An enlightened minority already exists, but what the majority of the more active thinkers of our time still lack is an adequate conception of the nature of mental life and of the dynamics and economics of personality.

Modern developments in the physical theory of matter have led physicists to take an interest in metaphysics. Various suggestions have been made as to the advisability of physicists studying philosophy and philosophers physics. To a psycho-analyst it seems highly desirable that both physicists and philosophers should interest themselves in the psychological reality of their own mental organization if they really wish to know how it works and how it may influence their apprehension of facts and their formulation of theories.

V. THE NEO-REALISTIC HUMANISM IMPLICIT IN PSYCHO-ANALYSIS

The *Lebensanschauung* implicit in psycho-analysis is a neo-realistic humanism. This outlook on life emerges from psycho-analytic theory and practice and is intrinsic to it. The prefix 'neo' distinguishes this outlook from older types of realism and humanism but does not indicate wherein the differences lie. It will be most convenient to discuss the characteristics of psycho-analytic realism and humanism separately.

(1) NEO-REALISM

i. PSYCHOLOGICAL REALITY: IMMEDIATE AND INFERRED

The distinctive feature of psycho-analytic realism is the recognition of psychic or subjective reality as well as of material or objective reality. It is a point of interest that some technical terms, *e.g.* 'reality-ego', still bear witness to the lingering influence of mechanistic prejudice in favour of external, or material reality. There are, however, few terms more ambiguous than 'psychic' or 'psychological reality'. Thus, the term is used in two senses, roughly corresponding to immediate and to inferred reality. Immediate psychological reality is that reality of which alone we have direct and intimate awareness, namely, conscious experience. It might even be said that the only reality which is absolute is present conscious experience; living is living in a present 'now', however vivid the influence of the past or the expectation of the future may be. Eternity as experienced is a quality of feeling, not a duration of time, though we also feel that a period of time that drags intolerably is endless.

Equal subjective reality must be accorded to every conscious experience. The criteria by which perception is distinguished from hallucination and delusion from factual conviction are not purely psychological, but psycho-biological and psycho-social criteria (see p. 99). Ordinary perceptual experience with its belief in the existential reality of self, other people, and things, more sophisticated rumination about the nature of reality, delusion, and dream, all alike have subjective reality as experiences regardless of the quantitative and qualitative character of the experience.

Like the perceptual data that are the source of knowledge of the outer world, the data requisite for understanding mental life are given in conscious experience but they do not explain themselves; the nature of mental life has to be inferred from these data in the same way that knowledge of the external world has been inferred from perceptual data. It is the psychological reality of unconscious mental processes inferred by Freud which is the foundation of psycho-analysis, on which all its subsequent development is based. Freud himself wrote (1929, p. 17): 'I can assure you that the acceptance of unconscious mental processes represents a decisive step towards a new orientation in the world and in science'. The concept of unconscious mentation was not itself originated by Freud. It already existed in various forms, but it was Freud who first formulated systematic working-hypotheses regarding the nature and inter-relations of unconscious and conscious processes from the data provided by his initial studies of dreams and neuroses by the method of 'free association'. Present-day theory represents the outcome of the research stimulated by these hypotheses. This theory is admittedly incomplete, it is controversial in many respects, but it is nevertheless a coherent and realistic theory of mental life.

There is nothing mystical about psycho-analytic realism. It is based upon common-sense empiricism, upon the acceptance of whatever seems to be inescapably real for man, *i.e.* of the mental and material conditions which evoke his active response. Its concern is not with metaphysical dilemmas regarding the knowability or unknowability of things in themselves but with the strictly practical question of what it is necessary for man to know, *i.e.* to infer to be real, in order to live. If psycho-analysts understand the word 'existent' in its ordinary everyday sense and ignore the ambiguities of its philosophical definitions, they will tend to agree with Cattell (1946, p. 101) that 'the only defensible meaning of real is existent'.

In regard to the external world, we know that perception offers us a highly selective report on the universe, a report in the first instance relevant to ourselves and strictly conditioned by our preparedness and ability to receive it. Conscious feelings and impulses offer us an equally selective report on unconscious mental life. Certain recurrences in our perceptual experience are attributed by us to a corresponding regularity in natural pheno-mena. Perceptual experience may misinterpret what is happen-ing, but it is usually right in its conviction that something is happening regularly and the response evoked is frequently ade-quate for survival. The inferences drawn by scientists about the happenings in the outer world with the aid of specialized tech-niques for highly refined and critical reality-testing, have given them enough understanding and control over certain classes of natural phenomena to prove that their theories are sufficiently accurate to serve as working-hypotheses for human beings to use for their own purposes. The control of mental processes hitherto achieved by psycho-analysts may be insignificant by comparison, but as a result of clinical experience they maintain that mental processes and mental organization have as good a claim to psychological reality as atomic organization has to physical reality. They also maintain that mental processes oper-ate in accordance with ultimately discoverable rules, in the same way that physical phenomena are governed by natural laws. Both types of law, natural and psychological, are no more than human explanations whose veracity in the end depends upon their pragmatic utility. It is not until adequate working-hypo-theses are established that intelligent control becomes potentially, if not immediately, possible. Control does not imply omnipotent mastery over natural law, but its intelligent utilization.

Unconscious psychological reality is inferred from the totality of personal experience, not from sensory perception alone. Con-sciousness is not limited to impressions of the outer world and reactions to external situations: it also offers the whole range of human impulses and feelings, of which some appear to be evoked by the current environment but others to arise spontaneously and to be irrelevant to the immediate circumstances. People's inter-pretations of their wishes and feelings differ in adaptive value, but even when their interpretations are a sound basis for action, the explanations they give to themselves or to other people are often grossly inaccurate. Conscious experience and behaviour only become thoroughly intelligible when they are considered in relation to their unconscious determinants.

ii. THE PROBLEM OF PSYCHOLOGICAL REALITY-TESTING

The difficulty of exploring unconscious mental life is due to its inaccessibility. There are circumstances in which unconscious processes become conscious but, ordinarily speaking, they can only be inferred from their effects. The greatest difficulty lies in the fact that these inferences cannot, as a rule, be submitted to the rigours of experimental verification as can the inferences of natural science. In so far as experiments have been devised (a number of these are described by Flugel, 1945) the results are mainly positive. So long as there is no agreed technique for the investigation of unconscious mentation and until some method of psychological reality-testing is developed as reliable as the external reality-testing of the natural sciences, even general acceptance of the reality of unconscious mental processes will not obviate the variety of inferences drawn about them. Indeed, clashes of inference are frequent in psycho-analysis itself, as witness the various secessions that have given rise to derivative but independent systems of thought and the controversy to-day regarding the work of Melanie Klein.

The worst stumbling-block for natural scientists is that psychological reality-testing involves those subjective factors whose influence the techniques of natural science are designed expressly to eliminate. But in the nature of the case personal equations cannot be excluded from an inquiry into mental life. It is poets and other artists, including mystics, who have hitherto shown the most lively sense of psychological reality, but the forms in which they express their insight, though true to feeling, are unsatisfactory as formulations of fact because they so often impart a pseudo-objectivity to purely subjective experience. The would-be tester of psychological reality has to cultivate the emotional sensibility of the artist and yet bring his intelligence to bear upon the data so provided in order to express subjective facts not merely in terms consonant with subjective experience itself but also in terms consonant with objective knowledge. No refinement of personal reality-sense can exclude the effects of individual resistance and bias: the most effective safeguard against these would seem to be provided by the pooling and comparison of results. Unfortunately, whenever diversity of opinion occurs, there is a strong tendency for the protagonists to champion their own opinions and forget the axiomatic relativity of knowledge and the subjective determinants of the appeal made to them by their own point of view.

The anxiety attendant upon the reduction of our established and habitual 'resistances' is the main factor that retards the development of subjective realism. We are mortally afraid to know ourselves and it is not death but anxiety which is the first and last enemy of psychological reality-testing.

iii. THE NON-MYSTICAL NATURE OF PSYCHOLOGICAL REALITY

The psycho-analytic conception of psychological reality does not involve any mystical assumptions. All the phenomena that, since the time of William James, have been called the 'varieties of religious experience' are subjectively real and there can be no doubt of their psychological importance. But, so far as investigation has shown up to the present, these experiences are capable of a purely psychological, as distinct from a mystical, explanation. This is a major difference between psycho-analysis and the views of Jung, for whom the 'full reality of the psychic' implies the 'sovereignty of the "mystical"', and who maintains that 'the polymorphism of primitive instinctive nature and the way of formation of personality confront each other as a pair of opposites called nature and spirit' (quoted from Jacobi, 1942, pp. 65, 61). It is Jung's mysticism that makes it possible for a Catholic writer (Witcutt, 1943, p. 5) to say: 'Freud and Adler stand to Jung in the same relation as the pre-Socratic philosophers stood to Socrates, theirs are the partial and one-sided theories absorbed and explained by the master's synthesis. That is to our advantage, because the theories of Freud and Adler were incompatible with Catholic teaching, whereas that of Jung may be with profit studied and in part absorbed by Catholic philosophy.' Melanie Klein's phraseology sometimes gives the impression that she is according to 'internal objects' the kind of pseudo-substantiality attaching to Jung's 'archetypes', but this may be an unintentional result of the emphasis she places on the subjective importance of animistic phantasies. However, it is impossible to emphasize too strongly that psychological reality is psychological and neither mystical nor material reality.

The material reality most intimately connected with experience is the brain. Concomitance of mental and cerebral activities has been postulated for some time, but it is very difficult to establish detailed correlations between mental events and brain events. Recent developments in brain surgery and electro-encephalography have opened new approaches to this problem from the physiological side. These were usefully summarized by a number of eminent research-workers in the 1949 series of broadcasts, 'The Physical Basis of Mind', opened by Sir Charles Sherrington (*The Listener*, 5 May 1949). Opinions of these authorities naturally differ, as do opinions of philosophers and psychologists. The simplest hypothesis about mental-cerebral relations, and one consonant with the findings of psycho-analysis, is that there is no duality of event; the events observed from outside the living brain and registered objectively, *e.g.* as electrical events, modifications of brain waves, are experienced subjectively by the person submitting to the experiments, as mental events. Ernest Jones says (1946, p. 12): 'I do not think the mind really exists as an entity', *i.e.* apart from the biological entity, the human being as a whole. He considers that our choice of 'mental' or 'somatic' phraseology is a matter of methodological convenience and that a common formula may be expressible only in mathematical terms. It is, indeed, difficult not to suspect that it is chiefly the strength of subjective prejudice which prevents more general acceptance of the unitary psycho-physical nature of the human being and the single event hypothesis of mental-cerebral activity. However, it has to be remembered that, even if there be only a single series of events, the fundamental duality still remains between the subjective experience of the event and its objective manifestation. It would appear in the highest degree improbable that the most delicate instrument will ever record anything but cerebral events, or that the most sensitive and highly trained subject of experiment will ever become conscious of anything but mental events.

A. N. Whitehead (1929, p. 44) seems to imply (wrongly) that the work of Freud tends to maintain an artificial separation between mind and body, and he himself assigns to every 'actual entity' a bi-polarity, a mental pole and a physical pole. The irreducible polarity in the daily life of human beings seems to be the subjective-objective polarity which justifies the empirical dual realism of psycho-analysis, its acceptance of both psychological and physical reality, immediate and inferred.

The dynamic significance of unconscious mental processes and the concentration of research upon them tends insensibly to the persuasion that they are somehow more real than conscious processes. The full psychological reality at any moment is the totality of activated processes, conscious and unconscious. Conscious experience is the aspect of the current synthesis of past and present experience of which we are aware, but it is certainly no less real than the aspects of which we are unaware. Failure to remember this fact results in the nihilistic reduction of human activities to 'nothing but' primary instinct gratification and to a wholly unrealistic impoverishment of human life. The transformations of instinct brought about by mental organization are as real as the primal impulses themselves. The aesthetic sensibility which may be called 'love of the eye' is not identical with the infantile 'lusts of the eye' that may ultimately motivate it and achieve modified expression in this sublimated form. They are, indeed, operative, but operative in the current psychological reality which is aesthetic appreciation. Probably many thwarted suckling wishes are gratified in the sublimated form of listening to music, but the adult lover of music would seldom experience any pleasure if he were offered a wet nurse instead of a symphony concert. The psychological fact is no longer that he wishes to be breast-fed but that he wishes to listen to music; or, perhaps more exactly, that he now wishes to be breast-fed by listening to music.

(2) Neo-humanism

i. INSTINCT

One of the main differences between psycho-analytical and older types of humanism is that the former is based upon a more balanced appreciation of the nature of human instinctual endowment. The failure of the older humanism, which Christian apologists continually emphasize (*e.g.* Murray, 1943), can be ascribed in part to its over-optimistic belief in the essential goodness of man. Neo-humanism recognizes that man is both malevolent and benevolent, and that his vices and his virtues are alike derived from what it is advisable to think of as ineradicable primary instincts. These instincts are neither moral nor immoral but amoral or pre-moral; morality is a product of mental organization. A second major difference is the psycho-analytic recognition of infantile sexuality with all its personal and cultural significance.

The primary instincts seem to be the part of human nature that cannot be changed. If they change at all, their alteration may take place in terms of long-scale evolutionary time rather than short-scale historical time. The evidence of history suggests that man's primary instinctual equipment has not changed appreciably since the beginning of recorded time. On the other hand, the mental organization of instinct and the modes of its expression do change and are modifiable. Personality is a pattern of instinct regulation, created in every individual in the course of his own development and influenced at every stage by current conditions. Even so, however, the ground plan of mental organization seems to be much less plastic than those who pin their faith on nurture and environmental influence would like to think.

Little as we know about psychological inheritance or the amount of mental organization that may be innate, the tendency to ego-differentiation would appear to be inborn, since some form of morality exists in all human groups known to us through history or cultural anthropology. Hence, although individual super-ego organizations may prove more or less modifiable, they cannot be liquidated, either in the individual or in the race. Conscience must be reckoned as constant a feature of human nature as instinctual impulses themselves, and human beings as inescapably moral. But conscience is no more uniform than any other human character; standards of value are always operative in individuals and in groups, but they are both varied and variable.

ii. MENTAL ORGANIZATION; ADAPTATION; PLEASURE AND PAIN

The ground plan of mental organization is familiar to us in the form of the threefold constitution of mind. This includes, firstly, the basic id, the totality of primary instinctual impulses conceived as unorganized in contrast to the ego-organization; secondly, the ego-organization itself, 'that part of the id which has been modified by the direct influence of the external world acting through the Pcpt.-Cs.' [1] (Freud, 1927, p. 29); thirdly, the differentiating grade in the ego, the super-ego organization.

Freud emphasized both the community of ego and id and the contrast between the organized ego and the unorganized id. He did in fact frequently suggest that the repressed is part of the id (cf. Isaacs, 1945, p. 62). For instance, he wrote (1927, p. 28): 'But the repressed merges into the id as well, and is simply a part of it'. And again (1933, p. 103): '. . . the repressed material merges into the rest of the id'. The clinical justification for the

[1] Freud's abbreviation of 'perceptual consciousness'.

concept of the id was discussed in Chapter IV (p. 112). To my mind the retention of the threefold constitution is necessary, however many sub-organizations we may become able to distinguish and however variable the relation of component systems to major organizations may prove to be (cf. Fairbairn, 1944, p. 82).

The present section is less concerned with the detail of mental organization and personality pattern than with the general conception of the threefold constitution which gives psycho-analytic humanism its specific character. It would in any case be gratuitous to enlarge upon the super-ego organization in view of the publication of Flugel's *Man, Morals and Society* (1945). This book is almost a super-ego encyclopaedia, since it includes practically everything that has been formulated concerning super-ego development and function.

It may be mentioned here, however, that although the super-ego organization is, in some respects, a bone of contention, it is also a topic upon which there is a considerable measure of general agreement. It is agreed, for instance, that super-ego organization is fully established at the close of the classical Oedipus phase and that it is created by introjection. Further, the importance of parental identifications is commonly accepted. In spite of differences of opinion regarding chronology, etc., no psycho-analyst denies the introjective origin of conscience or fails to see in it the means by which the child adopts parental standards for his own. Super-ego formation seems to act as a substitute for the inheritance of acquired characters, enabling the child to assimilate the cultural standards of his social environment, as mediated through his parents or other persons with whom there is close relationship in infancy.

There is equally general agreement that the character of the super-ego organization and the nature of its relations to the id and the operative ego are as much influenced by the child's own attitudes and reactions as by the real character of the persons around him. Whether the accentuated cruelty of an obsessional or manic-depressive conscience be attributed to arrested development or to defusion following regression, it is still the personal aggressivity of the individual which is held to be ultimately responsible.

There is also agreement that the major function of the super-ego organization is endopsychic control and modification of instinct. The automatic control of instinct effected by it is a labour-saving device comparable to other habit formations. There would clearly be definite value for the individual in an automatic control of instinct consonant with the requirements of the society in which he lived, but at the present day the super-ego is seldom attuned to current reality. This is partly because it embodies the attitudes towards instinct acquired in infancy, and partly because the attitudes so acquired are not only those necessary for survival in the individual's own infancy but also superstitious and traditional attitudes which may have been useful in earlier phases of human development but have now lost their utility. In a world so complex as ours it is no longer possible for any single person to obtain all the information required to form trustworthy opinions on every subject. However, it does not matter whether everyone knows everything about everything; what does matter is that as many people as possible should adopt a realistic attitude towards all human problems. It is precisely the archaic irrationalism of our conscience controls that prevents the adoption of such an attitude. The instinct-testing carried out through the super-ego organization not only prevents our being rational about external affairs but it ensures that we very seldom have any accurate appreciation even of our own motives. The key to realism in the ethical field appears to Waddington (1942) to be the development of a more realistic super-ego. This is a problem in which instruction is of secondary importance. Super-ego formation and modification are alike effected by introjection, and the character and attitude towards life of the parent or teacher and the nature of the child's relationship to him are of far greater significance in this connection than any teaching.

The modifiability and attunement of the super-ego organization to current reality seem to be related to the balance of its libidinal and aggressive trends and to the resulting character of its relation to the ego-organization. When libidinal systems are dominant and the relations between ego and super-ego are mainly identificatory, the conditions exist which promote both super-ego attunement and ego efficiency. When the super-ego organization is highly aggressive and the relation to the ego is prohibitive, a condition obtains in which the super-ego is recalcitrant to modification and the ego is impeded by inhibitions.

Human beings are strongly prejudiced in favour of identifying themselves with their most intimately familiar conscious selves; they shrink from recognizing that their conscious opinions, ambitions, and other preoccupations are not so supremely important as they habitually assume. However, as Freud's description of the difficult position of the ego clearly shows (see p. 133), we cannot avoid the conclusion that the conscious self is an agent and not an end of life and that the highest rôle to which it can legitimately aspire is not mastery but good management. The function of mental life as a whole is mediation and the ego's share in this is ordinarily described as external reality-testing and adaptation. But Freud made it very evident that this ego task is multi-polar, because the ego has not merely to react to the external circumstances but also to react in accordance with the conditions obtaining in the mental organization. Notwithstanding the trans-formations that man has effected in his environment, he did not invent either the universe or himself and his creative capacity is conditioned by the nature of both the universe and himself. In spite of all its arrogant attempts, the conscious self cannot decide omnipotently how it will live, it can only try to find out the conditions under which it can achieve satisfactory living. It can then do what it may to fulfil these conditions as intelligently as possible. Freedom and control are the result not of ignorant defiance but of intelligent utilization of natural and psycho-logical law.

Edward Glover's definition of reality-testing is as follows (1933b, p. 486): 'Efficient reality-testing, for any subject who has passed the age of puberty, is the capacity to retain psychic contact with the objects that promote gratification of instinct, including here both modified and residual infantile impulse'. Thus efficient reality-adaptation is consonant with both subjective and external reality; more often than not it represents a viable compromise between the demands of instinct, conscience, and environment. It is not freedom from conflict or guilt but the ability continually to resolve and transcend conflict and to liquidate guilt which is decisive for effective living. The freedom of the strongest and most stable operative self is fairly strictly conditioned both by its own constitution and by the economy of the total personality.

A second cause of the failure of the earlier humanism was its over-estimation of reason both in regard to its reliability and its provision of incentives to action. To-day, we are more aware of the limitations of human intelligence and the inherent relativity of human knowledge. Knowledge itself is not an incentive to action but a mental tool; the incentive to its use or neglect is derived from instinct. Nevertheless, psycho-analysis also regards human intelligence as man's chief guide to the psycho-social re-adaptation which is so imperative.

Primitive reality-testing, like the sensory-affective discrimination we assume to function in early infancy, was probably a matter of learning by trial and error through immediate pleasure and pain. Immediate pleasure and pain are the agencies still used in testing the capacity of animals to learn by experience. The development of intelligence has given cognitive discrimination a more important rôle in adult human life than affective discrimination. The ability to remember and to foresee has enabled man to create long-term standards of necessity and advisability which often supersede standards of immediate comfort and discomfort. The transition from spontaneous response guided by immediate pleasure and pain to deliberately considered response to what we judge to be the requirements of a situation is the transition from the pleasure principle to the reality principle in mental functioning described by Freud. The substitution is only partial; pain toleration varies widely from person to person and in the same person under different conditions. In general, however, the substitution of long-term intelligent as distinct from short-term affective assessment of the environment has meant that immediate pleasure and pain have ceased to be such reliable guides to the adult human in his dealings with the outer world as they are to the burnt child. But the prospect of eventual reward or punishment in one form or another continues to play no inconsiderable rôle in judgment of suitable behaviour.

In spite of all the phenomena of reversal and transvaluation of affects, pleasure and pain are on the whole more reliable indices of subjective than of external reality. People often are informed by their feelings about some of their dominant impulses. In normal people, the significance of strong feelings like intense love, virulent hate, acute jealousy, or terror, may be transparent. Although the more subtle blends of feeling and alterations of mood are cipher messages which the conscious self is often at a loss to decode, they are also potentially understandable. Quite generally, feeling-tone signalizes the fate of instinct, the relative success or failure of current adaptation. Happiness is a by-product of successful adaptation. It is elliptical to say that we pursue pleasure and avoid pain; as total persons we seek situations in which our impulses can find satisfactory expression and we avoid frustrating ones. It is only the short-sighted conscious self which tends to mistake the pleasurable consequence of performing its task adequately for the aim of its existence. The ego desire to be happy is, however, fully justified by the fact that happiness results from adaptation. Pathological euphoria apart, happiness, content, and serenity are signs of health, whereas persistent misery, discontent, apathy and boredom, unless actually justified by unfortunate circumstances, are signs of maladaptation and disease-proneness. Pain and grief are a part of the human lot but they enrich personality only in so far as they are overcome or transcended. No human being can avoid frustrations of divers kinds, and learning how best to cope with them should be a part of education, but usually too much stress is laid upon the educative and character-forming value of deprivation and sorrow and far too little upon the integrative influence of gratification, happiness, and content.

iii. THE PROBLEM OF INTEGRATION

The problem of adaptation is bound up with that of personal integration. The process of psycho-analysis throws a suggestive light on the kind of re-integration that is desirable for modern man. Freud (1933, p. 106) wrote that the object of psycho-analytic therapy is '. . . to strengthen the ego, to make it more independent of the super-ego, to widen its field of vision, and so to extend its organization that it can take over new portions of the id. Where id was, there shall ego be. It is reclamation work, like the draining of the Zuyder Zee.' This 'reclamation work' is fraught with anxiety for the reality-self and is usually opposed by conscience. The overcoming of the consequent resistances appears to become possible in so far as 'the patient tends to make the analyst into an "auxiliary super-ego" ' (Strachey, 1934, p. 138). With the support and sanction thus acquired the patient becomes more able to tolerate the interpretation of the various id-wishes directed towards the analyst in the transference. It may be said that the unconscious becomes conscious in proportion both to the diminution of anxiety and to the increase of anxiety-tolerance that are effected through the modification of the super-ego organization. In the process of psycho-analysis 'reclamation work' and super-ego modification are correlated. The psycho-analyst's attitude is the ego-supporting one that it is possible and desirable for the patient to tolerate the hitherto intolerable and gradually to become more aware of subjective realities that he had previously striven to ignore and that his conscience had probably been active in keeping from him. The ego is strengthened in proportion to the greater amounts of instinctual energy that are released from endopsychic durance and allowed to reinvigorate old or initiate new modes of expression. The degree of ego invigoration will be proportionate to the degree of super-ego modification and to the establishment of permissive rather than prohibitive relations between self and conscience. In the consulting-room the ethical standard is a standard of reality.

Since the severity and inhibitive power of conscience depends quantitatively upon the amount of infantile aggression turned against the self, recovery in analysis and ventilation in the transference situation of these early hostilities, without retaliation from the analyst, tends towards the production of more libidinal relations between conscience and self.

The working-through of infantile libidinal relationships in the transference reduces dissociations and promotes synthesis. It thus places hitherto useless or pathogenic quantities of libidinal energy at the disposal of the ego. This freeing of libidinal energy also increases the personal capacity for libidinization of aggression and its diversion to constructive ends. It is the libidinal impulses that are integrative; both personal and social integration and the successful control of aggression depend upon their adequate development and release.

The psycho-analytic process may fail or may achieve only partial success, but, where it succeeds, the re-integration it initiates brings about not only a release of energy for life purposes but a degree of harmonization between id, ego, and super-ego organizations. This may, in favourable cases, justify calling it at least a relative integration of the whole personality. Spheres of conflict and inimical relations between the mental systems will not be lacking, but the sphere of effective co-operation will be appreciably increased.

Even this skeletal account of the psycho-analytic process brings out the features of most general significance. These may be summarized as follows:

(*a*) The basis of therapeutic re-integration is realization. Subjective reality is not ignored but accepted for what it is, whatever its nature.

(*b*) Release of energy for life purposes and re-integration mean the increase of friendly relations between all the aspects of personality.

(c) The personal control of instinct, hitherto impaired by prohibition and dissociation, is improved by ego-synthesis and suitable use. Intelligent conformation to necessity is preferable to automatic control by fear. The waste of human energy through personal and social mismanagement of instinct is great.

(d) Libido is integrative: it is labile and capable of displacement to a great variety of creative interests. The optimum ratio between primary and displaced gratification is probably specific for each individual. Aggression is disintegrative, it is less labile but capable of libidinization and of diversion to constructive ends. Unexpended aggression turns against the self. The promotion of personal and of social integration alike demand the full development of libidinal capacity and the provision of suitable channels for the external discharge and utilization of aggression.

One of the first tasks for modern man is the revision of his attitude towards his primary instincts. Signs of this revision are already apparent in a saner attitude towards education and many other problems, including sexuality. There is always a danger of swinging from the tyranny of conscience to a tyranny of impulse, but the whole-time pursuit of sensual pleasure is no more completely satisfying than a life of absolute asceticism. One of the more ludicrous distortions of psycho-analysis was the popular notion that children ought never to be thwarted and that all repression was bad. It is, however, perfectly clear that in a social world many impulses must be prohibited in their primary form, and that children need help in enduring frustrations that are really necessary and in finding substitute ways of expressing themselves. It is not desirable that we should react from the despising of our instincts to their worship but it is eminently desirable that we should recognize them for what they are—the dynamo of psycho-social life. It is because humanity has not yet attained or regained a genuinely realistic attitude towards instinct that it has never achieved any stable civilization. What Freud (1930) called the 'discontents' engendered by civilization have never been successfully mitigated and, in consequence, we may still witness the final disruption of so-called Christian civilization.

Broadly speaking, there are two methods of personal and social instinct-control: firstly, prohibition relying upon force and fear, and, secondly, persuasion and explanation relying upon libidinal factors and intelligent co-operation. Probably both have always been employed to some extent, but there is no doubt that, on balance, control by fear has been the dominant method. There is also no doubt that the only stably integrative method is libidinal and intelligent. The more archaic the super-ego organization, the more it seems to function on the lines of 'go and see what baby is doing and tell him not to'. Like the Victorian parent it demands blind obedience and enjoins total prohibition under threat of dire punishment. Aim-inhibited expressions of instinct under such duress are often limited to reaction-formations as distinct from sublimation. In reaction-formation the aim of instinct is inverted, *e.g.* where infantile soiling-impulses are replaced by adult devotion to cleanliness. Reaction-formation is economically a more expensive process than sublimation, in which the primary impulse achieves expression, although in modified form.

Human dread of instinct and of infantile propensities is reinforced by identifying them with dreaded and disgusting id aspects of the parents. The basic rôle of anxiety and fear in personal instinct control is paralleled by the rôle of propitiation and aversion in primitive religions. Jane Harrison was convinced of the existence of such a primitive stage in Greek religion and wrote (1908, p. 7): 'It can, I think, be shown that what Plutarch regards as superstition was in the sixth and even the fifth century before the Christian era the *real* religion of the main bulk of the people, a religion not of cheerful tendance but of fear and deprecation ... we have evidence, drawn not from the terminology of religion, but from the certain facts of ritual, evidence which shows beyond a possibility of doubt that the Greeks of the classical period recognized two different classes of rites, one of the nature of "service" addressed to the Olympians, and the other of the nature of "riddance" or "aversion" addressed to an order of beings wholly alien ... and this second class of rites ... is primitive and lies at the very root and base of Greek religion.'

If integration is favoured by libidinal methods of control it might seem paradoxical that Christianity should have failed in its civilizing mission in spite of its assumption that 'God is love'. This failure may, perhaps, be due in part to the idealization which plays so important a rôle in Christianity. It would seem to be a fact that the type of personal integration promoted by

Christianity is a partial integration in which conscience and reality-self are firmly allied against instinct, and which, by its very nature, perpetuates mental civil war.

iv. IDEALIZATION-DENIGRATION

In the past, all too little attention has been paid to the process of idealization, and it has not been sufficiently well recognized that it is a dual process of idealization-denigration. It is commonly taken for granted that man's ideals are his noblest creation and it is far too readily overlooked that humanity has paid for its aspiration to the super-human, or angelic, by the simultaneous development of sub-human, or diabolical, propensities. These degraded trends are often called 'bestial' but man's degradation is specifically human: human behaviour exhibits depths and refinements of lust and cruelty never attained in the animal world. It would seem to be a fact that man's most odious behaviour is usually brought into play in the service of his most cherished ideals, as witness the Inquisition and all the wars of religion and 'ideology'. Many people have deplored the cruelties practised in the name of religion, but very few seem to have realized how firmly the conjunction of cruelty and piety is rooted in the nature of idealization. It is for this reason that it is so necessary to distinguish between genuinely good, *i.e.* really satisfying and loveworthy objects, whether external or introjected, and idealized objects. The real unworthiness of the latter is disguised by overcompensatory libidinization, and their real deficiencies impel a correspondingly exaggerated denigration of the subject himself or of some other object. Money-Kyrle's interesting paper (1944, p. 166) on political ethics seems to pay insufficient attention to this matter.

The aetiology of this dual process of idealization-denigration is by no means fully established. From the study of perverts and psychotics, Edward Glover concludes that idealization occurs much earlier than has usually been supposed, *e.g.* in relation to 'part-objects'. He says (1938, p. 96): 'These primitive idealizations have in my opinion a specially close relation to anal sadism . . . these early idealizations have a considerable reassurance value and can take part in the process of "libidinizing" anxiety objects'. Susan Isaacs (1945, p. 62) gives reasons for considering that '. . . at certain stages of development and under some conditions, idealization *may* contribute something to the stability of the immature ego'. Clearly, idealization could not have become such an established human habit if it were devoid of all adaptive value. As a weapon of defence, however, it is liable to prove a two-edged sword. It is a mode of mental behaviour which, possibly more than any other, militates against psychological reality-sense. Although it may have its appropriate uses at certain stages of development, it may belong to those categories of mental behaviour which the adult human must learn to transcend.

It would seem that the possibility of idealization-denigration is based upon the intense all-or-none reactions of infancy, the alternations of complete content with absolute dissatisfaction, and the consequent tendency to the initial organization of relatively separate and distinct libidinal and aggressive nuclear ego-object systems. But these early reactions are realistic in the sense that no situation is likely to be felt as blissful that is not really satisfying, at least to some extent, and no situation atrocious that is not really painful or frustrating in some degree. But, in idealization, pleasurable experiences are revived in relation to a situation which is really painful. The evidence from adults seems to point to idealization-denigration as a method of overcoming intolerable ambivalence. The same evidence suggests that it is very frequently employed in the period of life when the reality ego-systems are acquiring definite organization. Self-consciousness and the potentially unbearable recognition that the same person may be both hateful and lovable develop together. The process would appear to be in essence a regressive solution of ambivalent conflict intimately related to the toil and trouble of acquiring sphincter control. This accords with Glover's view quoted above concerning its specially close relation to anal sadism. Susan Isaacs also writes (1945 p. 62): 'One essential element in idealization is this *controlling* of the idealized object and of its counterpart, the terrifyingly bad one, and of all mental processes relating to them'. The emphasis on control is highly suggestive since love of power, desire for mastery, and the exercise of authority over others are all strongly tinged with anal sadism and seem to be closely allied with anxieties about security of bowel control.

In adults it is never easy to distinguish between primary anal tendencies and those reinforced by regression. It would appear, however, that idealization-denigration can reach its greatest heights in the phase of classical Oedipus conflict, and it is these idealizations which re-emerge in the characteristic romanticism and religious preoccupations of adolescence. In the Christian tradition aim-inhibited self-sacrificing love is idealized as God and sadistic erotism becomes the Devil. Owing in part to the permeation of European culture by this Christian tradition, the Oedipus conflict tends to issue in a personality pattern in which the frustrated and forbidden primary impulses are identified with the denigrated infantile and parental erotic and sadistic selves. The idealized asexual parents and idealized selves form a prohibitive control system in the super-ego organization. In extreme cases the conscious self is left in the position of the rope in a tug of war: the opponents are irreconcilable and victory must go to one side or the other unless the rope parts. Occurrences like the conversion of St. Augustine and his transformation from libertine to saint indicate a change in the ego-relationship from identification with the id to identification with the super-ego.

Control systems are developed in all cultures, but it is in the Christian tradition, more particularly the Protestant and Puritan tradition, that the sexual instinct has suffered the maximum denigration. This may be one of the reasons why the Industrial Revolution began in Britain and why commercialism with its anal profit-motive and its jungle methods first became dominant in north-western Europe and the U.S.A. The idealization which makes possible the love of God can hardly occur in the absence of fairly strong libidinal trends. Some of the saints, indeed, have been such great lovers that their love of God embraced all His children, as, for example, St. Francis of Assisi. In less well-endowed persons, where the infantile hatred of the parents is not turned against the self, love of God too often leads to withdrawal and dislike of one's fellows. Hence, although the religious apologists are right in considering the profit-motive to be less integrative than the love of God, the Christian integration, by its very nature, cannot resolve the conflict between super-ego and id or materially aid the libidinization of aggression. The lives of the saints are filled with accounts of id vengeance exacted in such forms as bodily ill health and persecution by the Devil.

Religious idealization is considered here only in relation to the economics of personal integration, and many aspects bearing on this have had, perforce, to be omitted. The point it is sought to make is that the type of integration achieved through idealization-denigration can only be partial because it depends upon the maintenance of a super-ego and ego coalition against the id; it perpetuates warfare against instinct and does nothing to make durable peace with it. Idealization does not effect any true libidinization of aggression and the disillusioned idealist frequently becomes an equally unrealistic cynic. The psychological squalor of life between the wars was, in part, a consequence of profound disillusionment. Reaction-formations are similarly precarious in that the aggression behind them tends to come to the fore: as in the case of the woman of whom someone wrote, 'She spent her life in the service of others; you could always tell the others by their hunted expression'.

Man's idealism has been the most potent agent of his cultural development, but he has paid a heavy price for it, since the impairment of reality sense inseparable from idealization probably accounts in part for the instability inherent in human civilization. In a world in which so many people are looking for peace ideals to substitute for war ideals it is as well to point out that ideals have their disadvantages, and that intelligently realistic standards of personal and social necessity are to be preferred. But the transition from idealism to realism can only be effected gradually. The next step in mental development may be this gradual transcendence of idealism (and/or cynicism) by realism and the development of personal integrative democracy under intelligent ego management in place of super-ego or id autocracy. Human beings have not only evolved ideals of love but have also developed an everyday capacity for stable affection, sympathetic understanding, toleration, and even appreciation of their mutual idiosyncrasies. It is the growth of these genuine relationships of fellowship that are most likely to favour the modes of co-operation and of constructive use of aggression that would issue in more stable social integration. Neither personal nor social integration will ever be absolute; the family will always remain a fountainhead of aggressive as well as of libidinal relationships.

V. STANDARDS OF NORMALITY

The state of the world is evidence that modern man is neither psychologically nor socially healthy, although the present crisis may herald convalescence. In a state of universal ill health it is not easy to establish precise standards of normality. Since man is a psycho-social being, the criteria of personal normality are not purely psychological but psycho-social. In consequence, the standard of normality at any one period of history or in any given social group will inevitably vary. It will, however, always involve reference, in principle, to personal integration and social adaptation. Ernest Jones (1942, p. 7) writes: '. . . We surmise that the psychological problem of normality must ultimately reside in the capacity to endure—in the ability to hold wishes in suspension without either renouncing them or "reacting" to them in defensive ways. Freedom and self-control are thus seen to be really the same thing, though both are badly misused concepts. We reach the conclusion that the nearest attainable criterion of normality is fearlessness. The most normal person is, like Siegfried, "*angst-frei*", but we must be clear that we mean by this not merely manifest courage, but the absence of all the deep reactions that mask unconscious apprehensiveness. Where these are absent we have the willing or even joyful acceptance of life, with all its visitations and chances, that distinguishes the free personality of one who is master of himself.' This sets a very high, possibly unattainable, standard of normality, but a standard seldom achieved by the majority of so-called normal people to-day. It is a standard which implies the attainment of psychological realism and personal integration of the total rather than of the more usual partial type.

VI. CONCLUSION

The neo-realistic humanism implicit in psycho-analysis does not open up any prospects of personal or social perfection. It does not under-estimate the difficulty of the psycho-social problems confronting modern man. Its attitude is neither optimistic nor pessimistic; it tries to view these problems impartially in the perspective of man's mental and social development. The positive contribution of psycho-analysis is a conception of human nature which not only throws light on the origins of these psycho-social problems but also indicates some of the directions in which their solution may possibly be found.

CHAPTER VI

PSYCHO-ANALYSIS AND INTEGRATIVE LIVING [1]

I. INTRODUCTION

THE term 'integration' may easily become something of a catchword, but it conveys perhaps better than any other term the sense of wholeness resulting from the organization of dynamic components, a living unity engendered by the harmonious patterning of variety. Integration, in its application to personality, is a strictly relative term. Individuals react at any given moment as functional wholes, but these functional wholes are more or less temporary and vary, according to psycho-social circumstances, within limits imposed by the total personality. Applied to the living but more permanent total pattern of mental organization, the term integration conveys the meaning of a stable and unified personality, a microcosm of harmoniously interrelated systems, as contrasted with a schizoid micro-chaos of mutually discordant sub-organizations.

Integration is a term that is useful both in metapsychology and in personology, and one for which there appears to be no adequate synonym. It is indispensable in metapsychology and its use in personology is confirmed by habit. The term 'personal integrity' is too closely associated with conventional morality to be a satisfactory one, but it will sometimes be used in this chapter as a personological synonym for integration of the total personality.

It may be noted here that an American psycho-analyst, Joseph J. Michaels, has arrived independently at similar conclusions about the concept of integration in psycho-analysis. These are summarized in the following quotation (1945, p. 54): 'In the theory of psycho-analysis, the conception of integration probably finds its most complex expression and elaboration. Although this conception is not expressly stated, it is implicit

---

[1] Reprinted, slightly revised and expanded, from 'Notes on Psycho-analysis and Integrative Living' (1947), *Int. J. Psycho-Anal.* xxviii, p. 57. The original paper was dedicated to Ella Sharpe, 'who wanted this paper to be written'.

and inherent in the system as a whole and in its component parts. It seems as if Freud took for granted the conception of integration and built upon it extensively, and even though one does not find a specific description of it as such, nevertheless one can observe its implications permeating all the branches of psycho-analytical knowledge.'

The development of personality-pattern is brought about through synthesis and dissociation. It is moulded by the varied sequence of experience, that is, by all the relationships effected, whatever their nature. It is, therefore, highly improbable that even the best integrated personality should be free from dissociated components or lack tendencies to disintegration. Primary instincts cannot be eradicated and the effects of experience cannot be nullified, though they may be modified. Hence, integrative living is a continual resolution of conflict, and integration is a constant, creative transcendence of disintegrative trends. Therapeutic success and failure both point to the difficulty of such transcendence, but indicate the possibility that human beings might achieve more satisfactory degrees of personal integrity than are common to-day if they could overcome their profound dread of understanding and accepting themselves, and develop a more enlightened psychological reality-sense.

The pressure of world affairs is compelling attention to the practical importance of psychology and sociology. Personal and social conditions are interdependent, and understanding of the psycho-social factors which favour the development and maintenance of personal integrity may help towards the establishment of the principles of social organization which would be conducive to world integration. Whereas philosophy and theology have sought to provide logical explanations of man and the universe, it has, until recently, been the province of religion and ethics to supply 'values' and to direct the conduct of life. In their strictly personal aspect, religions offer plans or methods of integration and ethics purport to supply the rules of integrative living. It is, therefore, desirable to consider to what extent the implications of psycho-analysis accord with the recommendations of religion and ethics and how far they diverge from them. It is naturally impossible here to consider all the major religions of the world or all the numerous ethical systems and philosophies. All that can be attempted is a brief consideration of some aspects of

Christianity and the Christian ethic, since they have been most influential in the development of that Western European civilization which is our most immediate concern.

The limitations of this chapter and the strictly tentative nature of its conclusions should be borne in mind throughout. It is confined to general principles and leaves out all questions of detailed applications. The omissions include the vital current problem of how far and by what means the individual can improve his reality-sense without specialist aid. The views of any one individual on the subjects discussed can only be personal estimates and must, therefore, be selective and fallible: the author is a psycho-analyst and not a philosopher or a theologian. The preceding chapter (Chapter V) is in no sense an attempt to formulate a systematic philosophy of psycho-analysis: it is only an attempt to indicate an attitude to life inherent in it, and, therefore, at most, to suggest a type of empirical philosophy with which the findings of psycho-analysis would be consonant. In the same perspective-seeking way, this chapter discusses certain implications of psycho-analysis relevant to the gradual development of a positive ethics of human necessity and the equally gradual establishment of more integrative ways of living. It would appear that it is still mainly to people with some working knowledge of psycho-analysis that we must look for any assessment of the positive and creative human values inherent in it, or for the recognition of many implications that could with advantage be utilized by thinkers in other fields. Psycho-analytic thought is already widely disseminated and will continue to spread, but its constructive significance for human life, as distinct from its revolutionary impact upon human thought and its detailed application in specific fields, has not yet been fully appreciated.

II. PERSONALITY TYPES

(1) DESIDERATA OF CLASSIFICATION

Differences in mode of integration and in habitual behaviour are correlated with variation in personality-pattern. Any psychological approach to the problems of religion and ethics must therefore include a consideration of personality types. Personology is, by definition, the study of the total personality (see p. 124).

It follows that any satisfactory classification of types must take into account both the dynamics and the economics of personality-pattern. It must include motives but cannot be content merely with allotting them to primary instinctual sources; on the contrary, it must consider motives in operation through the network of relationships canalized by experience. In terms of metapsychology, classification must allow for qualitative and quantitative variation in instinctual endowment and for degrees of instinct-modification but must assess these in relation to their distribution in the mental organization, *i.e.* to their mode of integration. Moreover, the pattern of personality is so intimately affected by the sequence of experience, and its basic or ground pattern is so largely determined by infantile experience, that any adequate classification must clearly take account of developmental factors. As knowledge of mental heredity becomes more exact, classification may also become genetic in the strict sense of the term. Individual and group differences may prove to be related to differences in genotype, as suggested by Bowlby (1940), to whose work reference will be made later.

(2) PSYCHOLOGICAL HEREDITY

Little exact knowledge is yet available about psychological heredity. In a survey of the evidence provided by the study of twins, H. G. van der Waals (1948, p. 52) concludes: 'The supposition of an innate basic character on an hereditary basis is strongly supported by the results of the investigation of twins'. However, Endre Peto's psycho-analytic study of a pair of identical twins led him (1946, p. 128) to conclude that 'the inheritance of psychic qualities presents an exceedingly difficult problem about which it is hard to reach a decision, and that the influence of environmental conditions cannot be over-estimated.'

Clearly genotypic differences may exist both in instinctual endowment and in organizational trends, and, therefore, there may be innate predispositions to certain kinds of experience and to particular modes of integration. Writing of the primal phantasies that are important determinants in symptom formation, Freud inquired, 'How is it to be explained that the same phantasies are always formed with the same content?' and answered himself by saying, 'I believe that these *primal phantasies* (as I should like to name these, and certainly some others also) are a phylogenetic possession' (1929, pp. 310-11). Later he wrote (1927, p. 48): 'Through the forming of the ideal, all the traces left behind in the id by biological developments and by the vicissitudes gone through by the human race are taken over by the ego and lived through again by it in each individual. Owing to the way in which it is formed, the ego-ideal has a great many points of contact with the phylogenetic endowment of each individual —his archaic heritage.' He also said (Freud, 1937, pp. 305, 306): 'We have no reason to dispute the existence and importance of primal, congenital ego variations. The single fact is decisive that every individual selects only certain of the possible defence-mechanisms and invariably employs those which he has selected . . . and it does not imply a mystical over-estimation of heredity if we think it credible that, even before the ego exists, its subsequent lines of development, tendencies, and reactions are already determined.'

Irrespective of the question of their relation to a 'Collective Unconscious', Jung's archetypes appear as alternative descriptions, on the one hand, of subjective primal phantasies and, on the other, of objective organizational trends. Thus, Michael Fordham writes (1945, p. 225): 'The collective unconscious is a hypothesis, inasmuch as it is the place from which the archetypes emerge. The actual archetypes are facts of experience, whatever may be thought of their nature.' Jung himself wrote (1928, p. 139): 'The Archetypes do not consist of inherited ideas but of inherited predispositions to reaction'. Thus, Freud's primal phantasies, Jung's archetypes, and some of the phantasies regarded by Melanie Klein as typical of early phases of development, alike suggest the possible existence of innate predispositions to particular experiences. But only if there existed one single human genotype, which is an incredible assumption to any biologist, would all innate dispositions be identical for all human beings. While some organizational trends, such as the tendency to super-ego formation, seem to have become universal, the proclivity to one or other specific mode of integration may prove to be due, in part or wholly, to innate difference. If this should be the case, it would help to explain the hitherto insoluble riddle of choice of psychosis, neurosis, or normal character pattern.

In the language of genetics, living individuals are phenotypes; they are resultants of the interaction between their innate potentialities (genotype) and the actual circumstances of their lives. Even if the existence of a relatively small number of geno-types were ever to be established, classification would still have to remain sufficiently plastic to allow for the near-infinity of phenotypes, that is, of personal variations. Whatever groupings are ultimately adopted, 'pure' types are likely to be an insignificant minority and 'mixed' types to be the rule. Like the nomenclature of instincts, that of types will be a conceptual labelling of classes whose members exhibit certain major similarities, and the description of any given personality will never be exhausted by correct allocation to an appropriate class. Moreover, people are not independent or insulated psychological entities, they are interdependent and interacting psycho-social beings; hence the ultimate desideratum is a psycho-social classification of human types. It will be evident that, in the meantime, a purely psychological classification of personality types is both theoretically and practically an important first step and a step which is probably indispensable.

(3) Standards of Normality: Adequacy of Integration as a Criterion of Mental Health

In dealing with the problem of typing, psycho-analysts are hampered to some extent by their closer association with disease than with health, but they are also hindered by the intrinsic relativity of standards of normality. Hollitscher (1943) discussed the logical aspects of concepts of mental illness and mental health. In everyday life, the actual working criterion of health is almost bound to be an average standard, a more or less statistical norm of viable adaptation to a particular social setting at a given period of history. Clearly, adaptation to unhealthy conditions in a sick world may yield average normality but it is equally clear that this may be achieved at the cost of impairment of personal integrity. Naturally this possibility is more evident now than it was before the First World War. Since 1914, evidence has accumulated that modern Western civilization rests on insecure foundations and it would be a singularly obtuse psycho-analyst who regarded global war as a sign of world health or failed to recognize that we are now living in a transitional and unstable period.

The social conditions under which Freud grew to maturity may have seemed stable enough to demand their acceptance as a task of reality-adaptation, but *Civilization and Its Discontents* (Freud,

1930b) is, in effect, a devastating critique of a moribund society. There has never been much substance in the complaint that psycho-analysis deliberately ignores the social determinants of personality, although these are sometimes under-emphasized or not clearly recognized as such. Nor is there much truth in the Communist thesis that psycho-analysts are invariably social re-actionaries. In a recent novel the Communist heroine labours under the delusion that two years' analysis would convert her to Toryism, and says (Morley, 1946, p. 98), 'I take issue with the bourgeois psycho-analyst. His object is to reconcile the individual to existing society—an aim so narrow that it shows a complete disregard for objective reality.' The objective reality to-day is that existing society all over the world is in a state of metamorphosis. The task of the analyst remains what it always has been, namely, to help his patients to come to terms with themselves, and, in so doing, to achieve as favourable a psycho-social adaptation as their own personalities and actual conditions permit.

It is inevitable, in a world changing so rapidly as ours, that social criteria of adaptation should themselves be in a state of flux: the everyday average normality is no longer the same as it was fifty, or even five, years ago. But if social and psycho-social criteria of normality are temporarily unreliable, there yet exists for psycho-analysts a useful, though perforce still relative standard of mental health, namely, the standard of personal integrity. This is not, of course, a standard limited to psycho-analysts and analytical psychologists, but one widely accepted throughout the ages: it is, for example, the economic equivalent of the balanced life advocated by Confucius. It is true that ego-differentiation militates against integration because it tends to obstruct the development of psychological reality-sense and to interfere with the appreciation of external reality. But, when everything has been said about the opposing factors, integration remains the libidinal aim of humanity, the goal of psychological development for all those who wish to live and who are not dominated by the urge to destroy themselves or others. John Dorsey, who equates psychological reality with 'meaning', and integration with comprehensive ego-toleration of meaning, posits the same standard of health from a slightly different angle. He writes (1943, p. 149): 'An individual's optimal mental health is defined as his capacity to express all of himself to his own best interests. Motivation for the unreserved acceptance of psychic reality is optimal mental health.'

Each person will describe integration according to his own preferred conceptions, but the many differences in conception are differences in evaluation and description of the one class or type of psychological event or condition. The phenomenon that Jung calls 'integration of the personality', or more simply, 'finding the self', is the same kind of phenomenon that psycho-analysts refer to as 'integration of the total personality'. (The term 'integration' has not been borrowed without acknowledgement. It was in use among psycho-analysts prior to Jung's publication of *The Integration of the Personality* (1940), *e.g.* an early paper of the present writer's entitled 'Some Problems in the Integration of Women' (*Int. J. Psycho-Anal.*, 1932, vol. xiii, p. 446).) The self is a total self not to be equated with the reality-ego. Integration is described by Jung as a *'unio oppositorum'*, individuation through harmonization of ego with personal and collective unconscious: psycho-analysts think of it as a threefold harmonization of id, super-ego, and ego systems. Freud himself said (1937, footnote, p. 382): 'It is impossible to define mental health except in terms of metapsychology'. What appears to Jung as tension between nature and spirit usually corresponds, for psycho-analysts, to tension between id and super-ego, and the agent of integration appears to them to be the creative libido.

The relation between the type of personal unification achieved by the great Saints and total integration will be discussed later. Here, it need only be stated that the psycho-analytic conception of integration as a threefold working harmonization of the total personality must be distinguished from the many idealist confusions of integrity with perfection of one kind or another. It must also be distinguished from a series of partial integrations, for example, from the ego super-ego alliance against the id favoured by traditional inhibitory morality and Puritanism. It would often seem that the average standard of modern Western normality has been an average of psychological impoverishment. This average not seldom corresponds to a viable degree of ego-stability dearly purchased at the cost of a host of major and minor impairments of zest in living. For Hartmann (1939b, pp. 319, 320), adaptation and synthesis are the basis of an 'evolutionary' concept of health, and he notes that 'successful efforts at adaptation towards specific external situations may in indirect ways lead at the same time to inhibitions in adaptation affecting the organism'.

It will be clear that, in discussing standards, average normality and mental health should not be equated. There is a psychological criterion of health in degree or adequacy of integration; this is a relative standard since integration at its highest can only be relative and has continually to be maintained or re-attained. It is, however, a positive, dynamic, and economic standard; it draws no artificially sharp distinction between health and disease and it allows for the probability that there may be more than one type of adequate integration. It should, perhaps, be repeated, since integration of the total personality tends to be confused with ego-stability, that the former is a total or ultra-egoistic concept. Clearly, however, the stability and efficiency of the reality or operative ego will tend to vary with the adequacy of total integration. The higher the degree of personal integrity attained the stronger and richer the reality-ego will be, and the more capable of life-fulfilling adaptation even in face of adverse circumstances.

(4) Views of Jung, Experimental Psychologists, and Others

In regard to the problem of classification itself psycho-analysts have, as yet, achieved nothing comparable in scope to Jung's *Psychological Types* (1923). These types are based on what Jung considers to be the two fundamental mechanisms of Extraversion and Introversion and the four basic functions of Thinking, Feeling, Sensation, and Intuition. Only the initial extravert-introvert antithesis seems to have been at all widely used by psychologists. American workers invented the term 'ambivert' to describe persons who could not be labelled definitely extravert or introvert, *i.e.* persons whom psycho-analysts would think of as making a more balanced use of mechanisms of projection and introjection. However, Jung himself posits a compensating relation between conscious and unconscious. Fordham says (1945, p. 227): 'According to him, there is no introvert without an extraverted unconscious, there is no extravert without an introverted unconscious'. A series of war-time tests that proved useful in predicting liability to break-down under Service conditions was based on the hypothesis that, in neurotics, there is an increased tendency for interest to be deflected from the environment on to the self (Bennett and Slater, 1945).

In his *Handbook of Social Psychology*, Kimball Young (1946, p. 148) gives a summary of views on personality types, and in a later book, *Personality and Problems of Adjustment* (Young, 1947, pp. 276-336), he devoted a chapter each to 'Theories of Personality' and 'Types of Personality'. These contain more detailed accounts of current approaches. His own views are indicated by the following quotations from these chapters: (p. 300) 'Once more we must be careful not to fall into the particularist fallacy and try to interpret such phenomena as individual variability in terms of one dimension only, but always recall the three factors: the constitutional, the personal-social, and the cultural'; (p. 328) 'One thing is clear: the concept of type is related to the entire matter of the organization of mentality and of overt behaviour'; (p. 333) 'We have not yet hit upon the differentiating criteria of personality make-up'.

In this country, the methods initiated by Spearman have been developed by Burt and others in relation to emotional factor analysis (Burt, 1939, 1940). The Presidential Address delivered by Godfrey Thomson to the British Psychological Society at Durham, 1946, surveyed recent work in factorial analysis. In the field of trait analysis the work of Raymond Cattell of Harvard on personality structure and measurement is of a kind that merits serious attention from psycho-analysts, in spite of his very true observation (1946, p. 100) that 'clinical and general psychologists, especially when irritated by the difficulties of statistics, have been known to say that the "unitary traits" obtained by factor analysis are mere mathematical entities having no necessary relation to psychologically real functional unities'. It would be interesting and might be very useful to compare Bowlby's series of diagnostic traits (Bowlby, 1940, p. 201 *et seq.*) with trait series obtained experimentally. The work of British experimental psychologists on 'schemata' (see Oldfield and Zangwill, 1942, 1943) clearly has relevance to character as well as to intelligence. The 'schemata' attested by experiment appear to be closely akin to the mental systems posited in metapsychology by inference from clinical experience. H. J. Eysenck (1947, p. ix) has reported the results of intensive collaboration between psychiatrists and psychologists in the effort 'to discover the main dimensions of personality, and to define them operationally, *i.e.* by means of strictly experimental, quantitative procedures'.

(5) Psycho-Analytical Views

Turning to psycho-analysis itself, the earlier libidinal character-typing has not yet been brought up to date nor fully related to the economics of personality-pattern. Freud (1932c, p. 278) made a beginning when he distinguished three main libidinal types and three mixed types 'according as the subject's libido is mainly allocated to one or another region of the mental apparatus'. Edward Glover (1932c) made a developmental classification of mental disorders on the basis of his theory of the multiple nuclear origin of the ego-organization which could, with advantage, be expanded in relation to variations in normal development. Ernest Jones' 'Love and Morality' (1937) is a dynamic and economic study of contrast in personality-pattern.

Research on mental-hospital patients led John Bowlby to the conclusion that Kretschmerian typology is useful in psychiatric diagnosis and prognosis. He considers that variations between health and illness are not merely matters of degree but also of kind, and states (1940, p 10): 'The qualitative distinction which is believed to be vital is that between the affective and schizophrenic psychoses'. This qualitative difference appears to Bowlby to hold good not only for psychotics but also for psycho-neurotics and abnormal and normal character-types. He therefore proposes a vertical classification of syntonic and schizoid personality types (corresponding to Kretschmer's cyclothymes and schizothymes), each containing a number of recognizable sub-types, ranging from normal to psychotic. The genetic evidence available suggests to him that the main groups may be genotypically distinct, though the sub-types may be determined by the course of development. Bowlby recognizes the occurrence of mixed types and does not claim that his two main groups exclude the possible existence of other major genotypes. He realizes that the whole problem demands further investigation, particularly research on 'normal' subjects.

Bowlby himself regards vertical classification as an alternative to the linear classification, in terms of developmental stages and depth of regression, initiated by Abraham. However, the two systems may prove to be complementary rather than mutually exclusive. The linear classification is essentially dynamic since it is based on instinct vicissitude, whereas the vertical classification is fundamentally economic. The crucial difference between syntone and schizoid would appear to be a difference in mental organization. This is borne out by Bowlby's own conclusion (1940, p. 190): 'The truth is that whatever else it may be, the psychic mechanism which distinguishes the schizoid from the syntone is not simply a splitting of the mind. It is my belief that it is *a particular form of splitting which is distinctive.*' A particular form of splitting in disease carries with it the implication of a particular mode of integration in health. It is possible that the syntonic mode is phylogenetically younger than the schizoid. Both are 'immature' modes, if relative strength of ego-organization and optimum degree of personal integrity be taken as features of 'maturity'. In general, the difference in mode of organization seems to turn on relative id-dominance in the schizoid and archaic super-ego dominance in the syntone, neither of which favour ego-stability. Even if the mode of integration be innately determined, the individual personality-pattern will still have its own linear developmental history.

Apart from systematic research, everyday experience shows that a wide range of character variation is to be found among people well enough adapted to rate as 'normal'. Freud rightly insisted that, whatever the basis of classification, the resultant types 'should embrace all the variations which according to our practical standards fall within the category of the normal. In their extreme developments, however, they may well approximate to clinical pictures and so help to bridge the gulf which is assumed to exist between the normal and the pathological' (1932c, pp. 278-9). Persons who give the impression of being really whole and full of life are still the exception rather than the rule. Irrespective of those minor 'symptoms of the normal' that psychoanalysts regard as safety-valves, health insurance rather than disease, many people met with in ordinary life automatically remind us of types familiar in the consulting-room. Thus, a man who likes his life to run on tram-lines and becomes fussed and irritable if meals are not punctual, will probably be considered by any practising analyst as quite likely to be obsessional in personality-type. But, unless the analyst is unusually rash, he will not thereupon diagnose this man as a pathological case of obsessional neurosis. On the contrary, psycho-analysts actually behave in these matters rather as if they took for granted that their patients represent only more or less extreme examples of types common among the omnibus class of practical or average normality.

(6) 'GENITAL PRIMACY', PSYCHOLOGICAL MATURITY, AND PERSONAL INTEGRITY

Psycho-analysts assume that, among other diversities, normal persons will show great variations in their relationships to their fellows. Abraham's view (1925) that the normal adult reaches a genital stage of libidinal development in which genital sexual primacy is accompanied by capacity for personal object-love still throws a useful light on the problem of psychological maturity. It is illuminating because it suggests that Abraham's genital type corresponds, in terms of personality-pattern, to a favourable mode of integration in which libidinization of infantile hostility is maximal rather than minimal, and in which genital sexuality is fully synthesized with the reality-ego organization. People are more reasonable about sex than they used to be, but there is an inevitable lag between knowing and becoming. Persons whose genital impulses are fully ego-syntonic are still comparatively rare. It is permissible to assume that ego-syntonic genitality is more amenable to intelligent reality-adaptation and that it carries with it an increased ability for personal love of the sexual partner. 'Falling in love' is a special phenomenon, usually involving idealization of the beloved (ideal-transference), but it seems likely that the psychologically mature adult should be capable of passionate love, that is, of an effective synthesis of personal affection and sensual passion. 'Genital love' might be considered to be the outcome of such synthesis, an outcome which can engender an enduring sentiment of affection which will persist when the original passion is spent. However, Michael Balint (1948, p. 38) thinks 'genital love' in man is a misnomer for an artefact of civilization. He writes: 'Man, that neotenic embryo, never reaches full maturity, he remains an embryo in his anatomical structure, in his emotional behaviour towards his elders and betters—and in his love life. What we call "genital love" is a fusion of disagreeing elements: genital satisfaction and pre-genital tenderness.' According to Abraham, the hysteric develops object-love but with exclusion of the genitals: frigidity in women and impairment of potency in men are common enough in people not otherwise markedly neurotic. But experience testifies that the opposite condition, genital potency with incapacity for personal appreciation of the sexual partner, is by no means uncommon: it is, perhaps, more frequent among men, where its development may have been aided by the long tradition of 'feminine inferiority'. Such incapacity to feel genuine affection and personal friendship for members of the opposite sex is evidently closely related to the splitting of sensuality from affection and their allocation to different hetero-sexual objects described by Freud (1912, *Collected Papers*, iv, p. 203).

Although he disclaimed any such intention, Abraham seems to have set a genital standard of maturation which is relevant to personal integration and not only to sexual development. Such normal maturity is likely to be the outcome of a predominantly positive Oedipus situation, issuing in a favourable post-Oedipal economic distribution of parental relationships. In one such favourable distribution, the ego is strengthened and enabled to retain control of a good deal of infantile aggression and libidinal capacity through identification with the sexual rival, and the super-ego is libidinized by identification with the love-object. On the other hand, where mental and environmental conditions are sufficiently favourable, more evenly balanced hetero-homosexual and even predominantly homosexual Oedipus situations can be resolved without giving rise to overt illness or delinquency in the adult. Certainly, the post-Oedipal distribution of identificatory relationships can vary widely without obvious pathological consequences. Nevertheless, it is also clear that it is only a fortunate few who enter on adult life with their genital potential intact and fully ego-syntonic. The majority suffer damage in varying degree through dissociation and regression, inadequate libidinization, and tension-promoting distributions of identificatory relationships. These conditions may never result in illness or prevent the subject from making a reasonable success of life, judged by average standards, but the impairment of function may, nevertheless, be appreciable in a host of major and minor psychological impediments to vigorous and joyful living.

It is difficult to see how genital sexuality can become fully and generally ego-syntonic until the mental facts of infantile sexuality are as clearly recognized and taken for granted as are the physiological facts of infantile development. So long as the parental conception of infantile life excludes sexuality, the infant will remain under pressure to deny it himself. The cultural scales are thus weighted in favour of dissociation of sexual impulses rather than in favour of their ego-synthesis. The different evaluation of infantile sexuality is a crucial difference between psycho-analysts and members of derivative Schools. The psycho-analytical conception of infantile sexuality is its oldest cause of offence and the one that may easily endure the longest. It has instigated more deviations and new Schools among those unable to tolerate its psychological reality than any other single factor. To psycho-analysts, the clinical evidence appears to admit of no compromise, and infantile sexuality must therefore remain a stumbling-block until such time as its key significance can be more widely appreciated. The importance of realism about infantile life is discussed further in the section on ethics.

(7) CONCLUSION

It is evident that a satisfactory classification of personality-types that will be at once genetic, dynamic, and economic, and useful in practical life, cannot be achieved easily or quickly. Its formulation should not be hurried, in spite of its obvious desirability. Once psycho-analysts have completed their own groundwork and have arrived at working hypotheses regarding the principles of type differentiation, they will be well advised to compare and collate their results with those of experimental psychologists, social psychologists, and sociologists. The ultimate classification of human types must be psycho-social if it is to contribute to the solution of problems of social organization on lines more favourable to individual and group adaptation. Differences of terminology will tend to cloud the issues but, whatever form of words or mathematical expression is preferred by different workers, any conclusion which has a fair degree of probability will ultimately prove to be consonant with other reliable findings. Mutual interpretation between workers in various fields will not always be easy, but it should become increasingly possible. Marion Milner (1945) made a pioneer attempt to interpret 'internal objects' in terms of general psychology. Psycho-social classification may eventually correlate with anatomical and physiological classifications, but development and modification of types at the psycho-social level is bound to be more rapid and multifarious than changes at a biological level.

A generation or two might suffice to bring about an appreciable change in the distribution of psycho-social types. Although our Western civilization has, during more recent times, favoured the development of immature and poorly integrated personalities, a century of healthier psycho-social conditions might go some way to correct this adverse balance.

This brief discussion of classification is given as a preface to the remainder of the paper for two reasons. In the first place, the diversity of types and the variety of individuals are clearly relevant to the personal significance of religion and to the application of any general principles of behaviour to the personal conduct of life. It is, for instance, self-evident that a routine which may be life-saving and rewarding to an obsessional character may be little short of murderous to a creative artist. In the second place, diagnostic terms will be used in this chapter in a characterological rather than in a pathological sense. Terms such as 'manic-depressive' or 'obsessional' will refer to persons who are not necessarily ill in the clinical sense, but whose mental pattern and *modus vivendi* seem to resemble those of persons exhibiting the corresponding diseases. Further research alone can show whether Bowlby's vertical classification by genotype is right or wrong, but in the meantime clinical terminology pre-judges the issue less than the use of terminology implying the definite acceptance of genetic assumptions.

III. RELIGION AS A METHOD OF INTEGRATION

(1) The 'Problem of Religion'

In his *Man, Morals and Society* (1945), Flugel devotes a chapter to the 'Problem of Religion', in which he summarizes the main contributions of psycho-analysis and discusses some points of convergence and divergence between Freud and Jung. He notes the parallel drawn by Pfister between the aims of the Christian 'cure of souls' and those of psycho-analytical therapy and combines the views of Freud and Philpott (1942) in his estimate of the Atonement. He writes (1945, pp. 274-5): 'Notwithstanding the magnificence of its vision and the nobility of its purpose, Christianity (like the other great religions) has been in most respects a failure, and this in spite of its nominal and worldly triumphs. It has failed both to remove internal guilt and to abolish external aggression—largely, as we have seen in this book, two aspects of the same problem. . . . The great weakness of Christianity would seem to be that it has indicated neither a suitable outlet for the energies of aggressive extraverted individuals nor an adequate and positive goal for social and political endeavour; indeed, by its attitude of indifference to the larger social problems, it fostered the divorce between ethics and politics which many thinkers have in recent years deplored . . . recent events have made it clear in which direction the next step in religious development must lie. The religious emotions must be largely or entirely secularized and be put in the service of humanity. The religion of humanity is surely the religion of the nearer future.'

Finally, Flugel discusses (1945, p. 277) Cattell's proposed 'substitution of the group "Theopsyche" for the God of revealed religion'. He writes (*op. cit.* pp. 279-81) that 'Humanity or the Theopsyche serves as a sublimation for the primitive feelings relating to the mother or the idea of brotherhood rather than for those relating to the father. The Western world, with its strongly patriarchal traditions, will perhaps not easily forgo the father. How to cater for the archetypal need for a father-figure in a world society is indeed a problem. . . . Men must abandon the last shred of that longed-for but illusory "omnipotence" to which, even after the relinquishing of magic, they sought to cling through their relation with a divine ruler of the universe. . . . If there is a purpose in evolution, we have no means of understanding it except in and through the mind of man. There is no guidance as to the nature of this purpose and our place in it save such as we ourselves provide through the free use of human faculty.'

(2) The Vitality of Christianity

Flugel's conclusions will be referred to later, but some consideration of the present status of religion may be advisable here. One gains the impression that psycho-analysts and scientists in general are often too ready to assume that Christianity is steadily and rapidly losing ground, an assumption not wholly consistent with available evidence. For instance, Latourette's *Advance Through Storm* (1946), the seventh and latest volume of his *History of the Expansion of Christianity*, shows that the years 1914-44 were years of continued expansion, at any rate in the mission field. In Europe, in spite of the increasing secularization of culture and the avowedly anti-religious campaigns which reduced Christians in some countries to the status of persecuted minorities, Latourette believes there has been some advance, although a slowing-down by comparison with the nineteenth century. In a review of this book (*Sunday Times*, 23 June, 1946) the Dean of St. Paul's said: 'Even in Europe, where the reaction against Christianity has been most marked, there are signs that the Christian religion has a power of resurgence unsuspected by its enemies. The Church was not destroyed either in Russia or Germany, and the drive towards unity expressed in the Oecumenical movement gathered strength during the dark days of the threat of war and even in the war itself.' Since the war, the World Council of Churches has held its first Assembly (Amsterdam, 1948). During the war the Russian Church regained official toleration, although an anti-Catholic campaign is now in full swing in Eastern Europe. Christians were active in all the resistance movements, and in Western Europe are still more, rather than less, influential in politics than they were during the pre-war years. The fact that, according to Latourette, Roman Catholics constitute the largest single denominational group in the United States (twenty-three millions) and the recent creation of more than thirty new Cardinals do not point to any diminution in the vitality of Catholicism.

Times of trouble naturally and inevitably tend to rouse latent religious attitudes in individuals. It has been said, for instance, that there are no atheists in a bomber, and while this may not be literally true, it underlines the human proclivity for turning to God in danger and distress. Recent years have seen a revulsion from materialism and a growing conviction of the failure of the nineteenth-century brand of humanism, and there has been a swing of the pendulum back from impersonal and scientific to personal and religious interests. Rosamund Murray's book, *The Good Pagan's Failure* (1943), illustrates this trend, and there are many people in somewhat similar case to its author who see no alternative between a psychologically unrealistic humanism and Christianity.

The appeal of Christianity has also been increased by changes internal to itself that have come about during the last few decades. For example, modern Protestantism can no longer be accused of failure to realize its social responsibilities. The late Archbishop Temple, who championed the movement for unity among Christian Churches, also had at heart the welfare of the common man and laboured unceasingly in the rather stony vineyard of social reorganization according to Christian principles. The difference between Christian Socialist trends and many secular types of collectivism derives from their regard for personality. If human beings are all the children of God and equal before Him, the personality of every individual demands respect and must be given due consideration. John MacMurray (1935, p. 229) goes so far as to say that the goal of religion is 'the creation of a human society, universal in its extent, based upon the communion of persons'. Christian experiments in neighbourhood relationships are under way as illustrated, for example, in Joseph McCulloch's *Medway Adventure* (1946). The Catholic Church as a whole is regarded by many people as still reactionary, but Catholic writers like Jacques Maritain and S. B. Frank are socially progressive. Such writers may not affect the official policies of the Church, but they are popular and influential within the widening circle of their readers. Indeed, voices may even be heard to-day protesting against the over-socialization of Christianity and insisting that the primary task of religion is the fostering of man's relation to God and not the betterment of his earthly conditions.

Asceticism has an acknowledged rôle in the spiritual life and extreme forms of it are sometimes practised. The Catholic Church, however, unlike the Puritans and the gloomier Protestant sects, has never disdained to recognize and use the senses for its own purposes: the Seven Deadly Sins are not all sins of the flesh. The relations between the sexes are strictly regulated, but when the required conditions are observed, the Catholic can enjoy marriage and intercourse as sacraments (see Gerald Vann, 1944, p. 48 *et seq.*). In recent years many Protestants have changed their views regarding the anti-sensual and anti-emotional bias of the Puritan tradition and have begun to appreciate its life-denying implications (as witness Sidney Dark's *Passing of the Puritan*, 1946). The Anglican mystic and publicist, Evelyn Underhill, was a convincing exponent of the sacramental view of life.

An emotional resurgence in Christianity has expressed itself both in a revival of interest in mysticism and in revolt against purely formal institutionalism. It has come home to many people that religion is a matter of the spirit and not of the letter of the law, a way of living based upon experience of God, permeating the whole life, and not a lip-serving habit of Sunday observance dissociated from everyday life. On the Continent these trends owe much to Kierkegaard, Karl Barthe, and Emil Brunner. The subjectivist Existentialism now fashionable in France in some ways appears to be the philosophic parallel to Surrealism in art; it has many aspects and many atheist exponents who differ among themselves, but it also retains from Kierkegaard its avowedly religious expressions, *e.g.* the personalism of Berdyaev. For most Christian mystics, *e.g.* the Catholic S. B. Frank and the Anglican Evelyn Underhill, there is no real conflict between mysticism and institutionalism, only a recognition that the latter must be quickened by the spirit and enlightened by a renewal of understanding of the significance of Church organization and ritual. Quoting Baron von Hügel, Arthur Hopkinson writes (1946, p. 17): 'To use his own words, there are "Three Means of Religious Apprehension": the first, institutional and authoritative; the second, intellectual and ethical; the third, mystical and experimental. These are the three elements in religion.'

There is also a revival on the intellectual plane, one expression of which amongst Protestants and also among non-sectarian critics of materialism, is neo-Thomism. St. Thomas Aquinas has never ceased to be the official philosopher of the Catholic Church, and the views of Jacques Maritain are said to be adaptations of Thomism to modern conditions. Neo-Thomists are to be found among critics of psycho-analysis. In reply to criticism of his chapter on religion in *Mind, Medicine and Man* (1943), Zilboorg writes (1944, p. 94) that he tried 'to demonstrate that the strictest adherent to Catholic theology and to the philosophy of St. Thomas can and ought to accept the principles of psycho-analytic theory and practice, and that in accepting these he would not have to violate his theology or do any injury to his faith'. In an earlier paper Zilboorg wrote (1939a, p. 488) of Thomist critics: 'They fail to observe the major principle of St. Thomas which saved Aristotle from being re-forgotten after he had been re-discovered. This principle represents perhaps the greatest contribution of St. Thomas. He adapted Aristotle to the prevailing apologetics by means of a new postulate: that which is true in philosophy may not be true in theology and *vice versa*. By confusing soul with psyche or psychic apparatus . . . the opponents of psycho-analysis found themselves unable to apply the Thomistic principle to the Freudian studies and unable to comprehend that what is true in psychology may not be true in traditional apologetics, Catholic, Protestant, or secular, and *vice versa*—that the psychic apparatus is not the soul and the soul is not the psyche.'

The Thomist argument, however, can be a dangerous sophistry unless it is clearly realized that the 'soul' is a subjective, personological concept, whereas the 'psychic apparatus' is an objective, metapsychological concept. But any psychological definition of the 'soul' runs counter to the argument itself, which is based on the assumption that the 'soul' is not mental but spiritual and, therefore, as a concept, it is a theological concept. The subjective facts of experience are of a different order to the inferred probabilities of objective psychology. It is now appreciated that each level of organization has its own laws and that psychological phenomena cannot be adequately described in physical or chemical terms. But the underlying assumption is that the different systems of objective knowledge concerned are mutually consistent and not mutually contradictory. A fact of experience, such as a truth of subjective theology or mysticism, will differ from an objective concept of philosophy, but the truths of a theology which claims to be objective should be consistent with objective philosophy, scientific theory, and all the other objective constructions of human intelligence. It was noted elsewhere (p. 163) that Catholics themselves find the theories of Jung acceptable but not those of Freud or Adler.

Another intellectual resurgence in religion takes forms which might be grouped as evolutionary and which seek to reconcile science and religion. Religious thinkers of this type have found much support in the latest theories of modern physics. They accept the 'historical process' but regard the development of religion from early primitive to advanced forms as the story of the gradual unfolding of man's God-given capacity to appreciate Eternal Truth. They contend, in brief, that religion cannot be explained by reference to its primitive origins and phases of growth, but that these earlier stages can be understood only in the light of subsequent developments. On this view, animism cannot explain Christianity but Christianity can illuminate the problems of primitive animism. Evelyn Underhill, for whom psychology was a good servant but a bad master, took this point of view. She criticized theology for the obscurity of its language, but she endorsed the doctrines and ritual of Christianity as accepted by the Church of England.

There are also Christians who take yet a further step in the direction of a fresh interpretation of Christianity. For Albert Schweitzer, the historical truth about the teaching of Jesus is that it is permeated by the mistaken conception that the end of the world was at hand. The credibility of the older Gospels, Mark and Matthew, is increased for Schweitzer by the fact that they report this mistaken conviction and thus show that Jesus shared the 'eschatological Messianic' expectations of the late Judaism into which he was born. Schweitzer's arguments are given in full in two books, *The Mystery of the Kingdom of God* (trans. 1925) and *The Quest of the Historical Jesus* (trans. 1910), but are summarized in his autobiography, *My Life and Thought* (1931) (trans. 1933, 6th imp. 1946). He concludes (1933, p. 67): 'We have, therefore, to reconcile ourselves to the fact that His religion of love appeared as part of a world-view which expected a speedy end of the world. Clothed in the ideas in which He announced it, we cannot make it our own; we must re-clothe it in those of our modern world-view. . . . We are obliged, that is, to admit the evident fact that religious truth varies from age to age.' But (*op. cit.* pp. 67-8): "So far as its essential spiritual and ethical nature is concerned, Christianity's religious truth remains the same through the centuries. The variations belong only to the outward form which it assumes in the ideas belonging to different world-views.'

In Schweitzer's view, the essence of Christianity, as distinct from the formalized religion of dogma and ritual, is its spiritual and personal ethic of active love. Thus he writes (*op. cit.* p. 69): 'The subject of all His preaching is love'. Christianity is better served by (*op. cit.* p. 74) 'devotion to Jesus' religion of love than by acquiescence in all the articles of belief. If the Church has the spirit of Jesus, there is room in her for any form of Christian piety, even for that which claims unrestricted liberty.'

A socially minded British Christian, writing under the name of John Hadham, says (1944, p. 86): 'I profoundly believe that the New Age will not be firmly established until it has found the spiritual formula which will give it unity, harmony, power and purpose. I profoundly believe that this new formula will be a re-interpretation in terms of new knowledge and new thought-forms of the Christian faith.' John MacMurray holds that religion is still very immature, but that (1935, p. 240): 'The development of religion is in its substance the integration of human society'. He writes further (p. 243): 'The maturity of religion waits on the development of consciousness, upon the universal sharing of a maturity of consciousness which has been already achieved as the individual consciousness of one religious genius'. MacMurray believes that 'religion has not yet reached maturity because we have not yet understood Jesus'. In his view, the 'specific task of religion' is 'to integrate the community of mankind'. These opinions may appear to be rather one-sided, since personal integration and social integration are interdependent factors in what field theorists might call the human life-space. But although MacMurray regards isolationary individualism as anti-religious, he is none the less a respecter of persons, as is shown by his views on education. He has outgrown the Puritan tradition and insists on the need for educating the senses and the emotions as well as the intellect.

In the last year or two, differences of opinion in the Anglican Church have sharpened, almost to the point of cleavage. The essential points at issue are the bearing of modern science in general, and biblical research in particular, on the theology of Christianity. Bishop Barnes, whose book, *The Rise of Christianity* (1947), has given rise to lively discussions, is prepared to sacrifice the supernatural elements in Christian doctrine, *e.g.* most of the miracles, including the Immaculate Conception and the Resurrection, to further a re-birth of Christianity consonant with modern knowledge. For Bishop Barnes (1947, p. vii), when 'mistaken assumptions of the pre-scientific, pre-critical era' are repudiated, 'there emerges, I submit, a lovely and satisfying faith which contains the essentials of the great Christian tradition'. After describing the failure of the Churches to adhere to the teaching of Jesus, he continues (1947, p. 337): 'But after failure the search for religious reality begins anew. Out of apparently dead formulae and empty ritual the Spirit of Christ emerges as buds in springtime appear on what seemed lifeless twigs.' The late Congregationalist, J. C. Cadoux, expressed views akin to those of Bishop Barnes in his *Life of Jesus* (1948).

Opposing, more orthodox, views are expressed by Canon Richardson in his *Christian Apologetics* (1947) and in a broadcast discussion with Bishop Barnes (*The Listener*, 2 September 1948). He contends that to attempt to reconcile the natural sciences and religion is to begin at the wrong end, because theology, like the other distinctively human sciences, is an independent, empirical science with its own approach, methods, and categories of investigation. He writes (Richardson, 1947, p. 57): 'Theology as a science stands or falls with the category of revelation; if there is no distinctively Christian revelation in history, the special categories of theology will not be needed'. Canon Richardson adopts the so-called modern, though in fact, as he says, Augustinian, theory of general and special revelation in place of the traditional antithesis of natural and revealed knowledge. All truth is general revelation but the special revelation of Christianity is 'mediated through history', though not (1947, p. 118) 'as a body of propositional truths contained in an infallible Scripture' but (p. 139) 'through the long series of events of Jewish history which culminated in Christ and His Church, as these events were interpreted by the prophets and apostles through whose witness the Bible came to be written'. In regard to miracles, Richardson says (1947, p. 176): 'Briefly stated, our contention is that the biblical principle of historical interpretation necessitates the belief that Jesus was raised from the dead and that He worked the works of the Messiah, but it allows a wide variety of view concerning the details of particular incidents'. For another well-known Anglican publicist, C. S. Lewis (1947), the Incarnation is 'The Grand Miracle'.

Canon Richardson is aware that human or 'existential' sciences, *e.g.* history and theology, are bound to involve subjectively determined interpretation of their data according to the observer's 'faith principle'. He agrees with St. Augustine that faith is prerequisite to understanding, and thinks (1947, p. 230) 'reason becomes fruitful and capable of reaching a relatively reliable view of the universe and the purpose of man's existence in it, when it is guided by the insights of the Christian faith'. In his Gifford Lectures, the American neo-Lutheran, Reinhold Niebuhr, gives a Christian interpretation of *The Nature and Destiny of Man* (2 vols. 1941, 1943), based, as he says in his preface to the first volume, 'upon the conviction that there are resources in the Christian faith for an understanding of human nature which have been lost in modern culture'. Sir Walter Moberly has recently given definitions of theology and of 'authentic Christianity' which may be taken to represent the views of present-day Christians in university circles. According to him (Moberly, 1949, p. 282): 'Theology *is* the study of the self-revelation of the living God; that is, of a corporate experience of God in which, from start to finish, He in the initiator. . . . "God who at sundry times and in divers manners spake in time past unto the fathers by the prophets, hath in these last days spoken unto us by His Son." That is the theologian's basic presupposition.' And (1949, p. 103): 'The true Christian life consists not in keeping commandments, however stringent, nor in following principles, however lofty, nor even in the imitation of Christ. It is a life in grace—that is, of prayer and sacrament, of daily and hourly dependence on power from on high, a life lived within the context of the worshipping community and based on faith in the great acts of God in Christ recounted in the Bible—Incarnation, Redemption, Resurrection.'

This short review of signs of life in modern Christianity is only illustrative and very incomplete, but it will serve its purpose if it checks the too confident expectation of an early or inevitable demise of Christianity. Christianity may be challenged and on the defensive, but it is also challenging and on the offensive, *e.g.* the Mission to London, May 1949, and it is probably wiser to regard it as a psycho-social force which will retain vitality for a long time to come. Moreover, conceptions like Cattell's 'Theopsyche' are mainly intellectual in their appeal; in theory they may offer what appears to be ample provision for religious need, but in fact they lack the profundity of emotional appeal characteristic of Christianity. The probability that any such intellectual artefact will replace God is, perhaps, on a par with the likelihood that an artificial language, like Esperanto, or even a semi-artefact like Basic English, will ever become a living universal language.

If Christianity is not moribund but still full of vitality, the question of the form, or forms, in which it is likely to persist becomes important on account of their potentially different effects on the human life-situation. According to Arnold Toynbee (1948, pp. 242-3): 'The institutional element has historically, up to date, been dominant in the life of the Church herself in her traditional Catholic form, which, on the long historical view, is the form in which one has to look at her . . . and perhaps the subconscious purpose . . . of this heavy panoply of institutions in which the Church has clad herself is the very practical one of outlasting the toughest of the secular institutions of this world, including all the civilizations. If we survey all the institutions of which we have knowledge in the present and in the past, I think that the institutions created, or adopted and adapted, by Christianity are the toughest and the most enduring of any that we know, and are therefore the most likely to last—and outlast all the rest.

On the other hand, Latourette is convinced (by evidence that he adduces) that the main stream of Christianity is now passing through Protestantism, and he argues that Protestantism is most likely to be the source of future versions of Christianity, though the form of these cannot be foretold. He writes (Latourette, 1949, p. 161): 'Moreover, the Gospel can never be fully expressed in words. It began in a Life and as a Life. It continues and, from its nature, must continue primarily in lives.' Hence he suggests (Latourette, 1949, p. 193) 'that no one kind of Christianity can be regarded as normal or as final. The more stereotyped varieties, those most anchored to a cultural heritage of the past, will have the advantage of resistant tradition and structure, but the disadvantage of inflexibility and association with patterns that have been discarded elsewhere. Christianity will go in expanding influence through those forms which combine fidelity to the Gospel, the largest expression of the fruits of the spirit, and adaptability to changing environments.'

The issue is of primary importance to humanists on account of its bearing on the survival of freedom of conscience and liberty of thought. The Catholic Church may be the most open and active opponent of the Soviet ideology but there is little to choose between them in their essential intolerance and conviction of their absolute right to dominate and to enforce submission to their authority by any and all available means. Reinhold Niebuhr (1943, p. 229), applying the test of tolerance to Catholicism, says: 'It may vary its attitude slightly towards other versions of the Christian faith from time to time, but it is completely consistent and unyielding in its conviction that it alone possesses the truth and the whole truth'. Niebuhr (1943, p. 233) also remarks that failure to recognize the 'historically contingent' character of ritual has led Anglo-Catholicism 'to insist that its order is the only possible one for an oecumenical church. The logic of this sinful spiritual imperialism conforms to the logic of sin generally. It is the unconscious ignorance, and the conscious denial, of the finiteness of its own perspective.'

It is true that Protestantism is fissiparous and that its various sects have at different times exhibited intolerance in high degree, but it also appears to be a fact that the best minds in modern Protestantism stress the practice of both love and tolerance, and of humility (including intellectual humility), as essential to Christian living. In spite of the latent dangers inherent in religious life solutions, at the present day such Christianity is less a threat than a positive gain to humanity. A Christian who actually practises love and toleration in matters great and small and is alive to the prideful and persecutory trends to which organized religions have succumbed in the past, is a more desirable world-citizen than a fanatic of any persuasion, religious or materialist. Sir Walter Moberly (1949), using Toynbee's phraseology, advises university Christians to seek to become a 'creative' and not a 'dominant' minority. In religion, as in all the other spheres of human life, it is the anxiety-driven will to power over other persons that is among the most dangerous threats to humane living. Hence it is to be hoped that Latourette's forecast may prove true. But, to psycho-analysts, a gradual relative recession of Catholicism will not appear something that can be taken for granted; it is by no means certain that the psychological appeal of Catholicism and its sister Eastern Orthodoxies, is not more profound and many-sided than the appeal of any current form of Protestantism.

(3) THE PSYCHO-ANALYTICAL APPROACH: FREUD'S VIEWS ON RELIGION AND CHRISTIANITY

Some repetition will be unavoidable, but it would be superfluous to re-traverse in any detail the ground covered by Flugel (1945) and, even more recently, by Ernest Jones (1948). The psychological study of religion, however, and not least the study of Christianity, is only in its infancy. Understanding of its personal significance is still elementary. It appears, as Flugel says (1945, p. 261), that 'the attitude of man towards his Gods is determined to a large extent by displacement of his attitude towards his parents'. There are grounds also for assuming that the individual's appreciation of the nature of God will be affected by the quality of the attitudes projected on to Him. A God identified with a beloved ego-ideal will seems a very different God from one identified with hate-charged or sadistic super-ego components.

There is also reason to suppose that the intra-psychic mechanism of religious experience is to be found in ego relationships to ego ideal-systems and parental ideal-systems. It is a matter of interest that Cardinal Newman directly related God and conscience. In his *Apologia pro Vita Sua* he wrote (1890, p. 198): 'If I am asked why I believe in a God, I answer that it is because I believe in myself, for I feel it impossible to believe in my own existence (and of that fact I am quite sure) without believing also in the existence of Him, Who lives as a Personal, All-seeing, All-judging Being in my conscience'.

Such conceptions as these are fundamental, but they do not exhaust the dynamics and economics of mystical experience, nor do they completely account for the modifications of personality-pattern to which the 'spiritual life' may conduce. Psycho-analysis itself undoubtedly implies the possibility of more integrative living and, in favourable circumstances, it actualizes this possibility to some extent. A consideration of Christianity as a method of integration, albeit a method more often doomed to failure than to success, may throw some light on the general problem of integration and on the points of likeness and difference between Christian and psycho-analytic conceptions of personal 'wholeness'.

Some psycho-analysts, like Pfister, and many Freudian-influenced psycho-therapists like William Brown, combine their psychological insight with religious belief. Dr. Pfister's 'scientific testament', *Christianity and Fear* (1949), has just appeared in translation. The Dutch psycho-analyst, Max Levy-Suhl (1946, p. 119), considers 'that in psycho-analytic therapy and perhaps in psycho-therapy in general, processes of an ethical and religious kind work together and are indispensable'. Zilboorg's views on the compatibility of psycho-analysis and Catholicism have already been quoted, but his general approach is conveyed in the following passage (1944, p. 99): 'Instead of opposing religion, instead of rejecting it as unscientific or as a cultural neurosis (the use of the latter term is hardly more than a polite pseudo-scientific name-calling), I believe we shall understand it better and view it probably with greater sympathy, if we concentrate our attention on the study of its psycho-cultural function as one of man's fundamental ways of living and of meeting life'.

The majority of psycho-analysts tend to think that the biological and psycho-social conditions of human life, so far as they are known to them, justify the conception of religion, in both its personal and its social aspects, as a natural consequence of human development. This evolutionary conception of religion did not originate in psycho-analysis. The authority of divine revelation had been challenged by the natural scientists long before Freud published the *Future of an Illusion* (1928) and the post-Darwinian work on comparative religion and cultural anthropology (for example, the work of Tylor, Frazer, Westermarck, and others) had already made out a strong case for an evolutionary theory. The earlier work was mainly concerned with the objective invalidity of religious dogmas and myths, and with the primitive survival nature of ritual and ceremonial. The social aspect, the political and cultural function of religion and its rôle in history, also received much consideration. It was William James who first pointed out that, whatever the nature of dogmas and ritual, religious experience is undeniable as experience, and who first connected it with the realm of the subconscious. It is Freud, however, who gave us our first clues to the specific unconscious drives and infantile dilemmas which can manifest themselves in religious guise.

While Freud himself recognized the personal sources of religious belief in infantile helplessness and father-longing, he appears to have been far more interested in its public than in its private aspects, *i.e.* in its phylogeny than in its ontogeny, in ritual and dogma rather than in religious experience. Thus, both he and Reik were forcibly struck by the parallel between ritual and obsessional ceremonial and, in the *Future of an Illusion*, Freud leans to the conclusion that religion is the 'universal obsessional neurosis of humanity' (1928, p. 76). He says: 'To be sure this analogy does not exhaust the essence of religion' but 'it accords well with this that the true believer is in a high degree protected against the danger of certain neurotic afflictions; by accepting the universal neurosis he is spared the task of forming a personal neurosis' (*op. cit.* p. 77). In *Moses and Monotheism* (Freud, 1939, p. 117) this analogy has come to be 'rather in the nature of an axiom' and 'religious phenomena must of course be regarded as a part of mass psychology'. In this book, however, Freud dealt neither with a universal obsession nor with mass psychology, but with the development of Judaic monotheism in terms of Jewish group psychology (or rather, psycho-sociology) and, to a slighter extent, with its supersession by Christianity. Thus he writes (*op.*

cit. p. 148): 'We have treated here of only one case in the rich phenomenology of the religions and have not thrown any light on the others'.

Moses and Monotheism has been severely criticized. In a review in the *American Journal of Sociology* (1939, p. 475), Salomon A. Baron writes: 'Methodically, however, the work is open to most crucial objections. The extreme liberties admittedly taken by Freud with available biblical material is illustrative also of his utilization of the findings of modern anthropological and historical research. . . . This limitless arbitrariness in the selection and use of the little existing evidence renders the entire factual basis of Freud's reconstruction more than questionable.' Whatever the ultimate verdict on Freud's historical reconstruction may be, he is fully justified in stressing both the pre-eminently patriarchal character of Judaism and its persisting influence in Christianity. It is easy to recognize in many of the divisions within Christianity the factor of recurrent revolt against paternal authority. In this country, for instance, the Pope's refusal to sanction Henry VIII's first divorce and re-marriage was an important factor in bringing about the Reformation. The formal definition of Papal Infallibility, issued by the Vatican Council in 1870, appears as an attempt to reassert the divinely inspired omniscience of the Holy Father in face of the incoming tide of secularism and rationalism. Incidentally, the existence of the Essenes might be taken as corroborative evidence of possible Egyptian sources of Judaism. The *Encyclopædia Britannica* (11th ed., 1910, vol. ix, p. 778) describes the Essenes as 'a monastic order among the Jews prior to Christianity . . . our authorities agree in assigning them a dateless antiquity'. 'Before the rising of the sun they were to speak of nothing profane, but offered to it certain traditional forms of prayer as if beseeching it to rise. . . . Their most singular feature, perhaps, was their reverence for the sun ' (*op. cit.* p. 780). In his 'Preliminary Notes upon the Problem of Akhenaten' (1939), James Strachey describes the rôle of the sun in the first emergence of monotheism in the history of the human race.

It would not seem to be a matter of crucial significance whether Freud was right or wrong in his conception of the original form of the human group, in seeming to narrow down the origins of religion to ancestral patricide, or in positing the totem feast as the *fons et origo* of all ritual. Hypotheses regarding the earliest phases of social life, like those regarding the earliest phases of infantile life, are bound to be conjectural and insusceptible of proof other than inherent probability and conformity with hypotheses more amenable to positive demonstration. What does seem highly probable is that, whatever the exact conditions of primordial life, they were not lacking in opportunities for familial and tribal disagreements with fathers and leaders, siblings, and fellow-tribesmen: as is attested by a wealth of myths quite independent of psycho-analytic evidence. Anthropology supplies many records of the ceremonial slaying of kings and the more strictly utilitarian killing of the aged and infirm. The anecdotal history of familial and tribal vicissitudes, passed on from one generation to another by word of mouth as soon as speech became equal to this task, must gradually have crystallized into more or less stereotyped myths and legends, epics and sagas. The psychoanalytic evidence strongly suggests that the more crucial ancestral vicissitudes find psychological representation in infantile development. If indeed, as Freud himself suggests, the infantile peak of sexuality represents a primitive human or pre-human ancestral puberty, the inevitability and intensity of Oedipal conflicts become much less surprising. We are not entitled, in view of the current state of knowledge of genetics and heredity, especially mental heredity, to affirm positively that infantile psychology reflects accurately the prehistoric vicissitudes of human life. We are entitled to say that the course of infantile development seems to exhibit a certain parallel to reconstructions of the course of racial development, and that this assumption makes many infantile strains and stresses more intelligible. We are most fully justified by our clinical experience in asserting that the Oedipal and pre-Oedipal conflicts operating in the individual are of an importance which can hardly be exaggerated in the development of personal religion and, therefore, presumably also in the historical development of the great religions.

Oedipal paternal relations, albeit the dominant strand in Judaism, are only one set of threads in the tangled skein of infantile drives that may find expression in religion. Freud is justified, from his own point of view, in regarding Christianity as 'a cultural regression as compared with the older Jewish religion' because it 'was no longer strictly monotheistic, took over from the surrounding peoples numerous symbolical rites, re-established the great Mother Goddess and found room for many deities of polytheism in an easily recognizable disguise—though in sub-ordinate positions' (1939, p. 142). But he also feels bound to admit: 'and yet Christianity marked a progress in the history of religion; that is to say, in regard to the return of the repressed' (*op. cit.* p. 143) (see also Philpott, 1942).

(4) THE NATURE OF CHRISTIANITY AND ITS APPEAL

In effect, Christianity, though its spread is in part to be accounted for by political and social exigencies, owes the width of its appeal to individuals of all ages and races to the circum-stance that it partly corrected the one-sidedness of Judaism and included many more of the unconscious motivations that are potentially religious. If the history and doctrines of Christianity were studied from this angle it would probably be found that at some time, in one way or another, Christianity offers some solu-tion to every infantile problem and not only a solution of Oedipal guilt and hostility. It is true that redemption through the vicarious sacrifice of Christ, a doctrine emanating from St. Paul, is a cardinal tenet of every Christian sect and that the Cross seems very soon to have become the official symbol of Christianity. The work of St. Paul was admittedly decisive in the early transmission and development of Christian teaching and it may well be true that the Pauline influence in the institutionalizing of Christianity, particularly in the organization of the Western Church, was greater than that of Jesus himself. But, surely, only concentration on the social aspects of religion and on the expiation of blood guilt and primaeval hostility could have led Freud to pass over Jesus as the occasion rather than the originator of Christianity and to write: 'It can scarcely be chance that the violent death of another great man should become the starting-point for the creation of a new religion by Paul' (1939, p. 143).

The religious genius of Jesus expressed itself in the positive re-affirmation of the other aspect of Oedipal ambivalence, the love of the Father, already enjoined in the Mosaic commandment 'Thou shalt love the Lord thy God with all thine heart' (Deut. vi, 5). To this Jesus added the New Commandment 'love one another' (John xiv, 12). What launched Paul on 'his continua-tion of primaeval history' (Freud, 1939, p. 143) was his personal experience on the road to Damascus (Acts xxii, 6-11); the resulting change of heart converted him from an active persecutor of Christians to an Apostle of Christ. Paul's own rendering of the gospel of love is given in the thirteenth chapter of the First Epistle to the Corinthians, beginning 'Though I speak with the tongues of men and of angels, and have not charity, I am become as sounding brass, or a tinkling cymbal', and ending 'And now abideth faith, hope and charity, these three: but the greatest of these is charity'.

The Gospels preach a personal religion to all human beings as God's children, equal before Him. This teaching of Jesus was the result of his own experience. Despite the omniscience claimed by the Churches for Christ as the Son of God, the historical Jesus was a Jew, brought up in a patriarchal tradition, and his ideas, although revolutionary, retain the impress of this tradition in the form in which it was compatible with his own personal insight. His revolt was not against the Fatherhood of God, the patriarchal conception of Deity as such, but against the deadening influence of righteousness as obedience to law and conformity to ritual observance unquickened by personal love of a Heavenly Father, whose essence appeared to Jesus to be love. The Catholic Church still claims to be the only true representative on earth of the spiritual Church of Christ, but is presumably unaware that, in so doing, it is voicing the isolationist claim of its ancestral Jewry to be the Chosen People, in direct contradiction to the true catholicity of Jesus. At various times, down to to-day, people have wondered what Jesus would make of his Churches, and his Churches of Jesus, if he were born again in their time. It would seem that the historical Jesus sent his disciples out to preach glad tidings of life more abundant to individual persons rather than to found institutions. The recognition of the personal significance of Christianity has never been lost; it has remained alive through all the hazards of 2000 years of institutionalization and is again being stressed by many modern believers as the quintessence of Christianity.

Although the Churches never quenched the personal flame of love of God, yet in the course of their development of formal organization, dogma, and ritual, they restored and even at times surpassed the tyranny of law and external observance which Jesus had found so deadening in Jewry. Nevertheless, the psychological effects of their historical development were not wholly detrimental. The tracing of the various cultural influences that helped to mould Christian thought and practice is a fascinating study in itself, but it is their effect rather than their historical derivation that is of most immediate concern to psychology. The expansion of Christian doctrine and ritual, deemed by Freud to be regressive in that it involved abandonment of the highly selective monotheism of Jewry, brought about the greater psychological inclusiveness which endowed Christianity with its almost universal appeal. However instrumental political and economic motives may have been in engineering the world dissemination of Christianity, it could scarcely have established itself with the tenacity it has shown in so many of the fields of missionary effort had it not been for the depth and variety of its psychological appeal. In our own days, for instance, why should some educated Chinese, who are the heirs of a cultural tradition much older than that of Europe, adopt this 'barbarian' religion unless it offers them something not so adequately provided by their indigenous Confucianism or their earlier adopted Buddhism? Part of the answer, at any rate, is to be found in the Christian emphasis on personal love. The doctrine that 'God is Love' is reinforced by the doctrine of the Incarnation and by the greater ease, for many men and women, of themselves feeling love for God Incarnate in Christ Jesus. The Son of Man albeit Son of God offers a personal target for personal affection as well as a suitable object for certain types of identificatory relationship.

The Oedipus conflict involves mother-relations as well as father-relations, as Ernest Jones noted in his 'A Psycho-Analytic Study of the Holy Ghost' (1922). He considers that in the Christian solution (*op. cit.* p. 423): 'Object-love for the Mother is replaced by a regression to the original identification with her, so that incest is avoided and the Father pacified; further the opportunity is given of winning the Father's love by the adoption of a feminine attitude towards him. Peace of mind is purchased by means of a change in heart in the direction of a change in sex.' Incidentally, this solution is indicated in the equation of 'Mother Church' with the 'Body of Christ'. The quoted passage naturally refers to the male Christian; no such inversion is required of women. For women, as implied in such phrases as 'the bride of Christ', Christianity offers an aim-inhibited heterosexual solution of infantile father-love. The self-sacrificial love, exemplified by Christ on the Cross, which is the Christian ideal of love, has evident affinities with self-giving maternal love.

The complete relinquishment of infantile object-love for the mother is difficult of attainment and Ernest Jones recognizes in the doctrine of the Trinity the re-emergence of the primal mother-goddess in the mysterious disguise of the Holy Ghost and her more direct re-emergence in the Madonna. The Council of Nice repudiated the divinity of Mary, but later (Jones, 1922, p. 429), 'voices were increasingly raised in favour of according the Virgin Mary a loftier part in the hierarchy. This tendency won the day in the Catholic Church and may be said to be still proceeding, for it is hardly more than half a century since the last step was taken of pronouncing that she herself was also conceived immaculately. The human need for a Mother to worship was too strong, so that She had to be reinstated.' The Madonna and the women Saints provide objects for heterosexual mother-love in men and also cater for homosexual attitudes in women. How successfully they can do this is illustrated in Franz Werfel's *The Song of Bernadette* (1942). The breadth of its Oedipal appeal is, perhaps, one reason why the Catholic Church retains such formidable vitality to-day by comparison with some of its Protestant derivatives. It is correct, so far as unconscious determinants are concerned, to speak of heterosexual and homosexual attitudes towards religious objects, but it must be remembered that the sentiments developed undergo a varying but often a high degree of rarefaction and de-sexualization. The personal relation of the devotee to the object of his worship is one of emotional adoration for an ideal. On occasion, more primitive infantile longings re-emerge, as in the instance quoted by Evelyn Underhill (1927, p. 151) from Mallock's *Veil of the Temple*, of a clergyman 'whose litany led up to the fervent petition: "Hands of Mary, which drip with myrrh, fondle us" '.

The Catholic idealization of the Mother of God is balanced by a patriarchal subordination of the daughters of men and together they constitute a factor making for asceticism, particularly in the priesthood. But the Catholic Church as a whole has never disdained to use sensory avenues of appeal for religious ends. It is the Protestants, who deny any feminine attribute to the Godhead, who have carried the denigration of sensuality to its fullest extent, although this very denial has enabled them to allow women better public status, and even, in some cases, to permit them to function as ministers of religion. Among Protestants, sensuality may take its revenge in orgiastic 'revivals' and comparable emotional festivals.

In brief, there is little doubt of the significance of Oedipal drives in Christianity or of the continuing influence in the latter of patriarchal trends inherited from Judaism in spite of the re-emergence in Catholicism of matriarchal trends and the general advance in conceptions of human fraternity (see Flugel, 1945, p. 273). Ernest Jones (1948, p. 316) summarizes thus: 'The central conclusion based on psycho-analytic research is that *the religious life represents a dramatization on the cosmic plane of the emotions, fears, and longings which arose in the child's relation to his parents'*. When the nature of mysticism is considered, it will become clearer that while the Oedipal conflicts finally mould personal religion, they do not exhaust its infantile motivations. This is the case whether these pre-Oedipal motivations are regarded as primary or as secondarily re-evoked and modified by regression. At present the most reasonable view would appear to be that in religious motivations we have to deal with Oedipal conflicts and with pre-Oedipal situations whose interest has been reinforced and selectively accented as a result of regressive or partly regressive solutions of Oedipal conflict.

Theologians and students of comparative religion have emphasized the syncretism of Christianity, particularly in earlier formative centuries. By this is meant its capacity for absorbing and re-editing in its ritual a great variety of primitive rites and customs from different sources, the fertilization of its theology by the marriage of Greek and Palestinian-Oriental conceptions, and its adoption of a Roman pattern of organization. This formal syncretism is paralleled on the psychological side by the catholicity of its provision, not merely for the restraint but also for the sanctioned expression of infantile impulses which are otherwise taboo. The supreme instance of this is perhaps the Eucharist. By whatever name it is called this is the sacrament which is of cardinal importance to believing Christians of all creeds and denominations, the means of Holy Communion with Christ and fellow-Christians. The religious significance of the Eucharist is not adequately assessed by regarding it simply as a revival of the totem feast, although 'only in its tender and adoring sense, not in its aggressive sense' (Freud, 1939, p. 141). The Catholic Mass, perhaps, exhibits best the ultimate personal significance of the Sacrament. The Mass offers an almost exact parallel to the manic-depressive's relations to his idealized 'good object' and to the attitudes described by Melanie Klein (1935) as typical of a 'depressive position'. All Christian sects enjoin some form of baptismal re-birth and confirmatory initiation prior to admission to Communion, and stress the need of mental preparation and a right spirit in approaching the Sacrament. The Catholic must undergo a more or less immediate antecedent purification, *i.e.* he must confess, repent, and receive absolution: he must go to Mass fasting and must swallow the consecrated wafer whole. Every precaution is thus taken to preserve the idealized object from cannibalistic destruction. The Catholic reservation of the Host carries on the manic-depressive parallel. The spiritual renewal and worshipful refreshment, which is the gift of sacramental grace to the true believer, appears as a sublimated version of infantile suckling fulfilment, in the form of loving, uninjuring incorporation of the idealized object. It is, at the same time, the reward and the substitute for the relinquishment of Oedipal erotic aspirations.

For Christians the diabolical connotations of oral sadism and greed are unmistakably demonstrated in C. S. Lewis's *Screwtape Letters* (1942). Writing to his apprentice Wormwood, that accomplished fiend Screwtape says (*op. cit.* p. 45): 'To us a human is primarily food; our aim is the absorption of its will into ours, the increase of our own area of self-hood at its expense. But the obedience which the Enemy demands of men is quite a different thing. . . . We want cattle who can finally become food; He wants servants who can finally become sons. . . . Our war aim is a world in which Our Father below has drawn all other beings into himself; the Enemy wants a world full of beings united to him but still distinct.' The signature of Screwtape's final letter runs (*op. cit.* p 160): 'Your increasingly and ravenously affectionate uncle, Screwtape'. The late Archbishop of Canterbury, William Temple, gave the following definition of peace (1944, p. 39): 'Peace as the goal of our striving, that peace the makers of which are blessed, must be nothing less than this: Goodwill effectively maintained against every form of greed'.

It is important for the psychologist to become fully informed of the archaic-infantile content of dogma and ritual, but this should not lead him to overlook the provision made in ritual and prayer for the satisfaction of impulse and the recovery of otherwise lost instinctual energy in the believer. It soon becomes apparent that Christianity caters not only for obsessional characters but also for a much greater variety of psychological types.

As will be seen later, it can be argued that to a person of truly religious temperament, his religion is a sublimation rather than a disease. The distinguishing feature of Christianity is its emphasis on personal love: 'He that loveth not, knoweth not God; for God is love' (John iv, 8); 'In love the *whole* spiritual life of man consists' (Aquinas, *On Perfection*, Opusculum XVIII, cap. 1). This rôle of love in Christianity is most apparent in the accounts given by the mystics of their religious experience, to which some attention must now be given.

(5) The Nature of Mystical Experience

After all, it seems only logical to expect that the study of religious experience and of the methods employed to foster the 'spiritual life', *i.e.* mystical technique, would yield more exact knowledge of the personal significance of religion than inquiry into ritual and dogma, informative though these are. The difficulty is that a thorough study of mystical experience would be a lifework; the literature of Christian mysticism is voluminous and much of it is couched in language hard to understand. Baron von Hügel, a mystic's mystic in the sense in which one speaks of a novelist's novelist, wrote a book called *The Mystical Element in Religion as Studied in Saint Catherine of Genoa and Her Friends* (1909) which is considered by many religious people to be the greatest modern work on the subject, but is generally agreed, even by them, to be hard to follow. For present purposes I have used the work of the late Evelyn Underhill, a recognized authority in this country, who has the great advantage of writing simply and directly in everyday language. I have also referred to such modern non-technical publications as Sackville-West's *The Eagle and the Dove*, Almedingen's *Dom Bernard Clements*, S. B. Frank's *God with Us*, etc. It seemed that it would be easy for anyone like myself, not thoroughly conversant with the whole literature, to choose unrepresentative quotations from the sayings of mystics. Hence with a few exceptions, quotations from the writings of the Saints are re-quoted from the modern authorities, thus affording a better guarantee that they are representative than they would have had as first-hand choices of my own.

Mysticism is not limited to Christianity. Oriental mysticism, however, frequently though not invariably repudiates life and seeks peace in the annihilation of individuality over and above the surrender of personal self-will. Thus, the attainment of Nirvana seems to a psycho-analyst to involve the profoundest possible regression to pre-natal primary identification. In striking contrast, the main line of Christian mysticism is active rather than quietist. Consciousness of self may, indeed, be lost in ecstasy, but more frequently the 'creaturely sense' is retained in some degree. The Christian aim is less absorption into God than active participation in the Divine Life and utilization of the gifts of the Spirit for other people, through prayer and deeds. There is considerable variety of character and personality among the Saints, and corresponding diversity in their experience and in their technique, but, for those drawn to pursue it, the way of the Spirit seems to be a very positive way of life which bears positive fruit. It would appear, however, that 'strait is the gate and narrow is the way' and that 'many are called but few are chosen'.

The Christian Saints have all been great lovers of God. With one accord they insist on what, in theological terms, is called the 'prevenience' of God and is more simply described by Evelyn Underhill (1946, p. 110-11) in a definition of mysticism as ' Man's conscious Godward trend; the response of his small dependent spirit to the pressure and invitation of the real God, the magnet of the universe. Such a definition as that relieves us from narrow and exclusive conceptions; since God's demand on the soul is a universal truth experienced by different men in many different ways and degrees.' Human love of God begins in response to Divine Love. S. B. Frank writes (1946, p. 76): 'Religious experience is a special kind of experience the essence of which may be best defined as *communion*'.

It will spring to mind that this living communion initiated by God is paralleled by the infantile libidinal relationship with the mother. Primary identification and the infant's innate libidinal capacity are predisposing and determining factors in this relationship, but it cannot flower into a mutual communion unless initiated and sustained by maternal love. Whether a happy suckling period and innately high libidinal capacity are preconditions of adult love of God is one of those possibilities it may be very difficult to determine with any certainty. There is a passage in Book I of the *Confessions* of St. Augustine, which I have not seen quoted elsewhere, but which seems highly relevant in this connection. St. Augustine writes (1930 ed., pp. 17-18; Book I (VI) 7), in describing God's mercies in infancy: 'Thus there received me the comforts of woman's milk. For neither my mother nor my nurses stored their own breasts for me; but Thou didst bestow the food of my infancy through them, according to Thine ordinance, whereby Thou distributest Thy riches through the hidden springs of all things. Thou also gavest me to desire no more than Thou gavest; and to my nurses willingly to give me what Thou gavest them. For they, with an heaven-taught affection, willingly gave me what they abounded with from Thee. For this my good from them, was good for them.' It is possible for suckling experience to be so satisfactory that no later gratifications approach the same high level. In such circumstances mysticism might well provide the answer to needs which no adult human relationship could supply.

Some religious people retain throughout life conspicuously affectionate relationships with one or other of their parents. The outstanding historical example is that of St. Augustine and his mother, St. Monnica. In modern times a particularly close relation of mutual understanding and affection existed between the Anglo-Catholic Benedictine, Dom Bernard Clements, and his mother. His biographer writes (Almedingen, 1945, p. 7): 'There lived but one woman in his life, and she was his mother'. William Temple (1944, p. 5) wrote of 'my own father, of whom I say nothing except that he was and is, among men, the chief inspiration of my life'. However, it is impossible to say, at present, whether these relations are more common in religious families than in others or how common they are among the religious.

Persons to whom religion offers a working solution of their life-problems seldom appear in the consulting-room, whereas many appear who have failed to gain adequate help from religion. These ineffectively religious patients usually lament their loss of faith and their estrangement from God. Such states of mind are ordinarily found in conjunction with a high degree of unresolved infantile ambivalence, which may or may not be accompanied by conscious hatred of parents and parent-substitutes. It would seem, however, that the libidinization of parental relations achieved by some religious people is often, though not invariably, purchased at high cost. It may demand the sacrifice of all normal adult heterosexual relationships, and even the surrender of individual responsibility for a life under authority. Dom Bernard Clements not only lived a celibate life, but in his forties he was constrained to give up his independent parish and in due course to take the vow of absolute obedience to the Benedictine Rule. Discussing this step, Almedingen says (1945, p. 35): 'The freeing of a will in the undoubtedly harsh school of absolute submission is, indeed, as Donne said about another majestic truth— "Stone to philosophers, and milk to faith" '. It is difficult to read Dom Bernard's biography without being impressed, on the one hand, by the intensity and sincerity of his faith and, on the other, by the depressive-obsessional character of his personality.

No rapid survey can do justice to the depth and strength of feeling displayed by true lovers of God or to the richness of their imagery. Every aspect of infantile life seems to be included in the scope of their religious experience. Infantile suckling drives take a prominent place and appear in intellectual description as well as in personal worship and adoration. Thus, Evelyn Underhill writes that mysticism is (1946, p. 107), 'to use a favourite phrase of Baron von Hügel, a "metaphysical thirst". A mystic is not a person who practises unusual forms of prayer, but a person whose life is ruled by this thirst.' But thirst is not the only primary need to receive both direct and sublimated expression. In another place, Evelyn Underhill writes (1927, p. 157): 'Those have not been among the least of the saints who have recognized in the Beatific Vision itself some equivalent for the sense-conditioned experiences of men; and been humble enough to accept the supernatural with and through these its natural veils. "What do I love when I love Thee?" says St. Augustine. "I love a certain kind of light, and voice, and fragrance, and a kind of food and embrace, when I love my God: a light, melody, fragrance, food, embrace of the inner man. Where for my soul that shines which space does not contain, that sounds which time does not sweep away, that is fragrant which the breeze does not dispel, and that tastes sweet which when fed upon is not diminished, and that clings close which no satiety disparts." So too his English pupil (Julian of Norwich): "And we shall endlessly be all had in God, Him verily seeing and fully feeling, Him spiritually hearing and Him delectably smelling and sweetly swallowing". "For Thou", says Nicholas of Cusa, "dost abide where speech, sight, hearing, taste, touch, reason, knowledge and comprehension merge in one." '

St. Theresa's attitude towards God was at first quite consciously ambivalent. She refers to her 'hatred of our Lord, which I made so public', and says that her decision to become a nun was 'more influenced by servile fear than by love' (Sackville-West, 1943, p. 28). The influence of both aspects of her Oedipal conflict is apparent in many of her visions. Thus she saw the devil as 'a frightful little negro' (*op. cit.* p. 31) gnashing his teeth in despair at losing what he attempted to seize. 'She was one day in prayer when she found herself, without knowing how, plunged apparently into the infernal regions. The entrance was by a long, narrow pass like a furnace, very low and dark and close; the ground saturated with water and mud, exceedingly foul, sending forth pestilential odours and covered with loathe-some vermin. At the end was a hollow place in the wall like a cupboard, and in that she saw herself confined. She could neither sit nor lie down, there was no room; there was no light, only thick darkness . . . in hell it is the soul itself that tears itself in pieces, with an inward fire surpassing all torments and all pain' (p. 33). Of St. Theresa's book *The Interior Castle*, Sackville-West writes (1943, pp. 48-9): 'God himself had supplied the basic image around which she built her Castle. . . . The precincts were hor-rible indeed, "a mass of darkness and impurity, full of toads and vipers and other venomous animals"; but, once the infested entrance had been passed, God showed her "a most beautiful globe of crystal in the shape of a castle, with seven rooms, the seventh, situated in the centre, being occupied by the King of Glory, resplendent with the most exquisite brilliancy which shone through and adorned the adjoining rooms. The nearer these lay to the centre, the more did they partake of that won-drous light." '

Blissful experience, however, is not the element most empha-sized by Christian mystics, rather is it their overwhelming con-viction of the reality of God. To quote Evelyn Underhill again (1946, p. 110); 'St. Augustine's saying "God is the only reality and we are only real in so far as we are in His order and He in us" gives us in a phrase the central conviction of every mystic; and we notice at once its intensely objective character. Their concern is with God. He is. That is what matters; not the ecstatic feelings I may happen to have about Him. For mystics, God is the fact of facts.' Elsewhere she writes (1913, p. 228): 'The sense of intimate communion with a transcendent Person-ality—usually identified with the exalted Christ—is one of the best attested phenomena of Christian mysticism'. Frank writes (1946, p. 40): 'That which is immediately given us in the religious

221

experience is a reality which we apprehend, on the one hand, as something primary, as the deepest source and the absolute foundation of our being, and, on the other, as something absolutely valuable, giving us the supreme, perfect joy, satisfaction and delight'. Also (*op. cit.* 59-61): 'In religious experience we have a peculiar and clear combination of intimate nearness with remoteness, or, in philosophical language, of the greatest immanence (which in this case is actual possession, a mergence of the object of experience and ourself) with transcendence . . . it is an immanent experience of a transcendental reality . . . and it actually is such that we are aware of a living intimate contact with something that comes from afar, we are conscious that something taking place within us is an effect produced from without'.

The combination of the utmost intimacy with overwhelmingly mysterious unknowability characteristic of the sense of the 'Presence of God' will again correlate in the psycho-analyst's thinking with the probable experiences of infancy. Nor do the infantile drives leading to emphasis on the omniscience and omnipotence of God require much elaboration. Any psycho-analyst reading Berdyaev's *Slavery and Freedom* (1943) will probably appreciate anew how imperative it may be to allay anxieties of helplessness and bondage through the recovery of omnipotence and magical wish-fulfilment in God. As Dorsey says (1943, p. 148): 'Ideas of omnipotence (the necessary counterpart of the utter helplessness of our infanthood) are carried over into adult life because of our continued insecurity as adults'. In discussing Determinism, Wisdom says of the libertarian concept of freedom (1943, p. 146), 'Underlying it may be found the omnipotence of thought'.

Religious systems and religious persons vary in the emphasis they lay on the immanence or the transcendence of God. Quakers stress His immanence, whereas most Protestants tend rather to assert His transcendence. For instance, Canon Richardson (1947, p. 244) is convinced that 'faith is not a mystical but a rational activity, and to seek "religious experience" as an evidence for or as a consequence of Christian faith is the first false step in our religious life. Our knowledge of God is a mediated knowledge and the One Mediator is Christ the Word.' On the other hand, for the Catholic Dr. Frank (1946, pp. 26, 27), the Christian revelation is 'the revelation of God's *immanence* in the human soul. The revolutionary significance of Christ's message is in His showing that God is immediately near, within our reach, and that faith is *a direct knowledge of God*—a knowledge which may be clearer in babes than in the "scribes" versed in the Scriptures, the law and tradition.' The testimony of the Christian saints asserts both immanence and transcendence, a paradox which will seem inevitable and natural to anyone familiar with the mental mechanisms of introjection and projection and the difference between identificatory and definitive object-relationships. In the consulting-room we more often meet with immanent and transcendent devils in various forms than with experience of God. However, one woman known to the writer had two experiences in her late teens which illustrate both these aspects. In the first, while in great distress and confusion of mind, she was trying to submit herself and her problem to God in the sense of 'Thy Will be done', when she received a blessing; her consciousness was suffused with a feeling of peace and beatitude which seemed like the healing gift of a transcendent power. In the second experience she was faced with an exhausting task to which she felt inadequate. She spent a few minutes in concentrated prayer for strength. This time waves of energy seemed to well up within her, she went to the dreaded task refreshed and renewed, and carried it through without difficulty. At the time, she herself attributed both these blessings to the grace of God, but both can be interpreted in terms of modification of intra-psychic economy. The first can be thought of as an experience of definitive object-love relationship between ego and super-ego ideal, a revival of infantile beatitude, and the second as a release of id energy for sublimatory use sanctioned by the super-ego.

Nevertheless, it remains true of most believers that, as Evelyn Underhill says of contemplative prayer (1946, p. 51): 'No experienced Christian will be willing to allow that in such prayer he merely explores his own buried resources. He is aware, at least in his deepest and most surrendered moments, of real contact with a real spiritual order, however dimly and mysteriously known: and from this contact he does receive renewal of assurance and of life.' Her conception of the psychology of such prayer is given in the following passage (*op. cit.* pp. 52-3): 'We know in other departments of life that some of our greatest experiences and all our most fruitful intentions are undoubtedly prepared and matured in the subconscious deeps, and it is only their finished results that enter the conscious field. And this I believe to be true of the soul's deepest intercourse with God; abiding unbroken in

the depths of personality, and thence overflowing as a transform-
ing, strengthening and cleansing tide into the consciousness which
is sufficiently pure, humble and attentive to receive it.'

(6) The Economics of Mysticism: Sanctity and Integrity

Students who are sympathetic to religion often become too
evangelistic, whereas students who are antipathetic to religion
often tend to under-estimate its personal significance. There is
as much 'for' and 'against' special pleading in the sphere of the
psychology of religion as in politics. It is necessary to recognize
that, for persons of religious temperament, who are by no means
only obsessional types, religion can and sometimes does offer a
positive way of living. To the psycho-analyst, the economic aim
of Christianity tends to appear as the pursuit of ego and super-ego
ideal integration, although Christians themselves, particularly
mystical Christians, would maintain that it is the pursuit of total
integration. The Christian conception is summarized in the
following quotation from Evelyn Underhill, although this has
been abbreviated by the omission of some, not absolutely essential, passages (1946, pp. 114-18): 'The great Christian mystical
tradition . . . has a special quality which distinguishes it from
those who have responded to the attraction of God from within
other faiths. . . . It is different because it is based on the Incarnation, the redemptive self-giving of the Eternal Charity. The
Christian mystic tries to continue in his own life Christ's balanced
life of ceaseless communion with the Father and homely service
to the crowd . . . and the more profound his contemplation of God,
the more he loves the world and tries to serve it as a tool of the
divine creative love. . . . This acceptance of our whole life of
thought, feeling, and action, as material to be transformed and
used in our life towards God, is what Baron von Hügel meant by
"inclusive mysticism". It alone is truly Christian; because its
philosophic basis is the doctrine of the Incarnation, with its con-
tinuance in the Church and Sacraments. Its opposite, exclusive
mysticism, the attempt to ascend to the vision of God by turning
away from His creatures by an unmitigated other-worldliness, is
not Christian at all. . . . Finally, the thoroughly organic, deeply
human character of real mysticism is surely brought home to us
when we see how gradually a mystic grows, what hard work he is

called upon to do, and how many things he often has to suffer in getting rid of all that prevents him from swinging easily and peacefully between the Unseen and the Seen; how marked are the moral and psychological changes which must take place in him, and the different kinds of prayer which express his increasing communion with God.'

'Most people have heard of the "Mystic Way" with its three stages of Purgation, Illumination, and Union. Though this ancient formula, borrowed by Christian writers from the Neo-Platonists, cannot be applied rigidly to all cases, it does in a general sense describe the great phases of growth which gradually make our ordinary, faulty, earthbound human nature capable of communion with the Eternal God. All, indeed, have to pass through a process much like this on their way to the full living-out of any kind of life. The artist, explorer, scientist, philanthropist, must root out everything that conflicts with his vocation and impedes his progress—all forms of self-occupation, pride, ambition, love of comfort; all competing interests, pleasures, and affections—and such self-conquest is the very essence of the mystic's purgation. . . . The reward of this courage and single-mindedness, this stern training in detachment, is always a great increase in knowledge and understanding. . . . But the fullness and creative quality of the life to which he is called is only developed in him when he passes, and usually by way of great suffering, beyond this to a further stage: . . . The mystics are fond of this metaphor—"I live in the ocean of God as a fish in the sea". That is the life of union, of conscious abiding in God; the full expansion of man's spiritual possibilities, and full satisfaction of his deepest desires. It brings with it great creative power. Once more we come back for our best definition to St. Paul's "I live, yet not I".'

True sanctity is, indeed, very seldom achieved by human beings. Psychologists and others have been quick to seize on the pathological affinities of mysticism and the frequent failure of its practitioners to attain their goal. These aspects were intensively studied by Leuba, but it is he who writes of the great Christian mystics (1925, p. 128): 'All of them, so soon as unity was established in their consciousness, have spent themselves without stint in the service of their fellow men'. It is Leuba who considers that the satisfaction of their fundamental needs in relationship to God (p. 189) 'resulted in a substantial unification of personality. The

latter parts of the careers of our mystics show them able to manifest the whole energy of synthesized beings in the fulfilment of
tasks considered as assigned by God himself and achieved in close
collaboration, or even in union, with him.' Referring to life as
a symphony in which many instruments play their parts, Arthur
Hopkinson says (1946, p. 23): 'No body of men and women have
understood this orchestral view of life, or exercised more harmonizing influence in human relationships than the mystics.
. . . They were, for the most part, many-sided men and women;
some of them highly intellectual, many of them engrained with
institutionalism, and most of them people of practical wisdom
doing good service in their generation. They lived harmonized
lives, which contradict by facts the popular conception of mysticism as a vague and profitless form of religious emotion.' The
argument that the spiritual life, sincerely followed, is a way
of sublimation and sanctity, a rare but genuine type of integration rather than a disease, is certainly not without evidential
support.

There are, however, aspects of sanctity which are not so satisfactory. For instance, 'there is a definite type of ill health which
dogs the possessors of great mystical genius. . . . The psychic
pain and instability which accompany growth to new levels have
their reverberations in the bodily frame. . . . The lives of Suso,
St. Theresa, and others, provide well-known examples of this
bodily rebellion against growing spiritual stress; which mystical
writers accept as an inevitable part of the way' (Underhill, 1913,
pp. 174-5). The predisposition to the love of God may be given
by the earliest experiences of infancy, but, as it operates in the
adult mystic, the love of God is a love moulded and crystallized
by Oedipal idealization, and the 'spiritual life' wears the aspect
of a process of regression, prepared by the issue of the Oedipal
conflict but set in motion in the adult by voluntary self-frustra-
tion. As noted earlier, the lives of the Saints are filled with
accounts of id vengeance exacted in such forms as bodily ill health
and persecution by the Devil. Mystical literature indicates that
the solution by the Saints of their problems of aggression was
either masochistic and autoplastic, or projective, usually a combination of both. It is tempting to surmise that St. Theresa of
Avila would have died at a much earlier age had she not found a
sanctioned outlet for her strong aggressive drives in a public
career of convent reform.

The argument that sanctity and the life of union with God are psychoses must carry weight on account of the many pathological phenomena associated with mysticism, the evident psychopathic constitution of many mystics, and the clearly regressive nature of the 'mystic way'. There is much to be said, for instance, for the view that the superabundant energy, which is quite as characteristic of the Saints as their liability to ill health, is a manic phenomenon bound up with the denial of reality to anything but Divine Love. In the present state of knowledge, it must be admitted that sanctity may be a benign antithesis or counterpart of melancholia, and beatitude a very convincing form of euphoria. Schizoid affinities can also be adduced. But it is by no means certain that this is an altogether satisfactory diagnosis, at any rate in the case of the great Saints, in whom the effects of terminal 'unification' are most clearly apparent. In them the regressive progress seems to culminate in a positive re-integration which is, to say the least, an unexpected issue in psychosis.

There are two presumptive factors which might help to determine this result. It will be remembered that Freud emphasized the psychotic's denial of reality and finding of substitutes for it (1924c, *Collected Papers*, vol. ii, pp. 272-82) and that Federn more recently suggested that new psychotic reality is created by 'the gaining of reality by what has previously been mere thought' (Federn, 1943, reprint p. 42). It is quite true that the Saints deny full reality to anything but God and that they accord Him an altogether Supreme Reality. They are, however, not given to denying the phenomenal realities of everyday life and current conditions. They simply 'value' nothing but the Divine Love. Neither is it certain that, apart from the distortion effected by idealization, they create any wholly new reality. It may be that the infantile experience to which they regress and which is so clearly mirrored in the descriptions quoted above is historically real. 'Except ye become as little children, ye cannot enter the Kingdom of Heaven.' Perhaps the Saints enter the Kingdom of Heaven, after they have re-traversed the intervening developmental hells and purgatories, because they were peculiarly blessed in infancy. There is no positive proof, but it is possible that the re-integration of the Saints is successful because their 'spiritual' regression ends in the revival of satisfactory infantile experience: their subsequent idealization may derive from early sensory-affective enjoyment of actual blissful communion. The second factor is the high personal capacity of the Saints for active loving; this is well attested by the circumstantial evidence. The accounts of their lives may be inaccurate in many respects, but they are unanimous on this point, and such unanimity is probably not without some basis in fact. The term 'love' covers a wide range of human emotions and sentiments, some of which attain great refinement and sublimatory differentiation. Father D'Arcy has published a comprehensive and erudite book called *The Mind and Heart of Love* (1946), but a simple tale like *Silver Fountains* (Mackinder, 1946) will bring home to the reader the quality of the loving-kindness which is 'Christian charity'. The contrast between charity and the cruelty of formal piety is also strikingly illustrated in another novel, *A Woman of the Pharisees* (François Mauriac, trans. 1946). Loving-kindness is not the exclusive prerogative of Christians, but it seems to have been quite unusually well developed in the greatest Saints.

The unification of the Saints is a hierarchic theocentric type of integration dominated by the Love of God. It is selective in the sense that impulses and systems refractory to the love of God, and to His will, tend to be projected or to receive somato-plastic expression. Projection mechanisms are illustrated by the temptations of St. Anthony and the persecutions of many other Saints by convincingly objective Devils. Many of the bodily distresses of the Saints suggest conversion phenomena. What is remarkable about the integrity of the Saints is not its impairment by certain inevitable dissociations but its validity. Sanctity would appear to be a positive condition in which by far the greater part of the total personality is God-centred and effectively dominated by the love and will of God, as apprehended by the person concerned. It may not be too much to assume that sanctity is the sublimatory positive of infantile sexuality in the same way that neurosis is described as the negative of perversion. This way of thinking of it helps to explain both the rarity of its achievement and its status as a type of integration. It would seem that the price of sanctity is total sublimation of genital drives and total surrender of ego-direction to super-ego control. In the conduct of life, this surrender may take the form of obedience to spiritual and practical direction by superior ecclesiastical authority. The symbolic significance of surrendering personal initiative in order to become an instrument of the Divine Will need not be laboured here. The wholeness of the Saints is proportionate to the completeness of their sublimation and to the inclusiveness of their surrender to Supreme Reality, the incomprehensible and indescribable God who is, nevertheless, indubitably experienced as Love.

Even if the unification of the Saints is to be thought of as self-cure rather than disease, the impression remains that the integration of sanctity should, nevertheless, be regarded as a striking variation rather than as the end stage of the main line of human development. The true spiritual vocation is very rare and the findings of psycho-analysis suggest, very definitely, that the high road for the majority does not lead to super-ego autocracy and selective idealization, but to a more inclusive and democratic harmonization of id, ego, and super-ego systems, to the development of more comprehensive reality-sense, and to the more enlightened ego-direction of personal life.

(7) Intelligence and Religious Experience

We have outgrown the earlier naïve belief in the omnipotence of Reason, that modern Lucifer, and are more fully aware that intelligence is a subjectively conditioned and fallible instrument. But recognition of the fact that the ego is the executive manager and not the master of individual life does not in any way diminish the importance of its adaptive functions. The increase in understanding and ability to control themselves so needed by human beings to-day, can come about only through the general development of a more balanced psychological reality sense, through which awareness of subjective experience would become capable of intelligent interpretation as well as of direct description in its own terms.

Spiritual experience, in the main, seems to pertain to that level of directly convincing or self-evident awareness that is characteristic of first-hand perceptual experience of the outer world. This character accounts for Jung's hypothesis of the 'objective' psyche and its archetypes and for the mystic's conviction that religion is the only true realism. Intelligent appreciation of subjective experience, whether spiritual or perceptual, demands the application of conceptual thinking to the data of experience and not merely explanation of the experience at its own level in terms of what it feels like. It may be that spiritual experience is both informative and misleading in the same way as perceptual experience. Human intelligence in the form of conceptual thinking has corrected our perceptual impression that the sun rises and sets. It is to the same intelligence that we must look for the necessary correction and evaluation of religious experience. The experience is indubitable, and, in spite of the inadequacy of verbal description, its general character of overwhelming conviction of the Presence and Love of God (the Beatific Vision) is established beyond question. But, whereas Jungian theory would explain it as objective archetypal experience, psycho-analytic findings support the hypothesis that the experience involves definitive object-relationship between ego and loving super-ego ideal (so long as the 'creaturely sense' is retained) which may, or may not, resolve into the identificatory relationship of the 'unio mystica'.

Jung regards individuation (his technical term for the integrative process which results in 'finding the self') as the goal of life, but 'Jung has said that nobody is really cured "who did not regain his religious outlook"' (Gerhard Adler, 1945, p. 218). This suggests that Jung's twofold conception of psychic structure easily leads to failure to discriminate between various ways of 'finding the self', a failure against which psycho-analytic threefold conceptions are a more effective safeguard. It is likely that further research will support the view that the integration of sanctity with its idealization of super-ego love, its denigration of ego and id, and its repudiation of aggression, is economically a different phenomenon from the re-integration which comes about through increase in ego-ability to tolerate psychological reality and to accept with comparative serenity all the constituents of the total personality. It is this latter type of integration, which perforce includes but, in so doing, tends to modify idealization-denigration, that is the type that every psycho-analyst strives to initiate in his patients, whether he describes his aim in these or in other terms. The technique of psycho-analysis may display all the individual variations inseparable from the exercise of personal skill because practice is, after all, an art based on scientific principles. But such variations do not affect its fundamental implication that it is possible for men and women, albeit with countless reservations, to develop a more balanced reality-sense. This is equivalent to saying that it implies the possibility of integration through harmonization of the total personality.

Being and knowledge of life are not identical, and the application of knowledge to living requires wisdom, accurate empathy as well as accurate information. But it is a fact that knowledge, applied with only moderate wisdom, can increase ability to live and can reinforce integrative propensities. Knowledge is not the traveller; its function is to serve as a map of the country through which the human life-journey is made. Psycho-analytic terminology and matter-of-fact common sense are prosaic and it is easy to understand and sympathize with the preference of idealists for the more romantic and symbolically satisfying phraseology of Jung. Psycho-analysis, however, is not content to accept spiritual or 'archetypal' experience at its face-value as a subjective fact of an order inaccessible to cognition. On the contrary, it maintains that intelligence can and should be brought to bear on all the data of experience, and it is determined to further the objective knowledge of mental dynamics and economics in order to aid and safeguard the development of personal integrity. The assumption is that the more men know about themselves the better their chances will be of coming to life-promoting terms with themselves. Effective understanding of human nature will never be achieved without the application of intelligence to the full range of subjective experience. The fallibility of reason and its subjective conditioning should not dissuade us from its use, but should persuade us to use it to the full with all the safeguards that can be devised. These safeguards include the pooling and collation of our interim findings with those of as many other workers as possible.

IV. 'PSI' OR 'PARANORMAL' PHENOMENA

(1) PSYCHOLOGY AND ULTIMATE ISSUES

Certain kinds of explanation may appeal to psycho-analysts: for example, (a) that religious experience may be of an order comparable to perceptual experience and that it may, therefore, yield impressions that are misinterpretations of objective facts; and (b) that conviction of the objectivity of God may pertain to certain experiences of definitive object-relationship between ego and super-ego systems. Such explanations, however tentative and incomplete they may be, are consonant with many phenomena with which psycho-analysts have become familiar in situations that are not directly connected with religion. But purely psychological explanations of religious experience are very unlikely to be acceptable to convinced Christians, and psychoanalysts cannot hope to prove beyond many shadows of doubt that any description of the intra-psychic economy of mystical experience is completely exhaustive of such experience. To the mystic, psychology cannot explain away the overwhelming realness of Divinity any more than physiology can explain away the realness of mental life, and the mystic can argue that he has no more to fear from progress in knowledge of the psychology of religion than has the psychologist to fear from advances in brain physiology. Those who hold that man consists of body, mind, and spirit (or soul) usually seem to equate mind with consciousness or intelligence. Psychologists, as persons, have as much or as little right as other persons to express their opinions on ultimate issues, but as psychologists they have the right to speak with that modicum of authority accorded to specialists only on matters pertaining to psychology.

It was noted earlier that the Jungian concept of tension between nature and spirit corresponds, more often than not, to what psycho-analysts prefer to describe as tension between id and super-ego organizations. It should, however, be remembered that although Jungian theory is more acceptable to Catholics than is psycho-analysis, Jung's own arguments are in favour of the existence of objective psychic archetypes of divinity and are not arguments for or against the existence of God. Whatever the personal convictions of individual analysts, from Freud on the one hand to Pfister on the other, one must recognize that the findings of psycho-analysis, even when far more complete than they are at present, can explain only the psychology of religion and indicate the parallels between the comparative history of religion and the phylogeny and ontogeny of mental development. Psycho-analysis already has much to say about the psychological determination of conceptions of God and relationships to God. But psycho-analysis can offer no ultimate explanation of life and the universe, although it may affect the balance of probability between competitive theories. This matter has been discussed by Flugel (1945, pp. 263-5). As between science and religion, dogmatic assertion that evolution has come about by chance is no more justifiable than dogmatic assertion that it is the expression of Divine Will.

However much theologians may emphasize the limitations of the human mind and its inability to comprehend God, theological explanations seldom proceed far without attributing human motivations to God: human thinking is always human thinking. Many religious people have been driven to admit that the problem of suffering is intellectually insoluble on the premiss that 'God is Love'. Here the psycho-analyst is less completely baffled, since he can begin with the intellectually credible assumption that the primary function of pleasure and pain is self- and race-preservative, and he can thus view their later developments as secondary elaborations of a basically discriminatory rôle. All adults retain some unconscious beliefs in supernatural agencies; these are a heritage from infancy and possibly from our ancestors. Agnosticism seems the only fitting attitude for intelligence *vis-à-vis* ultimate issues, once it is realized that we can only think about them by analogy with human experience.

Primitive religious theories do not always lack a substratum of objective reality. There is biological justification for worshipping the sun and the earth as Father and Mother. The description of creation in Genesis (i, 2), 'the Spirit of God moved on the face of the waters', is a poetical version of modern scientific speculations that life began on this planet through the action of the sun on tidal waters. The conditions of primitive human life were probably such as strongly to favour the idealization of light and the denigration of darkness.

The would-be realist must admit that man and the universe are 'given' and not man-created, and that the ability of human beings to modify themselves and to change their environment is subject to conditions which are not of their own making. For psycho-analysis, acceptance of 'given facts' includes the acceptance of the dynamics and economics of mental life and should, in my opinion, also include the demotion of the reality-ego from mastery to management. However the balance of probability may alter, in view of the 'givenness' of life and the universe, it will always remain possible to argue that there is a real God (or some equivalent) with as much claim to objective reality as natural scientists accord the sun. It will also remain possible to assert that complete knowledge of the intra-psychic economy of religious experience could not diminish His reality any more than better understanding of the intra-psychic mechanisms of perception eliminates the sun. Moreover, psycho-analysts have good reason to appreciate the difference between intellectual convictions of probability and subjective certainties of emotional belief, and to recognize that the grounds of belief and unbelief are to be sought in the sphere of infantile relationships and not on the intellectual plane. Intellectual atheists often show by their emotions and behaviour that they retain an unconscious belief in God. Attitudes of mind, once established, can subsequently be modified and transcended, but they can never be eliminated: human thinking may transcend animism, but the latter will always be operative within it.

It would be a mistake to suppose that the study of psychology necessarily blunts emotions of awe and wonder. On the contrary, research in psycho-analysis is just as likely to increase as to diminish the impression that man is 'fearfully and wonderfully made'. The age-old argument from design is one that will carry some weight with any thoughtful psycho-analyst not temperamentally anti-religious. So will the argument, put forward by A. E. Taylor (1945) amongst others, that the assumption on which the most materialistic scientist works, that there are natural laws to be discovered, is a tacit admission of belief that there is unity and order inherent in the universe. Apart from such general considerations, intellectual assent or dissent from the probability of para-individual unities corresponding to the communion of saints or to the God of the mystics will be influenced by the degree of probability attached to inter-psychic, as distinct from intra-psychic, experience. The reliability of evidence for telepathy, survival, and such matters, is relevant here. It is, therefore, necessary to consider very briefly the scientific position regarding that field, variously labelled by different workers, but described with convenient brevity by Thouless as 'Psi' phenomena.

(2) TELEPATHY

In his Presidential Address to the Society for Psychical Research (reprinted in pamphlet form, 1945), Tyrrell distinguished three principal groups of Psi phenomena which he calls 'paranormal phenomena'. He says (1945, p. 2): 'There are three main groups of evidence: (1) Evidence for the acquisition of knowledge without the use of the ordinary channels of sense. (2) Evidence of communications purporting to come from the dead. (3) Evidence for certain types of physical phenomena alleged to occur in the presence of a particular type of medium.'

The first group covers telepathy and clairvoyance. Many spontaneous cases have been reported, but these are so difficult to verify that, in the main, they belong to the vast mass of anecdotal evidence which is viewed by scientists with justifiable misgiving. It will be remembered that the apparently telepathic dreams which came to Freud's notice (1922c) left him agnostic on the matter, except in so far as it seemed clear that any telepathic message received would be utilized by the dreamer for purposes of dream work in the same way and under very much the same conditions as an ordinary sensory stimulus. On the other hand, Ehrenwald reported two dreams which, he considered (1942, pp. 322-3), 'suggest that in certain circumstances the manifest dream content may contain elements of what we have termed hetero-psychic material, that is, motives that show striking congruence and temporal coincidence—without being due to chance—with corresponding features in the mind of another person. This is what we are bound to term telepathy. . . . Our cases have shown that such an event, even in individuals with what we have called a psychic disposition, is marked by special emotional significance of the particular dream motive to either the agent or the percipient—or to both of them.' In a later paper (1944), Ehrenwald summarizes the reports of Freud and other workers on possible instances of telepathy and suggests that the mental attitudes of patient and analyst in the analytic situation may be such as to favour telepathy in either direction. Judging by his own experience, he thinks that it may be telepathic influence that induces Freudian patients to dream Freudian dreams, Jungian patients to dream Jungian dreams, and so forth. However, it must be admitted that, in general, dreams lend themselves to a variety of interpretations, and the analyst's choice of interpretation is bound to be influenced by his own bias. Ehrenwald himself concludes that (1944, p. 62): 'The prerequisite of any future discussion of the problem must therefore be in the obtaining of further and if possible more conclusive factual observations of telepathy in the psycho-analytic situation than our approach has been able to afford'.

Ehrenwald has published a fuller discussion in his book *Telepathy and Medical Psychology* (1947a). He thinks that the Freudian conception of personality needs restatement along more teleological lines to do justice to the implications of telepathy. Quoting Goethe ('Supreme goal of human striving thou art person-ality') and Nicolas Berdyaev, Ehrenwald (1947a, p. 188) suggests 'that there is an ingrained tendency in our mental make-up which militates against the intrusion of hetero-psychic influences into our mind, a psychological diaphragm whose busi-ness it is to prevent the occurrence of telepathy, and which subjects such hetero-psychic material as may penetrate through the diaphragm to much the same forces of repression as were described by Freud. . . . Its failure to maintain its protective screen entails mental derangement. Its complete breakdown leads to the breakdown of the personality, whilst a transient permeability of the screen to certain patterns of psychological processes may lead to such occasional telepathic occurrences as we have seen during casual absent-mindedness or in states of minor emotional disturbance.' Personality thus becomes 'a dynamic principle concerned with the isolation of a self-con-tained psychological entity from the rest of the world, and safe-guarding its unity and coherence in the dimensions of both space and time'. To the present writer, in view of the purposive striv-ings engendered by all instinctual impulses and the synthetic function of the libido, the unmodified theory of psycho-analysis seems adequately teleological and the need for a new dynamic principle is less apparent, although the embryologist's 'organ-izers' and 'individuation fields' might be thought to afford a physiological parallel to Ehrenwald's 'personality principle'. His 'diaphragm' would, as he says, help to explain 'resistance' to telepathy, but it affords no solution of the credulity in regard to Psi phenomena which is scarcely less frequent than scepticism, at any rate among the general public.

Tyrrell considers that strong evidence for telepathy is pro-vided by the 'study of trance-mediumship extending over many years, notably with the American medium, Mrs. Piper, and the English medium, Mrs. Osborne Leonard'. However, it is neither the spontaneous nor the mediumistic evidence but the experimental study of telepathy that has given it status as a topic of scientific research. Much difference of opinion still exists among psychologists as to the validity and utility of the work, but the experimental study of telepathy has become a recognized scientific pursuit. Thus, in America, Duke University has created a special department for its study headed by Dr. Rhine, and Harvard University has devoted a special fund to this purpose. In this country, Trinity College, Cambridge, has instituted a Studentship in Psychical Research, first held by Whateley Carington; while Cambridge University has awarded a Doctorate on a thesis entitled 'Paranormal Cognition' (Bendit, 1943). Experimental research on telepathy is summarized by Tyrrell (1945) and described in much greater detail by the late Whateley Carington in his book *Telepathy* (1945). Both publications contain useful bibliographies. The aim of the experiments is, in the first instance, to establish the fact of telepathy. Rhine uses special cards, Carington uses drawings, and other test objects have occasionally been used, but the principle of most of the experiments is the same. Elaborate precautions having been taken to ensure that the subjects have no opportunity to receive information through sense channels, the experimenter chooses a series of test objects at random and the subjects or percipients guess what these are. Using appropriate statistical methods, the score of right guesses has been found to be significantly higher than would occur by chance. Many thousands of such experiments have been done in the last fifteen years. The experiments and the methods of statistical analysis have been subjected to much criticism, but the experimenters are themselves convinced that they have established telepathy as a fact of nature. Dr. Soal, of London University, repeated Rhine's experiments for five years without success but, on re-examining his results, discovered that two of his subjects displayed pre-cognition, since they guessed the card next ahead in the trial series more often they they should have done by chance, an occurrence which aligns with some of Dunne's views on Time.

Carington's experiments also showed, amongst other things, that telepathy does not diminish with distance, as would be the case with wireless or other forms of wave radiation. Carington noticed (1945, p. 66) that 'some subjects . . . appear to pick up an impression of the linear form of the original without succeeding in interpreting it directly. For example, one of the originals in my sixth experiment was a Bow Tie, and I was for a long time puzzled by a striking and highly significant outcrop of hourglasses in the drawings of these subjects, till it occurred to me that these were almost certainly misinterpreted Bows.' Such misinterpretation favours the view that telepathy is not a cognitive or intellectual process, but a matter of unconscious sympathy at a more primitive, even pre-verbal, sensory-affective level. A psycho-analyst would expect this, and it accords with the view of Thouless that telepathy represents a primitive means of gathering information, now largely superseded by perception. It also accords with Tyrrell's conclusion (1945, p. 14), that 'the real telepathy is buried deep in the region of the subconscious, and we can say very little about its nature'. We know that Freud found the ability of some fortune-tellers to read the unconscious wishes of their clients to be more positive evidence of telepathy than had been provided for him by dreams (Freud, 1933, p. 45 *et seq.*). The experimental work so far undertaken reveals nothing about personal dispositions to telepathy nor about the subjective significance of the test objects to either experimenter or percipients (but see p. 241).

In a discussion of objections and resistances, Carington (1945, p. 41 *et seq.*) attributes the rationalizations of some adverse critics to emotional resistance. He has not yet made up his mind (*op. cit.* p. 105) 'whether some specific repulsive or dissociative force must be postulated in order to account for the mechanisms commonly known as "repression" '. However, he puts forward a purely ideational association theory of telepathy (*op. cit.* p. 59). His view of mind is avowedly most influenced by Bertrand Russell, but in some ways approximates to psycho-analytical conceptions of mental organization, although he does not appear to be aware of this resemblance.

It may be admitted at once that Carington uses his theory to advantage, but this success seems to be due to the fact that he treats mental life implicitly as dynamic and association as a synthetic force, although he presents explicitly an ideational atomic conception of mind. He says (*op. cit.* p. 96): 'According to my present view, then, the mind consists of sensa and images, and of nothing else whatever'. He introduces the word 'psychon' to cover any sensum or group of sensa or images capable of behaving as one. He writes (*op. cit.* p. 97): 'I say, then, that the mind is a psychon system, or psychon structure, in very much the same sense that the body is a cell system, that a protein molecule is an atom system, or that a galaxy is a star system. The psychons are linked together into groups and sub-groups and patterns, and all these with each other, by the "forces" of association in much the same way that cells are linked by adhesive forces, atoms by electrical forces ("valency bonds"), or stars by gravitational forces.' He adds a footnote to the effect, 'I use the word "force" only for the sake of vividness. It does not refer to any "real thing" any more than it does in physics.'

This brief mention will be sufficient to show the resemblance between Carington's psychon structure and the psycho-analytical conception of mental processes and their organization. It also shows the equally striking difference due to Carington's failure to recognize the instinctual dynamism of mental life or to allow for the fact that perception and ideation are mental activities always involving more than sensa or images 'by themselves'. A psycho-analyst might consider that a closer study of psycho-analytic and other dynamic psychologies would have been a useful counter-balance to Carington's interest in philosophic theories of mind.

In regard to the evidence provided, one cannot doubt the honesty either of the work described or of Carington's own conviction that telepathy is a fact. The precautions taken against conscious or involuntary cheating certainly appear to be adequate: the present writer is not competent to assess the reliability of the statistical analysis. Caution is inspired, as Carington himself realizes, by the fear of reopening the way to the tyranny of superstition by accepting insufficiently proven facts.

Since this chapter was first written, the weight of the experimental evidence for Psi phenomena has been substantially increased by J. B. Rhine's publication, *The Reach of the Mind* (1948). Although much of the book describes the work done by Professor Rhine and his colleagues at Duke University, North Carolina, it is not a Departmental Report but a survey of the origins and growth of parapsychology. Rhine regards Psi phenomena as a successful challenge to materialist conceptions, and one which demands a return to 'psychocentric' as opposed to 'cerebrocentric' views of man and his relation to the Universe. His own philosophical leanings are towards 'neutral monism'.

Rhine distinguishes eight steps in the accumulation of evidence for psychocentrism and Psi phenomena, the first being the earlier experiments on telepathy, which, by 1930, had made it credible. The second step was taken by the establishment of extra-sensory perception (ESP, clairvoyance) through experiments with specially devised 'ESP' cards. These tests incidentally showed that much earlier work on telepathy had not discriminated between telepathy and clairvoyance, but, by 1940, further tests led to 'the working hypothesis that there is but one ESP, of which clairvoyance and telepathy are different manifestations' (*op. cit.* p. 46). The third step attested the extra-physical or non-physical nature of ESP by procedures showing that it is free from spatial dependence, and the fourth, its similar independence of time, through the discovery of pre-cognition. The fifth and most startling step is the hypothesis of psychokinesis (PK), *i.e.* of the existence of a mental energy which, in so far as it influences the fall of dice, must be thought of as convertible to physical energy. This resulted from 'the dice-work', first reported by Rhine in 1943, in which subjects concentrate on willing chosen numbers to turn up. The sixth step is the marshalling and consolidation of the positive evidence for the assumption that PK is not a brain-object but a non-physical relation. The seventh step is taken by the conclusion that 'ESP and PK are so closely related and so unified logically and experimentally that we can now think of both mind-matter interactions as one single fundamental two-way process' (*op. cit.* p. 107). The eighth step is the establishment of Psi capacities as normal functions of the total personality.

In contrast to Thouless and Ehrenwald, Rhine thinks Psi capacities are akin in nature to the higher mental faculties, *e.g.* creative imagination. Though they are independent of the space and time conditions tested, they are extremely sensitive to psychological conditions, *e.g.* the personality of the experimenter may have marked effects on his subject's performance. Drugs seem to affect Psi in the same way as other mental processes. There is anecdotal evidence that Psi experiences have been of use to the individuals concerned, but two principal factors stand in the way of any immediate practical application: (1) they are too 'erratic, unstable, and unpredictable' (*op. cit.* p. 108) to be dependable, and, in the case of PK, which is demonstrated only through its physical effects in the dice-work, 'the evidence shows only the faintest traces of the capacity' (*op. cit.* p. 98); (2) the characteristic ultimately responsible for all the other difficulties—'This key property of the Psi process is its unconsciousness' (*op. cit.* p. 156).

As with Carington, there can be no doubt of the sincerity of Rhine's conviction that experimental proof of the existence of Psi processes is now adequate, and their general acceptance a matter of time and the overcoming of various emotional resistances. Indeed, the statistical methods employed have been examined by competent mathematicians, *e.g.* the opinion of the

American Institute of Mathematical Statistics, 1937: 'If the Rhine investigation is to be fairly attacked, it must be on other than mathematical grounds' (*op. cit.* p. 132). The account of the experiments given, though naturally condensed, seems to indicate that every possible error that was thought of was adequately controlled. In short, the evidence demands very serious consideration and cannot lightly be dismissed as 'nonsense' or 'incredible'.

According to Thouless, an attitude of unbelief has now become unreasonable 'and it would be a waste of time to devise new researches to prove over again that the facts exist' (Thouless, 1948, p. 98). Thouless admits that there is as yet 'no foolproof method of experimenting that can be guaranteed to give positive results when applied by any experimenter to any experimental subject' (*op. cit.* p. 99). Rhine, however, reports that a number of investigations are now in progress on the personality conditioning of Psi performance. 'The method of attack is to use the techniques of clinical psychology to find out mental characteristics, both transient and enduring, that are associated with ESP in action' (Rhine, 1948, p. 122). Ehrenwald thinks that quantitative experimental methods must be supplemented by non-quantitative psychological investigation of spontaneous occurrences (Ehrenwald, 1947a, 1947b). Clearly, Psi work has reached a stage at which team investigation by workers with different backgrounds and training is greatly to be desired.

In view of the force of unconscious belief in the 'omnipotence of thought' and of the amazing subtlety of many of its disguises, a psycho-analyst may still be justified in hesitating to yield too readily to the increased pressure of experimental evidence. Further, it is well known, *e.g.* among biologists, that impeccable mathematics can, on occasion, make nonsense of natural phenomena; it is also possible that the highly artificial conditions of experiment introduce sources of error not yet apparent. However, there is no fundamental contradiction between the findings of psycho-analysis and telepathy, nor are phenomena such as 'fate-neuroses' inconsistent even with the assumption of PK. Psycho-analytical theory could accommodate 'hetero-psychic' along with 'auto-psychic' mental stimuli without any modification more basic than recognition of their existence. Psycho-analytical readers will recall that Federn (1938, p. 196) finds support in parapsychology for his assumption of the existence of

an undirected function in the central nervous system and his conclusion that 'the undirected function is the essence of the psyche'.

Thouless (1948, p. 100) argues that parapsychological facts
now seem 'odd' because current experimental psychological
theory is inadequate, but that they 'might be fitted into a
theoretical system which had to the existing system of psychological theory the relation which Heisenberg calls "enclosure" ',
citing in illustration the enclosure of the 'special case' laws of
Newtonian mechanics within the more general system of relativity. He suggests that the receptive phenomena, such as telepathy, 'may be regarded as a general type of cognition (*i.e.* of
the psyche becoming aware of events) of which sensory perception is the special case in which the psyche receives information
through the mediation of the sensory nervous apparatus. This
special case is undoubtedly the more familiar, perhaps because
cognition through the mediation of the sensory nervous system
is biologically superior as a means of the adjustment of the organism to its environment' (*op. cit.* p. 101). In his view, spontaneous
and experimentally induced phenomena represent evasions of
the inhibition to which the 'less efficient' cognitive function has
become subjected. Thouless rightly insists that (*op. cit.* p. 100)
'any suggestion as to theoretical clarification made now must
be highly speculative and altogether tentative'.

(3) OTHER 'PSI' PHENOMENA

Some of the evidence for 'poltergeist' phenomena and for
communications purporting to come from the dead, summarized
by Tyrrell (1945), is striking, but the impression remains that
work in this field has not, so far, materially increased the credibility of survival, etc. (Tyrrell published his views in book form
in *The Personality of Man*, 1946.) It would, however, be pre-
sumptuous to express a decided opinion without making a far
more thorough study of the whole subject. As Tyrrell says (1945,
p. 15): 'The researches of the Society for Psychical Research have
been endorsed by the support of a number of eminent men.
Clearly the research is not an attempt to reinstate the supernatural or to encourage superstition, as some critics try to make
out. It is an attempt to explore a new region of nature, which is
to be discovered by looking *within* the personality of man instead
of *without*.' Among the things which psycho-analysis has dis-

covered *within* personality are very strong subjective determinants of belief in immortality and in the omnipotence of thought. The gulf between natural and supernatural disappears if it is considered as the difference between perceptual and intra-psychic experience.

Anecdotal evidence of Psi phenomena not mentioned by Tyrrell is provided by the accounts of climbers who survive falls on the mountains, by aviators, and occasionally by subjects of dental anaesthesia. Some of these relate experiences of temporary externalization in which they observe their own bodies from without, falling through space or recumbent in the dentist's chair. There is also the problem of 'miraculous cures' which appear to involve almost instantaneous regeneration of bodily tissues; one such case has been described by Sackville-West (1943, pp. 166-7). The authenticity of such occurrences, if they be authentic, in no way proves that the orthodox religious explanation of them is valid. At present, more is known of the pathogenic somatic effects of conflict and frustration than of the therapeutic effects of libidinal release and gratification. Instantaneous relief of fatigue is, of course, not on a par with regeneration of tissues, but many people must have experienced minor miracles of mental and bodily refreshment effected, for instance, by the opening up of an unexpectedly beautiful view towards the end of a long and tiring walk. Edmund Bergler's papers (1934, 1935) suggest a 'natural' explanation of some other Psi phenomena.

(4) The 'Collective Unconscious' and the 'Group Mind'

Any increase in the probability of telepathy tends to raise the probability not merely of inter-psychic communication or communion at primitive levels of mental development but also of various types of inter-psychic organization at higher levels. To most psycho-analysts, Jung's conception of the 'Collective Unconscious' does not yet appear a strictly necessary or indispensable assumption. But it is not an assumption that can be summarily dismissed as entirely lacking in probability, although, as Flugel says (1945, p. 270), 'the majority of psychologists still display a justifiable scepticism'. Flugel notes, however (p. 269), that Freud's conception of mass memories 'brings his position into greater harmony with that of Jung' and his racial archetypes, although Freud does not provide any vehicle for mass memories such as is afforded to the archetypes by the Collective Unconscious. In *Moses and Monotheism* (1939, pp. 150-51) Freud wrote: 'The question arises in what form is the active tradition in the life of the peoples still extant. There is no such question with individuals, for here the matter is settled by the existence of memory traces of the past in the unconscious. . . . I hold that the concordance between the individual and the mass is in this point almost complete. The masses, too, retain an impression of the past in unconscious memory traces.'

Jungian conceptions of 'individuation' accord with the views of those sociologists who maintain that primitive man was group conscious rather than self conscious, and who interpret crowd psychology as a throw-back to earlier phases of development. Apropos of the question of the group mind, McDougall wrote (1929, p. 9): 'Some writers have assumed the reality of what is called the "collective consciousness" of a society, meaning thereby a unitary consciousness of a society over and above that of the individuals comprised within it. This conception . . . is provisionally rejected. But it is maintained that a society, when it enjoys a long life and becomes highly organized, acquires a structure and qualities which are largely independent of the qualities of the individuals who enter into its composition and take part for a brief time in its life. It becomes an organized system of forces which has a life of its own, tendencies of its own, a power of moulding all its component individuals, and a power of perpetuating itself as a self-identical system, subject only to slow and gradual change.'

The Gestalt field theorists recognize the dynamism of groups and that 'the whole is different from the sum of its parts' (Lewin, 1939, p. 885), but all that is left of the group mind in field theory is the recognition that the dynamism of the group whole is constituted by the dynamic interdependence of its members. Field theory is essentially a practical method of research in social psychology which employs diagrammatic representation and non-quantitative geometry ('topology'). Kurt Lewin (1939, p. 872) says: 'The field theoretical approach is intended to be a practical vehicle of research'. The central assumption on which the method is based and on which the 'fields' are constructed is as follows: 'The psychological environment has to be regarded functionally as a part of one interdependent field, the life-space, the other part of which is the person. This fundamental fact is the key-note of the field theoretical approach. In psychology it has become, in various forms, more and more recognized and can be expressed simply by the formula: Behaviour = Function of person and environment – Function of life-space' (Lewin, 1939, p. 878). The American psycho-analyst, French (1942), has made use of the field concept in his research work. There is certainly no support to be found among field theorists for conceptions of group animism. The Christian idea of the Spiritual Church constituted by the Communion of Saints is a conception of group animism involving both the living and the dead.

In popular opinion, and in the specialist opinion of the more enthusiastic exponents of particular views, it is often held to be supremely important to arrive at a final judgment on the issues raised by Psi phenomena. This seems a natural mistake in view of the strong subjective interests involved which tend to increase the anxieties of suspending judgment. No adult can voluntarily and directly change his emotional convictions or alter his personal inclination to certain beliefs, whatever their relation to his intellectual convictions and to his objective judgment on available evidence. But it is possible for many adults to distinguish between what they believe, or can infer that they unconsciously believe, and what they consider to be knowledge justified by evidence. The results of scientific investigation into Psi phenomena have not yet reached a stage at which they can be utilized as a factual basis for the conduct of life. However, whether we survive or not, and whether we are less psychically insulated from our fellows than we usually suppose, as human beings we are, in fact, interdependent and inter-related in our living. At the same time, however, we are also individual foci of vitality. The individual is a living being, whose psychological goal remains the attainment of optimum personal integrity. Our still rudimentary and empirical knowledge of human nature is already sufficient to indicate certain general principles of behaviour conducive to integrative living which seem unlikely to be radically affected by any future verdict on Psi phenomena.

V. ETHICS AS THE PRINCIPLES OF INTEGRATIVE LIVING

(1) INTRODUCTION

If integrity be the goal of personal life, the behaviour of men and women must be directed to its attainment, and the principles of ethics then become the principles of integrative living. It is clear that the personal and social aspects of ethics are inter-related and discussions of personal behaviour can never, therefore, be without relevance to problems of group and international behaviour. Although it is mainly the personal rather than the social aspect of ethics that will be considered in this section, brief reference may be made here to the similarity of their basic problems.

It would seem that optimal integration is as much the goal of world organization as it is of mental organization. The fundamental principles of governing nations and of bringing up children may indeed be identical, but their application will necessarily vary widely in different fields. In any given sphere of human activity, rules of conduct and stereotyped methods of procedure may be considered as efficiency devices comparable to the labour-saving automatism of personal habits. But, if group and personal habits are to promote and not to impede re-adaptation to new circumstances, then they must remain plastic enough to change with changing conditions. The modern slogan 'planning for freedom' refers primarily to the safeguarding of individual liberty within the rapidly expanding framework of social organization. It also indicates the need for finding a working balance between efficiency and adaptability, between stability and plasticity: a balance which has to be achieved alike in social and in mental organization. In his Reith Lectures, *Authority and the Individual*, Bertrand Russell (1949) discussed the problem of combining individual initiative and social order. As Wolters writes (1945, p. 496): 'We demand integration and adaptation; but an integration so complete that all responses are psychologically automatic has gone beyond maturity. The person is over-ripe. Variability must be preserved for adequate living.... When the capacity for development is lost, death has set in.' Hence, no 'rule of thumb' codes of conduct are likely to retain permanent validity. It is only the basic principles of behaviour that can remain constant and then only in so far as they express real and enduring necessities of human living.

(2) PHILOSOPHY AND ETHICS

Although this section is concerned with the implications of psycho-analysis regarding the conduct of personal life and with their relation to Christian ethics, no attempt can be made to summarize the vast literature of Western ethics and moral philosophy. Some idea of its extent may be obtained from Bertrand Russell's *History of Western Philosophy* (1946) and Albert Schweitzer's *Civilization and Ethics* (1946).

No two authors could differ more widely in personality and mental approach. It is, therefore, all the more striking that they agree in their general appraisement of the failure of Western philosophy to solve the problem of ethics, that is, to provide a logical or intellectually adequate basis for moral conduct. Thus, Bertrand Russell writes (1946, pp 98, 99): 'The pursuit of truth, when it is whole-hearted, must ignore moral considerations; we cannot know in advance that the truth will turn out to be what is thought edifying in a given society. . . . One of the defects of all philosophers since Plato is that their inquiries into ethics proceed on the assumption that they already know the conclusions to be reached.' Schweitzer writes (1946, pp. xii-xiii): 'The process by which Western thought has hitherto sought for a world-view is doomed to be fruitless. It has consisted simply in interpreting the world in the sense of world- and life-affirmation . . . in adopting an optimistic-ethical interpretation of the world. . . . It is only when one has clearly grasped the fact that Western thought has nothing else in mind than to establish for itself a world-view based on world- and life-affirmation and ethical in character, that one can realize how in its theory of knowledge, in its metaphysics, and in all its movements generally in the game of life, it is guided, consciously or unconsciously, by the effort to interpret the world in some way or other, and in some measure, in the sense of world- and life-affirmation and ethics.' In Schweitzer's view, Western thought has so far failed to achieve its end, not only because in its concentration on life-affirmation it ignores the tendency to life-negation so prominent in Oriental philosophy, but above all because the basis of ethics is not to be found in the world but only in the individual will-to-live.

(3) EVOLUTION AND ETHICS: PSYCHO-ANALYTICAL CONCEPTIONS

The growth of evolutionary and comparative theories of religion was accompanied by similar developments in the sphere
of ethics. The first contributions to a natural history of morality
long antedated the development of psycho-analysis, and were
hampered by inadequate conceptions of mental life. Some of the
views of later writers, in particular, Westermarck and Hobhouse,
though apparently uninfluenced by psycho-analysis, approximate to certain of its findings.

Westermarck concluded that moral judgments and conceptions are based on moral emotions, and his conception of the
nature of these emotions shows remarkable insight. He writes
(1906, ii, p. 738): 'We found that the moral emotions belong to a
wider class of emotions, which may be described as retributive;
that moral disapproval is a kind of resentment, akin to anger and
revenge, and that moral approval is a kind of retributive kindly
emotion, akin to gratitude'.

Writing of the fundamental and unchanging interests of man,
Hobhouse says (1915, p. 10): 'All these permanent qualities,
which run through humanity and vary only in degree, belong to
his inherited structure. Broadly speaking, they are of the nature
of instincts, but instincts which have become highly plastic in
their mode of operation, and which need the stimulus of experience to call them forth and give them definite shape.' According
to Hobhouse, we move between the two poles of individual impulse and social tradition and there is always 'the modelling of
each new generation by the heavy hand of the past' (*op. cit.* p. 14).
Of morality itself he writes (*op. cit.* pp. 14-15): 'That the moral
standard of man is based on the character of man, though it
sounds like a truism, is a principle which has been but little understood in modern ethics. . . . Let us, then, understand that human
morality from the first rests on the antagonisms as well as the
sympathies, the corruptions and foibles as well as the excellences
of human nature.' Hobhouse realized (*op. cit.* p. 35) that 'the
relation between intellectual and moral advance is certainly not
simple or direct', but he lacked any conception of the intricacy
of mental organization which enforces multi-polar rather than
bi-polar adaptation.

Since the mid-nineteenth century the views of biologists on the relation between natural and moral law have undergone an almost complete reversal. T. H. Huxley saw morality as a reaction against the barbarity of nature, whereas his grandson, Julian Huxley, regards the course of evolution as supplying valid clues to the present and future direction of human development. He stresses the need for adaptive and dynamic as distinct from static personal ethics (Huxley, T. H. and J., 1947). A few modern biologists, notably Julian Huxley and Waddington, have sought to use the findings of psycho-analysis to elucidate the psychological problems of ethics. Thus, Julian Huxley traces the natural history of moral judgment to a 'proto-ethical mechanism' for coping with infantile ambivalence. According to him (*op. cit.* p. 110), 'Primitive love conquers primitive hate by saddling it with the burden of primal guilt; and with this the polarity of right and wrong becomes attached to our thoughts and actions'.

Waddington turned his attention to the bearing of mental organization on morality and concluded that the development of moral realism and scientific ethics was dependent upon more realistic super-ego development. Waddington's views appeared first as an essay in *Nature* (1942) accompanied by discussions to which the Editor did not invite any psycho-analyst to contribute. The book published later (*Science and Ethics*, Waddington *et al.*, 1942) contained a correspondence with Karen Stephen, which turned largely on the nature of the super-ego and of goodness, and a short contribution by Melanie Klein. The latter regards the infant's anxiety and love-promoted reaction against its own aggression as the root of morality, and considers that (*op. cit.* p. 87) 'in the depths of our minds our first longings to preserve and save our loved parents, and to reconcile ourselves with them, persist . . . whenever we have the feeling of moral goodness, in our unconscious minds this primary longing for reconciliation with the original objects of our love and hatred is fulfilled' (see also Klein, 1948b). Money-Kyrle subsequently published two papers, the second (1944) a revised edition of the first, in which he in turn sought to establish the primitive morality of concern for the 'good object' as a universal basis of ethics.

Although the whole of Freud's work is ultimately relevant to the conduct of life and he established the fundamental relations between ego-differentiation, morality, and guilt, he himself did not display any particular interest in ethics as such. Flugel's *Man, Morals and Society* (1945) is a comprehensive reference book to date on the variations in personal morality which can result from diversities in super-ego organization and inter-systemic relationships. There is a special chapter (p. 240) devoted to the 'Psychology of Moral Progress', in which eight tendencies or transitions are listed as characteristic of moral development. These are as follows:

(1) from egocentricity to sociality,
(2) from unconscious to conscious,
(3) from autism to realism,
(4) from moral inhibition to spontaneous 'goodness',
(5) from aggression to tolerance and love,
(6) from fear to security,
(7) from heteronomy to autonomy,
(8) from orectic (moral) judgment to cognitive (psychological) judgment.

These transitions (*op. cit.* p. 255) 'from one state or condition of a more primitive kind to another indicative of a higher state of evolution' have been criticized as affording criteria rather than as being actual stages of moral development, and the reality of moral progress has been questioned. From the economic aspect, however, Flugel's eight tendencies indicate transitions from less adequate to more adequate degrees of personal integrity.

Interest in the 'scientific' bases of ethics has continued to grow and three books which have appeared during the last two years may be mentioned here, though one of the authors, Lan Freed, disclaims that her views are 'ethical'. In her *Social Pragmatism* (1948) Lan Freed makes a critical survey of ethical theories; she emphasizes both the futility and the pathogenicity of 'moralism' and advocates purely rational standards of universal expediency as the only sound principles of action. On the influence of modern psychology in the ethical field, she writes (Freed, 1948, p. 122): 'Certainly the psychologists gave a sort of scientific backing to what the cynics had denied the existence of—conscience—but at the price of revealing it as something more akin to a pathological symptom than a proof of our kinship with the angels'. While she thinks psycho-analysis has much to its social credit, Lan Freed considers that its influence on the popular mind has been adverse to a return of 'respect for reason' from its modern eclipse because (1948, p. 124): 'Through lending a new kind of respectability to forms of irrationalism of which through the eighteenth and nineteenth centuries men of culture increasingly tended to be ashamed, its effect has been on the whole to foster and preserve old modes of thought which without the kind of oblique justification it lent them would have gradually succumbed under the assaults of reason'. Old modes of thought may be less easily vanquished than Lan Freed supposes, but negative effects have occurred, although these have been due in the main to regrettable and widespread misunderstanding of the nature and implications of psycho-analysis. The desirability of rational behaviour is self-evident, but Lan Freed tends to be over-optimistic about its universal practicability and too little impressed by the size and obduracy of the psycho-social problems involved.

In *Man for Himself*, Erich Fromm (1949) formulates a psychological basis for objective ethics which is a highly individual derivative of psycho-analysis. In his view, the moral problem of to-day is man's indifference to himself, and the possibility of a favourable solution (p. 250) 'rests upon his courage to be himself and to be for himself'. Fromm develops his own definition and classification of character-types, which cannot be detailed here. The emphasis throughout is personalist, and the need is stressed for the development of a 'productive orientation' (*i.e.* creative or integrative attitude to self and life), instead of 'unproductive orientations', particularly the modern 'marketing orientation' which has tended to depersonalize and to automatize the individual human being.

A third book, *Ethics for Unbelievers* (Amber Blanco White, 1949), is based four-square upon the psychology of Freud, its conclusion being that it is now (p. 218) 'possible to give both meaning and content to the idea of a scientific morality' and that there is, therefore, some hope of devising a rational 'moral code fitted to the actual needs and tasks of man'. Mrs. White refrains from attempting to impose any detailed code of ethics on her readers: her survey of the field is comprehensive and her approach so full of practical common sense as to render her book a useful source of information.

(4) SUPER-EGO ORGANIZATION AND ETHICAL REALISM

Social codes and personal standards necessarily interact, and so influence one another. Most psycho-analysts would agree that man has become a moral being because he is a psycho-social being, though they might argue that his sociality is, in the first instance, familial, and that he is first and foremost a family being. Few people are entirely free from familial or social anxiety in one form or another, or totally indifferent to public opinion. But psycho-analysis shows that personal morality is the result of super-ego development through which cultural standards are individualized and operate as mental controls of instinct. Super-ego control is effected by the diversion of instinctual drives from expressive to organizational uses.

Whatever the differences of opinion about earlier phases of development, there is general agreement among psycho-analysts that the basic organization of the super-ego is complete at the close of the Oedipus phase and the ground-plan of personality established by about the age of five years. The ethics of the individual are, therefore, based on values acquired in infancy, and his moral attitudes, however much they may be elaborated and modified in later life, will be rooted in attitudes developed in infancy. It is well known to psycho-analysts that the automatism of super-ego control too often results in measuring adult experience by an infantile foot-rule and in enforcing infantile adaptations wholly inappropriate to adult situations. It is evident, for instance, that Flugel's transition 'from orectic to cognitive judgment' can take place only if the super-ego is well enough attuned to reality to co-operate with adult intelligence. Action taken by an adult may be right in the sense that it is appropriate to the current situation, but it may be psychologically disastrous if it has to be taken in defiance of conscience, however absurd and irrational the latter's demands may seem.

The perseveration of infantile attitudes in conscience would be less disabling in later life if the super-ego itself developed on a basis of infantile realism, but this is seldom the case. The more usual warping and distortion of infantile reality-sense has many determinants in the infant's own anxieties, but too often gains ample support from outside. The most important environmental factor which militates against infantile realism is the tendency of ordinary civilized parents to ignore or actively to deny both infantile erotism and infantile death-wishes. This tendency is due to the need of adults to remain ignorant of these matters owing to their own inability to tolerate their long-forgotten infantile urges. Western tradition appears to favour what may best be described outright as a psychopathic type of super-ego development, an assumption that is in line with the conclusion reached by Ernest Jones (1933) regarding the defensive-perverse character of the phallic phase.

It was noted earlier (p. 177), that, under the pressure of Christian culture, the Oedipus conflict tends to issue in a personality-pattern in which the frustrated and forbidden primary impulses are identified with the denigrated infantile and parental erotic and sadistic selves. The idealized asexual parents and idealized selves form a prohibitive control system in the super-ego organization. In effect, the child often purchases a precarious ego security at a heavy cost of available instinctual energy. High charges of aggression, directed through the super-ego organization, keep in subjection the discredited impulses and the dissociated infantile ego systems. What can happen in the social sphere when a cultural super-ego tyranny is overthrown is amply illustrated in Fascism and Nazism. The rebel instincts attain dominance in their most inhumane and perverted forms and provide an exhibition of greed, lust, and cruelty never equalled in scale or in the deliberation of its planning. For such revolutionary evils, a reinstatement of super-ego authority is no cure nor any insurance against worse to come.

It would seem, therefore, that there can be little hope of any civilized fullness of living until the mental phenomena of infancy are as well understood and taken for granted as are the bodily events. If parents and nurses accepted the Oedipal and other mental crises with the sympathetic matter-of-factness they often display in regard to teething or learning to walk, sexuality and hostility could find a legitimate place in the developing reality-ego organization from the beginning, and the super-ego would become correspondingly humanized and better attuned to reality. Civilization has certainly nothing to fear from the spread of more exact knowledge regarding infantile life; on the contrary, it has a great deal for which to hope. The frustrations of infancy which are unavoidable are many, *e.g.* incest wishes are doomed to disappointment by physiological immaturity. But how much more easily these frustrations might be surmounted if their nature was better appreciated by parents, who could then help their children to dispense with the distortions of reality-sense which, at present, they so often reinforce. Similar arguments apply to the conflicts of later life, since every age has its own inevitable frustrations and its own possibilities of compensation. Fewer people would deplore old age, for instance, if they knew better how to insure themselves mentally against its obvious disadvantages.

If parents could be realistic about infantile problems and about their own relations to each other and to their children, this realism would act as a brake on Oedipal idealization. It would favour super-ego identification with more fully human parents rather than with phantastic asexual images endowed with omniscience and omnipotence. Humanization of the super-ego would facilitate personal integration, better relations between the generations and between the sexes, and so, in time, better relations between nations. This world would be a happier and saner place if a tithe of the love now directed to various ideals were directed to men and women. People of every type and colour are more alike than they are different, and clearer appreciation of basic similarities would help to foster the sense of human solidarity so needed to-day. The giving of factual information to children about adult sexual life is a step towards a saner way of life, but complete sanity about sex and aggression, a fuller measure of personal control, and ability to enjoy the rational use of all our instincts, must wait upon the growth of psychological reality-sense. This growth may be slow because of the urgency of the anxieties which have always made people resist new ideas and crucify their prophets; on the other hand, the extreme urgency of the present human situation may help to expedite it.

Clearly, where super-ego realism is concerned, parental knowledge of the facts of early development is not enough; it is the parents' emotional revulsion from infantile erotism and ferocity that are malformative in their effects. The infant does not introject what his parents happen to know about infantile life: he introjects their personal attitude towards it as revealed in their everyday relations with him. Neither a docile infant nor a lusty rebel is likely to tolerate, without conflict, impulses that are intolerable to his parents.

It is certain, however, that the most tolerant and understanding parents cannot do away with the many frustrations and crises in development that are inevitable in infancy. Anxiety, like other forms of pain and fear, is basically self-preservative and an incentive to growth and adaptation, although it tends to become self-defeating when exaggerated. But parent-child relationships are decisive in their selective influence on the child's potentialities and in the degree to which they favour progressive or regressive solutions of infant life-problems. The child who is loved has clearly the best chance to develop his own libidinal capacities, not only in personal relationships but in many other forms of active interest in living. The advantage to the child of being wanted is a psychological factor too little emphasized by population experts and eugenists. In the same way, the infant whose impulses and feelings are recognized and respected for what they are, has the best chance of coming to realistic terms with them himself. The advance to greater moral realism depends upon the extent and speed of increase in psychological knowledge and its application to the development and modification of personality. The degree to which one can hope to attain a 'scientific attitude' to ethical problems depends upon the degree to which one is, or can become, a moral realist. Any extensive development of moral realism is, therefore, likely to spread over a number of generations even in favourable circumstances. It would be definitely unwise to expect miracles of the first few generations, even of the most successfully analysed parents and their children.

(5) Integrity and Control by Use

The recommendations that psycho-analysis can already make in regard to the upbringing of children cannot be considered in detail here. There are no invariable or infallible rules, though there are general principles and a certain amount of more specific guidance as to the handling of critical life-situations common to all infants. In every case the principles have to be applied to a particular infant in a particular setting, and no ready-made programme will suffice. The general principles of integrative development are, in the main, the same as those which govern therapeutic re-integration which were briefly discussed earlier (pp. 171-3).

i. LIBIDINAL CONTROL IN RELATION TO THE DEVELOPMENT OF LIBIDINAL CAPACITY; LIBIDINIZATION

Personal integrity is a libidinal end which is attained in the main only by libidinal means. Libidinal control, however, does not imply absence of all preventive controls and prohibitions; it implies rather a common-sense regime in which spontaneity is restricted only when this is demonstrably necessary. Although innate libidinal potentials almost certainly vary from individual to individual, it remains true that love and friendliness tend to evoke love and friendliness. Libidinal control means satisfying the need for love without pandering to it, and, on occasion, using preventive restraint without retaliation. The essential capacity which has to be encouraged to develop in the interest of personal integrity is the capacity for active loving. This was rightly stressed some years ago by Balint (1936). Where this capacity is well established, libidinal disappointments can be better tolerated because substitute relationships are more readily formed and aggression is more susceptible to libidinization.

The relation of libidinization to those other fusions of libido and aggression, sadism and masochism, has not yet been adequately explored, either in its personal or its metapsychological aspects. Sadism and masochism seem to be primary fusions of impulse, whereas libidinization is more usually applied to the establishment of libidinal dominance in a system of ambivalent relationships. Speaking purely descriptively, it would seem that libidinization implies the tempering of aggression by libido, whereas sadism and masochism involve the modification of libido by aggression. Primitive sadism seems to be concentrated on the achievement of the instinctual aim (erotic or food-seeking) to which the aggression is adjuvant.

Libidinization seems to be the most effective and the most directly integrative method of dealing with aggression, but it depends for success upon well-developed active libidinal trends and the absence of relatively stronger hostile and sadistic trends. The working balance of trends may change with the course of experience, depending on the responses elicited by the varying conditions of life.

A well-integrated adult may be comparatively slow to wrath and averse from vindictive reprisals, but he will take steps to protect himself against proven enemies and will not pretend to like people whom he dislikes. Infants, young children, and immature adults are more volcanic in their responses. Their capacity for libidinization is correspondingly more dependent upon the behaviour of the personal objects of their ambivalent relationships. These persons must prove to them by experience that they are, in fact, more love-worthy than hate-worthy. Granted a favourable libidinizing trend, it is not likely nor even desirable, that the whole of any individual's aggression can be completely libidinized. What is obvious is that people usually need no encouragement to develop anxiety and aggression or to distort their reality-sense. They need every encouragement to develop their libidinal potential to the point at which they can deal responsibly with their disintegrative trends and can tolerate a greater degree of realism in regard to themselves and other people.

Personal attitudes towards life are not generated by intellectual convictions: intellectual convictions are rather pointers to emotional attitudes and beliefs. Optimism does not depend, for example, upon an intellectual conviction that God, man, or nature are benevolent; it depends upon conscious or unconscious affective belief, or faith, derived from experience of loving-kindness. Such faith makes possible intellectual convictions of the goodness of God or life. No conceptual system, as such, can make life worth living or the reverse; the sense of worth-whileness and the sense of futility are equally dependent upon the adaptation of the personality.

People who see no hope for the brotherhood of man except in recognition of the common Fatherhood of God, or, for that matter, the common Motherhood of Nature, usually ignore the fact that family relations are the fountain-head of personal and social hate as well as of personal and social love. The maintenance of friendly relations within the family circle is often aided by projection of inter-familial enmities on to outsiders. Mechanisms of projection would have co-operated with environmental factors in sharpening the contrast between primitive tribal loyalty and hostility to strangers which Bertrand Russell regards as instinctive in man (Russell, 1949, p. 15). Family idealists have a degree of justification inasmuch as faith in life and friendly attitudes towards one's fellows are ultimately determined by adequate experience of libidinal relationships in infancy and childhood. The child who never succeeds in developing a mutually affectionate relationship with either parent is not very likely to overflow with charity towards his fellows when he grows up. On the other hand, a child innately well endowed and born to loving parents is blessed in his infancy and may in later life become a blessing to others.

Love and fear usually work together in promoting the control and modification of instinct, but if control aims at willing and intelligent co-operation rather than at blind obedience under threat, love is to be fostered rather than fear. The test of person-ality-pattern is much the same as the test which is now being applied to civilization: how far does it afford secondary outlets for interests frustrated in their primary intent, *i.e.* how far does it minimize discontent by providing new content? Zilboorg writes (1939b, p. 354): 'The measure of civilization is not in what is repressed in the individual, but rather in what is recaptured and gratified after repression'. Dollard writes (1939, p. 62): 'But socialization is by no means a completely frustrating experience. The seeming obvious intent of social organization is to maximize gratification, to permit of all possible impulse expression which is consistent with group survival.' The integrative rôle of prohibi-tion would seem to lie in stemming expressions of instinct that are personally and socially maladaptive. In the same way, it is legitimate to employ force where this is the only means of pre-venting maladaptive behaviour. It should be emphasized, how-ever, that prohibition and force are transitional means of preven-tion and that the only method which is permanently integrative and curative is the alternative disposal of the frustrated impulses.

The growth of libidinal capacity and the domestication of aggression are only two aspects of personal development, but it is more convenient to discuss them separately. Libido is essentially creative, expansive, and relational; unless actively dis-couraged, the overcoming of infantile erotic frustrations without impairment of adult sexual potential should not prove to be an insoluble problem for most children. The chief aids to the suc-cessful overcoming of frustration are to be found in compensatory relationships of affection and new interests symbolizing those that have to be relinquished. Apart from lack of affection and other directly 'blighting' influences, the chief sources of active discouragement usually arise from lack of realism in adults and from failure to suit adult requirements to infantile capacity. Once the primary libidinal impulses can be accepted and re-spected as the root from which springs the whole garden of human creativity and affection, a major source of discouragement will be removed.

One or other feature of the recapitulation theory has been criticized by biologists, but the hypothesis that the Oedipal phase represents an ancestral age of puberty accounts for the infantile climax of sexual development better than any other so far advanced.

The twofold classification of instincts tends to minimize the actual importance of self-preservation in individual development rather unduly and diverts attention from consideration of the possible influence of ancestral occupations and habits of life, as distinct from family relationships, etc., on modern interests and pursuits. For example, acquisitive tendencies may still be facilitated by ancestral food-gathering; hunting certainly continues to be a lively passion, which also finds expression in purely intellectual fields, in conjunction with other trends such as curiosity, desire for mastery, and so on. There are probably not a few Nimrods among the more ardent research workers in all branches of knowledge. The bodily effects of man's adoption of an upright gait are appreciated by anatomists and physiologists, but the psychological effects are still imperfectly understood, in spite of the fact that every physically normal child still has to learn to walk erect. It is tempting to surmise that our ancestors had something of a struggle to keep themselves upright in the earlier stages of this postural change and that human 'Excelsior' idealism may still be fostered by this originally utilitarian effort.

ii. DOMESTICATION OF AGGRESSION: ITS PREVENTIVE AND
     AUXILIARY USES

Libidinal impulses are generally considered to be more labile than destructive impulses, but this is not the only reason why the domestication of aggression is inherently more difficult than the fostering of libidinal capacity. The situations in which destructive impulses arise so often involve a twofold frustration. Thus it is not only a matter of dealing with aggression mobilized by libidinal frustration and anxiety, but also of coping with the ensuing frustration of primary destructive urges. We readily accept the fact that libidinal frustration is painful and is resented, but we still tend to overlook the corresponding fact that frustration of destructive trends is equally unpleasant; proto-revenge is doubtless sweet, even to an infant, and infantile helplessness plays as decisive a rôle in enforcing the frustration of aggressive wishes as it does of libidinal ones. The infant is just as incapable of gratifying what may appear to the onlooker to be whole-hearted wishes to murder as he is of fulfilling his positive Oedipal desires. If the painfulness of this inability to destroy and the intensity of primitive affects are taken into account, it becomes easier to understand that infants readily become anxious about aggres-

sive tendencies before they develop any degree of emotiona
sophistication. It becomes credible that even very early frustra
tions should evoke intense reactions, and that these should reviv
in later situations in forms corresponding to the phase of develop
ment then current. The 'typical depressive phantasies' woul
then represent the final crystallization of a process which begin
in infancy, proceeds through the ensuing phases of early develop
ment, and is completed by regression following Oedipal conflict
(see Controversial issues and proto-morality, p. 274).

The disposal of frustrated aggression is, indeed, among th
hardest and chanciest of personal and social tasks. Where th
individual is concerned, frustrated aggression that achieves n
secondary outlet is, in the main, disintegrative in its effects o
personality-pattern. It is absorbed unmodified in the psychi
economy, usually reinforcing super-ego sadism and hostility. I
the main only, because such statements have to be qualified b
recognition of the probability that a certain quantity of aggres
sion is necessary to the institution and maintenance of som
indispensable types of mental defence, *e.g.* repression. Hence
that modicum of in-turned aggression which prevents the con
tinued expression of drives in ways that have become futile o
dangerous, serves a useful purpose and is basic to the develop
ment of mental organization.

Most civilized persons, however, labour under a surplus rathe
than a deficit of in-turned aggression. Personal stability is usuall
favoured by ample provision for the expression of aggression
albeit in displaced and modified forms. But it is evidently a
over-simplification to contrast the interests of the individual anc
the group by saying, without qualification, that the free expres
sion of aggression is integrative for the individual but disintegra
tive for his group. Certainly, no society could maintain itsel
which permitted its members free and untrammelled expressio
of their aggressive impulses. The most primitive groups alway
institute social controls of murder and personal violence, just a
they do of sexual relationships; the instability of 'capitalism' ca
be related to its failure to control the jungle savagery of 'exploita
tion' which is the rule when 'business is business'. But societies
like individuals, are continually threatened by the surplus o
frustrated aggression which accumulates in all members who d
not achieve adequate secondary methods of expression, particu
larly where their aggression is continually exacerbated by othe

orms of privation. In primitive tribes, communal participation n the infliction of cruel punishments probably acts as a safeguard o social stability (see Dollard *et al.*, 1939, p. 123 *et seq.*). One obstacle to the humane reform of penal codes, *e.g.* to the abolition of hanging in this country, is to be sought in the unconscious reluctance of law-abiding citizens to be deprived of vicarious satisfaction of repressed impulses to violence. The interests which used to draw crowds to public executions have not ceased to operate because people are now hanged in relative privacy; they have simply been deprived of an age-long customary outlet. This surplus aggressive tension on occasion explodes in revolution or in war. The increase in stability in a nation at war is a temporary effect, usually followed by a period of instability. This aftermath is due not only to the practical hardships which, in one form or another, accrue even to victors in war, but above all to the fact that aggression has again become accustomed to more or less direct outlet, whether in actual combat or in more purely emotional and verbal hatred of the enemy. It is much easier to rouse the dogs of war than to persuade them to sleep again.

It is often convenient, but always disastrous, to forget that instinctual energy, once mobilized, has to be expended or 'bound'. What is not discharged more or less directly or in mitigated symbolic form through muscular or mental motility, in work or play, will inevitably expend itself in modifying the psychic economy and in producing somatic effects other than voluntary action. While, on the one hand, mental organization may be said to result from the toleration of frustration, it is clear, on the other hand, that adequate integration may be rendered impossible by excessive frustration. It is well known that there are persons whose energies are so absorbed in (mental) economic vicious circles that their capacity for effective action is reduced to a minimum, and also that there are persons so intolerant of inaction that they go to pieces unless they are habitually busier than bees. For every individual there is, presumably, an optimum balance between the amount of energy that is needed and can usefully be employed in mental organization and the amount which is better expressed in action or thought.

The optimum ratio between energy used in organization and energy expressed in motility, whilst specific for each individual, will tend to vary about an average characteristic for each personality-type. Thus, it is usual for compulsive anxiety types to discharge large amounts of energy in a fairly constant stream of activity, although the activity may vary according to the individual from unproductive symptomatic behaviour to the productive and successful discharge of professional duties. Manic-depressives, on the other hand, whether they are sick or well, usually tend to show an oscillating rhythm and to alternate periods of inactivity with periods of intense activity. Though 'do as you would be done by' may be a sound general principle of conduct, it is a principle that can be applied satisfactorily only if due regard be paid both to type and to individual differences. If one is schizoid-hysteric in type and one's neighbour is a manic-depressive or paranoid obsessional character, it will seldom be useful to treat him precisely as one would prefer to be treated oneself, or to expect him to share one's tastes and find satisfaction in the way of living that has the greatest appeal for oneself.

It seems probable that surplus libido is more readily dealt with in the mental organization than is surplus aggression. The charges of hostility that can be used to advantage in the mental economy are relatively low compared with the total amount of hostility often generated. In a great many people, integration would be favoured by a freer discharge of aggression than they habitually allow themselves. It is desirable, particularly with immature persons of all ages, to provide legitimate channels for the expression of hostility, while at the same time avoiding unnecessary frustration and wanton exacerbation of anxiety and aggression.

The question of types obviously has to be considered in this connection also. Some types favour libidinization more than others do; the process is, in a sense, one of emotional compromise and comes more naturally to some schizoids and hysterics than it does to persistent dichotomists like manic-depressives and obsessionals. Any form of compromise is difficult for an obsessional: he has to see things in black and white, to hate and then to love, to quarrel and make it up afterwards. Generally, the most an obsessional can achieve is a certain moderation in the expression of his feelings in personal relationships and an improvement in discrimination as to the persons and situations that are really inimical or friendly to him. The 'militant constructiveness' cited by Money-Kyrle (1944, p. 168) as a normal attitude certainly represents a healthy and effective fusion of libido, aggression, and self-preservation, though the militancy sometimes tends to outrun the constructiveness. This 'militant constructiveness' is, however, attainable only by persons capable of distinguishing the intermediate degrees of moral brightness between black and white and not by persons who are constrained to regard other people only in terms of the depth of their blackness or the brilliance of their whiteness. Intellectual and emotional detachment, whether displayed in relation to objective or subjective problems, to other people or to oneself, is another end-product of infantile ambivalence which can be very useful, but may become dangerous and life-thwarting if libidinization is inadequate. Mechanistic materialism is an example of the nihilism to which a too destructive detachment may lead. The part-product of modified aggression that is of incomparable personal and social value is a sense of humour.

A greater capacity for libidinization usually implies a lesser need for direct expression of aggression, because this finds correspondingly more outlet in mitigated and displaced forms. We, in this country, are undoubtedly wise in holding fast to our freedom of speech and our cherished privilege of grousing at Governments. One reason why our party members do not shoot, knife, or beat each other up, is probably the opportunity they have of blackguarding each other to their mutual satisfaction in the House of Commons. Safety-valves will be needed in all walks of life so long as the majority of men and women tend to be over-frustrated and under-provided with outlets either for creativity or for modified and unmodified aggression. The unifying effect of a common enemy upon a nation at war is a well-recognized fact, but the logical conclusion that a nation at peace tends to labour under a certain surcharge of unexpressed hostility is, as yet, less of a commonplace. It is also understood that idealism is strongly activated in war and can effectively sustain war-effort in soldiers and civilians alike, but it is not yet equally well understood that, after victory, the same idealism tends to militate against peace. We hear much less of the inevitable substitution of peace-time objects of denigration for enemy devils than we do of the need for ideals of peace to substitute for ideals of war, though the evidence of the devil-substitution is abundant. It is publicly and privately deplored that victory is followed by a renewal amongst allies of squabbles, suspicions, and disruptive tensions that remain in abeyance whilst the fight is on, but it is far less openly acknowledged that victory in war and inter-allied and social discontents in peace are dynamized by the same forces. Idealization, by its very nature, is inimical to peace because it is inseparable from denigration and always involves a dual distortion of reality. Realism alone is favourable to peace. The rôle of sadism and masochism in this connection is discussed by Edward Glover in the new edition of his *War, Sadism and Pacifism* (1947a).

Libidinization may be the most effective way of modifying aggression, but relatively unmodified aggression can serve integrative ends. The use of aggression, in the mental economy and in social organization, in the necessary prevention of such types of behaviour as really threaten well-being and stability, is clearly an integrative use. Prevention by persuasion is always to be preferred to prevention by force, but there are occasions, in both personal and public life, in which force has to be used as a legitimate means of prevention. Democratic societies are right in setting high value on tolerance, freedom of speech and association, etc. But the fate of the Social Democrats in inter-war Germany is a warning against excessive toleration of forms of intolerance which aim at the deliberate abolition of all free institutions.

The preventive use of aggression is negative, except in so far as it is protective and its results conduce to further positive developments. The most usual directly positive function of aggression seems to be the reinforcement and intensification of instinctual aims other than those that are destructive in intent. A close alliance between hate and aggression certainly exists to-day, and, under primitive conditions, it may have been necessary to survival. It seems clear, however, that in the animal world aggression is by no means invariably associated with hostility. The hunting carnivore is a ferocious beast, but it is questionable whether he could be said to hate his prey (unless it escapes him). It would seem more legitimate to describe his ferocity as appetitive, or greedy; as primordial sadism rather than hostility. The animal's aggression is clearly mobilized in the service of his food-finding and hunger-appeasing self-preservative impulses. Animal matings often appear rough and violent to human observers, but there is no good reason to suppose that anything is involved in such behaviour other than sexual urgency, leading to the ruthless overcoming of obstacles.

The inference from animal behaviour is rather to the effect

that aggression has natural and positive auxiliary functions and is 'normally' used in reinforcing other drives, in supplying impetus to surmount obstacles, and in fortifying the perseverance required for any long-term programme of achievement. In libidinization, a more or less permanent libidinal preponderance is assumed. A libidinized relationship, for instance, is one in which ambivalent conflict is adequately solved in favour of dominance of libidinal attitudes towards the person concerned. But the stronger the libidinal personal relationship, or the major life-interest, the greater the amount of free or mobile aggression these can absorb in auxiliary employment. This is another reason why it is so important for individual and social welfare that people should make suitable friends and find work that can both engage and develop their personal interests.

Popular conceptions of 'escapism' usually combine sense with nonsense. Inevitable frustrations are best accepted as such; it is a waste of life either to kick perpetually against the pricks or to submit inertly to every blow of fate and flee for refuge and consolation to some realm of pure phantasy. But such frustrations can be 'escaped' after acceptance if compensations can be found and the initial protest safely utilized. Where conditions permit, the aggression mobilized by unavoidable frustration can energize the search for ways of overcoming deprivation through the forming of new relationships and fresh channels of expression. Acceptance of life entails acceptance of defeat in many directions and on many occasions, but a truly sthenic acceptance will build upon ruins and pursue fulfilment in one direction after another. Re-adaptation of this kind will be piloted by libidinal interests, and self-preservation may supply strong incentives, but a large part of the necessary staying-power will be derived from aggression. This kind of dynamic and progressive re-adaptation is most favoured where aggression can become conscious and be allowed to play its auxiliary part in and through the ego-organization.

Conscious anger, which can be canalized to productive use, is an enormously energizing factor. Psycho-analysts take it for granted that capacity for hatred is as normal as capacity for love. Both are usually capable of displacement from personal objects to general aims. Any civilization founded on respect for persons and concern for their welfare probably demands a considerable shift or expansion of love and hate from persons to tendencies. The Christian, for instance, is enjoined to hate the sin, but not the sinner. All too often, however, conflicts of ideals lead to the bitterest inter-personal hostilities because the personal reality of the opponents is swamped by mutual denigration; they cease to be fellow-persons holding different opinions, and become devils to one another.

Aggression, like any other instinct, is a pre-moral source of vitality, which can be used for any number of different purposes but can only be controlled effectively by being used. Anyone who has been analysed will tend to feel that fear of instinct has become second nature to men and women, along with guilt about infantile sadism and erotism. Modification of this attitude in the direction of greater realism is not easy, because mastery of these anxieties involves facing all the apprehended risks and dangers; it means owning and doing one's best to assimilate aspects of the self that are usually ego-dystonic, tolerating aggression and shouldering the burden of infantile guilt, instead of trying to 'root it out' or 'lose' it. The burden of guilt and the remorse associated with it are often lightened, without conscious insight, by unconsciously determined programmes of reparation and creation, but the most stable solutions are those which dispose of aggression through the ego-organization and render it available for adaptive purposes. Ego-strength can be estimated, not only in terms of libidinal capacity and self-preservative adaptive plasticity, but also in terms of power of aggressive origin harnessed to life-fulfilling ends.

Human beings have most justification for fearing instincts which are frustrated and achieve no personally or socially acceptable outlet, because these are the personal and social pathogenic factors. It is perhaps even more true of aggression than of other impulses, that prevention of primary methods of expression, however necessary this may be, is an interim measure, liable to prove disastrous if no proper provision is made for suitable alternative outlets. It remains true that personal and social integrity can be assured only by libidinal dominance, but such libidinal primacy can be achieved only in so far as problems of aggression find adequate solution. The 'Four Freedoms', if they could be established, would render the social task easier by reducing the continual exacerbation of anxiety and aggression which is now almost the rule. But freedom from personal anxiety about aggression, and from the threat to social stability and realistic world-organization represented by surplus frustrated aggression, can only emerge as more individuals acquire confidence in their ability to control their own impulses by using them effectively. Prophylactic prevention is better than cure, but prohibitive prevention can lead either to health or to disease according to the presence or absence of permissible and acceptable alternatives. Civilized living can offer plenty of scope for domesticated uses of aggression, but, so long as human beings feel constrained to apologize for having any aggressive impulses at all, aggression will not be taken for granted and properly catered for as an essential component of human nature. If aggression be regarded as the turning outwards of a Death instinct, the argument for effective external expression becomes all the stronger.

iii. IDENTIFICATION AND OBJECT-LOVE (see also p. 138 *et seq.*)

It is customary to decry 'narcissism' by comparison with object-love, although it is clear that integration cannot be achieved without the use of considerable quantities of libidinal energy in mental organization. Inter-systemic libidinal relationships, *e.g.* between ego and ego-ideal, are the heritage of former external object-relationships, but mental harmony in the adult often seems to be correlated with adequate self-love. It is people who live on fairly good terms with themselves who are most likely to live on good terms with their neighbours. A person of ample libidinal capacity can afford the mental expense of libido needed to maintain adequate self-love without impoverishing his current external relationships. Helene Deutsch (1946, p. 147 *et seq.*) described the positive and protective rôle of narcissism in women. Alice Balint (1945, p. 319) thought that, for the growing child, 'identification constitutes the bridge that leads across from naked self-love to getting to love reality'. Henry Harper Adams (1947, p. 106) termed a state of harmonious relationship between ego and super-ego 'narcissistic equilibrium'. He remarks on the omnibus nature of the term 'narcissism' and the need for differential definitions. Indeed the significance of Federn's views on narcissism (*e.g.* Federn, 1928) is becoming more apparent with the passage of time. Even the less well-endowed 'narcissist', whose object-interests are weaker, is not doomed to a prison of ego-centricity. If he is at all capable of putting himself in other people's shoes, *i.e.* of projective identification, he can still expand his interests considerably. There are many people for whom identification proves a basis for more satisfactory relationships than object-love (compare Balint, M. (1948, p. 39), on the social implications of heterosexual and homosexual love). Introjection of 'bad' relationships is not a completely adaptive process, because the ensuing identification of one or other aspect of the personality with the hated person promotes inter-systemic tension and not harmony, as is most clearly illustrated in melancholia. But identification has integrative effects other than those which result from the introjection of libidinal object-relationships which plays such an important rôle in the natural cure of grief and loss. Ego-identification, often accompanied by admiring conscious imitation, is usually a helpful solution of heterosexual rivalry and a good substitute for homosexual object-love. These varied personal functions of identification give it high social value and it seems likely that it favours the development of a sense of human fellowship quite as much as object-love.

Object-relations are essentially discriminatory; the number of individuals for whom any one man or woman can develop sentiments of personal affection varies greatly but it is not unlimited. Object-love expands by repeated displacement, but its natural tendency is to concentrate on one person after another and to single out the beloved; it carries with it a tendency to isolationism and to the evocation of competitive jealousy and all the other forms of envy, hatred, and malice in relation to intruders and outsiders. Even where displacement occurs from a personal object to a class of objects, or to a 'cause', the selectivity of object-interest often remains evident. Personal likes and dislikes will always remain selective and will certainly never cease to develop and to influence behaviour. War-experience attests, however, that fellow-feeling can be strong enough to override personal and national attractions and antipathies. The need for the development of a greater sense of human fellowship and solidarity is apparent; the possibility of such development is given in the basic similarities of human beings and the community of their most urgent needs; its actualization will depend upon many factors, including advance in realism, but it will never materialize without the aid of sympathetic imagination. Sympathetic imagination combines intelligent appreciation with empathy. Hence, fellow-feeling probably has its securest basis in projective identification, although it has other essential roots in various modifications of definitive object-relationship.

iv. SUBLIMATION: THE PILOT FUNCTION OF IDEALS

Instinctual energy that is not directly discharged, absorbed in the mental economy, or diverted to symptom formation, finds expression in reaction-formations or in some of the heterogeneous activities commonly included under the omnibus term 'sublimation'. Generally speaking, in reaction-formation, super-ego and ego alliance against the id permits the expression of the dystonic impulse only through its opposite. The strength of the id interest and the difficulty of suppressing it may be gauged from the anxiety, often the fury, evinced by the subject if the appropriate reactive behaviour is thwarted. The classical example is the fanatical housewife whose abode is not a comfortable home but a temple of human sacrifice to cleanliness and order. In sublimation, again generally speaking, the primary impulses are not finally thwarted but only diverted from their primary channels to secondary, tertiary, and quaternary avenues of expression, varying in degree of displacement and mental 'distance' from the original aims and objects. The success and the stabilizing effect of sublimation depend upon the amount of instinctual energy that flows through the alternative channels with the concurrence of the total personality. There are innumerable degrees of failure and success, from inability to achieve any lasting or truly adaptive mode of expression, through activities of varying efficiency which meet with different kinds of interference, to the more stable grades of habitual and satisfying activity.

It is clear that sublimation is not merely desirable in the interests of society, but indispensable to the development of personal integrity. In spite of all the variations in capacity for sublimation linked with differences in tolerance of primary frustrations and anxieties, no one can hope to achieve any appreciable degree of personal integrity without some symbolic outlet for desires which are, by their very nature, unrealizable in their original forms and without some method of liquidating infantile (and possibly racial and communal) guilt. Every primitive culture known to us offers such outlets, and the beginnings of sublimation reach back into the mists of pre-history. It is common knowledge in the consulting-room that hobbies and cultural interests are usually items favourable to prognosis. The patients least able to benefit by treatment are often those so full of bitterness about primary frustrations, both infantile and adult, that they continue to rebel with fury against the acceptance of substitutes and 'second-best' gratifications. They persist in seeking to dictate their own terms to life, any other course seeming to them unconditional surrender to outrageous injustice.

The means of livelihood available to-day differ as widely in their psychological values as they do in their economic and other rewards. Agriculture is an arduous way of life, with many natural hazards as well as risks and difficulties due to the times, but, in spite of all its modern complications, it continues to offer a way of life profoundly satisfying in its human values. Many professions, for instance medicine, offer similar possibilities of integrative living. In industry the transition from handicraft to machine production took place without any regard for the preservation of human values, although to-day it is recognized that industrial civilization implies both psychological and material welfare. The 'humanization of industry' has become an urgent current problem.

It seems to be a valid generalization that sublimination always involves the diversion of instinctual energy from primary to secondary channels of expression, the displacement often being effected through the symbolism of the new activity. But 'sublimation' clearly covers a number of different processes of many grades and types, that are by no means identical either dynamically or economically. In 'A critique of the theory of sublimation' Harry B. Lee drew attention to a certain lag in psycho-analytical thinking about sublimation. He considers (1939, p. 269) 'that the evolutionary character of psycho-analysis as a science has failed to impress itself upon this aspect of the theory, and that Freud's generalizations about sublimation have remained untested and unverified; through not regarding the concept with a perpetual tentativeness, we have neglected to revise it in accordance with metapsychological standards'. Lee is favourably impressed by the work done by Melanie Klein and Ella Sharpe in this field. Utilizing their work in a later paper, 'A theory concerning free creation in the inventive arts', he concludes that the artist's sublimation (Lee, 1940, p. 293) 'is the artist's *vis medicatrix naturae*, compounded of synergistic and serial unconscious mental processes through which he transcends the miseries of recurrent mobile depressions'. This hypothesis is strikingly consonant with the views expressed by Ella Sharpe (1946) on the psychology of Shakespeare.

At the same time, the early conceptions of sublimation as symbolic gratification of infantile erotic wishes should not be too lightly dismissed. Although they are no longer adequate they are not, therefore, due for discard but for revision, amplification, and co-ordination with more recent conceptions. For instance, it is probably quite true that, for the artist, the production of a work of art often has the significance of having a baby, but this does not preclude the creative activity from serving many other purposes simultaneously; it is quite evident that the newer hypotheses throw more light on the particular psychological conditions in which symbolic parturition occurs. Economic considerations alone make it likely that every well-defined personality-type has its preferred sublimatory trends. We are certainly not yet in a position to assume that all creative artists are manic-depressives, but evidence is accumulating that creative art may be a most-favoured form of manic-depressive sublimation and 're-instatement of the ideal'.

It is in relation to sublimation and cultural development that ideals seem to play their most positive rôle. The negative aspects and the dangers of idealization have been, if anything, over-emphasized in this and the preceding chapter. The reason is that, hitherto, the positive aspects have been consistently over-accented, whereas the reverse picture, the concomitant denigration, impairment of reality-sense, and failure to libidinize aggression, has been almost totally ignored. Over-valuation of ideals is just as disastrous to any prospect of personal or social integrity as cynical under-valuation. The realist must accept ideals and their opposites as psychological facts and try to assess their advantages and their disadvantages. Insight into the process of idealization-denigration must deepen if any gradual transcendence of irrational idealism or materialism by a more integrative realism is to come about. Men and women are not going to lose their idealist and counter-trends any more than they are going to lose their consciences. To give up the pursuit of an ideal in favour of a worth-while but more realizable aim is a difficult task because it involves heavy frustrations as well as anxiety risks. It often means giving up the hope of re-living infantile gratifications in all their absolutist bliss, giving up the illusion of omnipotence for the acceptance of personal limitation, and foregoing the certainty of revelation for the relativity of human knowledge.

Nevertheless, it is in the field of sublimation that idealization has most greatly enriched human life, although this enrichment has not as yet compensated for all the misery it has brought in its train. It is probable, however, that ideals have been the main pilots of creativity in sublimation. Obsessional undoing and manic reparative and reinstating drives function as incentives to sublimation through their connection with libidinal ideals. Creativity which liquidates guilt is enhanced, in spite of the desolating gulf between vision and performance experienced by all inspired artists. At the same time, it would appear that creativity is impeded and stunted if it be limited to compulsive reparation, *i.e.* if its aim be restoration rather than creation. This is, however, only another way of saying that creative power varies directly with libidinal strength and its preponderance over destructivity. Sheer necessity for survival is itself a prolific mother of invention. Communal sublimations, *e.g.* the emergence of primitive agriculture and metal-working, or modern industrialism itself, are presumably always over-determined and are not susceptible of expression in any very simple form of instinct or relationship equation.

(6) VALUES

So far, it is chiefly the dynamic and economic aspects of instinct-control and morality that have been considered. The personological aspect of "values" and their development must now briefly be discussed.

i. DEFINITIONS AND STANDARDS

Human values reflect the complexity of the human psyche. Value is an abstract concept, used in various senses and capable of a variety of definitions. Most of these definitions have in common a scale of assessment of worth, whether the values in question are ethical, monetary, artistic, intellectual, or belong to any other category. Every individual will be influenced by the standards of value that prevail around him, but every individual's scale of worth will also be intimately personal, the outcome of his own specific life-experience. Judgments of objective worth (in relation to objective standards) can be made in any field, but judgments of subjective worth are always related to personal feeling and need. The ultimate source of personal values is to be sought in the sphere of instinct and emotion; the subjective valuation of other people, for example, is determined by the significance to us of our relations with them and may have little to do with any objective estimate of their characters.

Moral values in the narrow sense are characterized by two special features, their absolutism for the person who entertains them and their tendency to exhibit a sharp polarity between good and evil, in spite of the evident fact that everyone is good and bad by any definition of these terms. The definition of goodness and badness, *e.g.* the definition of 'the good life', has been fruitful in controversy and weak in logic because the dependence of human values upon human nature has not been understood and knowledge of human nature has not been adequate. Definitions of good, for instance, alternate between hypotheses based on conceptions of Absolute Goodness as an attribute of God and relativist theories which see good and bad as fundamentally artificial human conventions, devoid of any trustworthy criteria.

Moral standards differ in various parts of the world and in various epochs, but they differ in essentials less than might be expected. This suggests that the most fundamental problems of personal development and social organization are the same for all human beings at every time and in every place. Many virtues are virtues all over the world and many vices are universally recognized as vices, though some virtues and vices are differently estimated under different conditions. Thus, the poverty which St. Francis preached as a virtue could conveniently be regarded by nineteenth-century industrialists as a crime justifying all the human degradation of 'cheap labour'. The estimation of physical courage and martial prowess has been consistently higher in Europe than in China.

ii. NATURAL HISTORY OF VALUES

(*a*) *Primary need (pleasure-pain) values: id and infantile ego standards.* Cultural variations, however, do not obscure the essential natural history of values. There is little dispute that the most primitive standard of goodness is satisfaction of need, instinctual gratification in a satisfying relationship which evokes pleasurable experience; pleasurable experience, moreover, which we presume exhibits at first little or no gradation but constitutes an 'all-or-none' affective absolute. Similarly, the primitive standard of badness is related to the painful absolute of frustration.

Gradations in pleasure and pain become appreciable as mental organization proceeds. The gratification standard, which is an immediate pleasure-pain standard of direct correspondence to need, is not lost during later development, though it may be superseded or even inverted. It re-emerges in many adult forms of happiness and discontent, such as aesthetic pleasure and pain. With the development of conscious memory and foresight, antici-pation of pleasure and pain supplement and may eventually override immediate pleasure and pain as guides to behaviour. Conduct is now governed by variations on the themes of hope of reward and fear of punishment. These anticipatory standards continue to operate throughout life, and have been even more ruthlessly exploited in the moral and religious 'persuasion' of adults than in the upbringing of the young.

In thinking about the infant's 'good' and 'bad' experiences we still assume, with Freud, that erotic and self-preservative needs are simultaneously gratified in one total experience, *e.g.* that oral libidinal impulses and hunger are satisfied together in happy suckling. The absolutism of initial pleasure-pain values may be linked with the absolutism of survival needs; their urgency in the infant may be connected with the lesser certainty of fulfilment arising from utter dependence upon environmental co-operation. Untended infants die.

(*b*) *Moral values and their development; super-ego standards; cultural pressures; controversial issues and proto-morality.* Our willingness to use the term 'moral' or the term 'guilt' in reference to infantile experience will naturally depend upon our conception of the origin and course of super-ego development. In the present state of knowledge, it may be preferable to reserve these terms for the 'values' which result from the inter-relation of id, definitive ego, and super-ego organizations. There is probably no doubt in the mind of any psycho-analyst that the terms may be correctly used from the close of the Oedipus phase onwards. There can also be little objection to the use of terms such as 'proto-moral' or 'proto-ethical' for feelings of the infant which influence him to differen-tiate his values and to develop standards other than those of immediate gratification-pleasure and immediate frustration-pain.

Morality, like any other human characteristic, is an affair of reciprocity between the individual and his environment and there is little doubt that most infants are subjected to moralistic cultural pressure from a very early age. Mothers and nurses use freely such words as 'naughty' and 'good' even to a babe in arms and, though the babe may register nothing but the feeling conveyed in the tone of voice and the gentleness or otherwise of its handling, it probably registers these very early.

The early gratifications which make life possible for the infant usually occur under conditions that the observer would describe as 'being loved', and early frustrations under conditions that the same observer would call being 'alone and helpless, not loved'. Whatever the precise nature of the infant's own feelings they are quite certainly very different in these two different conditions, and it is also certain that infants can develop acute anxieties when they are left alone. It is not at all difficult, therefore, to imagine a natural transition from anxiety when the mother is not there to anxiety when she is there, but not in a 'loving' mood. The mother's own character and reactions must inevitably give impetus to the baby to adapt his behaviour to her conscious and unconscious requirements. These earliest adaptations need involve no premature emotional or cognitive development; they would be rather of the nature of conditioning by results, similar to the 'learning' of animals in many laboratory experiments, which show that behaviour which results in pleasurable experience tends to be facilitated and behaviour that results in pain, inhibited. This early 'conditioning' would pave the way for later differentiation of values other than immediate pleasure and pain. When these almost automatic adaptations are supplemented by conscious cognition, the child will be driven by force of experience to recognize that gratifications themselves fall into two groups. These are, firstly, the permissible, which win approval and are 'good' (pleasant and safe), and, secondly, the reprehensible and forbidden, which win disapproval, are 'naughty' or 'bad' (unsafe though immediately pleasant) and may lead to various distressful consequences. The child who has learned to distinguish between what is approved and what is disapproved is already a proto-moral being.

Adaptation to the specific family environment is promoted by growing discrimination between the permissible and the forbidden. Realistic discrimination between the possible and the impossible, actually dangerous or actually safe, is often less encouraged by family standards. Early values are solidly based on experience of real pleasure and pain, but, as development proceeds, values subsequently differentiated tend to diverge from reality to the extent that the family ethics fail to coincide with actual needs and facts. The more arbitrary and irrational the family standards are, the less incentive the child has to become intelligently realistic about his own behaviour. Where the demands made on him are also fluctuating and inconsistent, he may even find it very difficult to be sure of what is 'naughty' and what is 'good', and will thus become predisposed to doubt his own judgment for the rest of his life.

Irrational ethical injunctions produce similar effects on the development of moral judgment as does the giving of false information on intellectual development. In any case, the subjective incentives to reality-distortion are many and strong, and it is, therefore, very undesirable to confuse a young child in his efforts to orient himself in this bewildering world by telling him either ethical or factual lies. Children can be quite ruthlessly logical, and if they find that items of information or advice they receive from their elders are incompatible, they may cease to believe anything they are told. In very favourable cases, such early scepticism may act as an incentive to finding things out for themselves and result later in an aptitude for research work, but such an outcome is by no means invariable. In any case an early and well-founded loss of confidence in the veracity and sincerity of adults is a handicap to the child in the development of human relationships. To many children, it is a constantly recurring puzzle that adults not only frequently contradict themselves, but so often say one thing and do another.

The cultural pressure to develop moral standards has been mentioned first because so much attention has recently been paid to the subjective, particularly the animistic, determinants of proto-ethics. There is, consequently, some risk of overlooking the fact that, although personal morality is an individual resultant, the human infant is not born into a moral vacuum. He is born to parents already possessing their own version of prevalent cultural standards. These standards exert from the first a directly selective influence on the child's gradual differentiation of values and not only on mental organization through introjection and projection. The baby is an active agent, not an inert doll, and he may succeed in imposing quite a number of his own wishes on his attendants. The fact remains, however, that his life regime is dictated to him, rather than dictated by him. The values entertained by his parents are a set of values offered to him, with which he must come to terms. He may accept, reject, or compromise with these ready-made values, but he cannot avoid becoming aware of them and reacting to them.

Melanie Klein's views on the origin of personal ethics are given their simplest and most concise expression in her contribution to *Science and Ethics* (Waddington *et al.*, 1942). The impetus to moral development, 'to self-condemnation, which is the root of conscience', is given by 'the child's own feelings of revulsion against his own aggressive tendencies—a revulsion which he experiences unconsciously as early as in the first few months of life' (*op. cit.* p. 184). 'The child's overwhelming fear of losing the people he loves and most needs initiates in his mind not only the impulse to restrain his aggression but also a drive to preserve the very objects whom he attacks in phantasy, to put them right and to make amends for the injuries he may have inflicted on them. . . . When the imperatives: "Thou shalt not kill" (primarily the loved object), and "Thou shalt save from destruction" (again the loved objects, and in the first place from the infant's own aggression)— when these laws have taken root in the mind, an ethical pattern is set up which is universal and the rudiment of all ethical systems, notwithstanding the fact that it is capable of manifold variations and distortions, and even of complete reversal' (*op. cit.* p. 85). (See also Klein, 1948b.)

If life is, at first, a succession of comparatively unrelated experiences, of alternating contrasts of absolute satisfaction and absolute distress, then proto-love and proto-hate are not originally associated, except in so far as one may oust the other. This happens if pleasant experience is suddenly interrupted and vice versa. Further, if early pleasurable experiences are accepted *in toto* and carry identificatory 'proto-me' feelings, whereas unpleasant experiences tend to be repudiated and to arouse larval 'not-me' feelings, the stage is set for a transition from anxieties about undifferentiated painful situations to anxieties about sadism and aggression in later, better differentiated situations. Some early painful experiences may never become associated with the definitive reality-ego; they may be non-associated rather than dissociated. In any case, early repudiation of, or revulsion from, unpleasant total situations would necessarily involve repudiation of the aggressive reactions which formed part of the painful undifferentiated whole.

Considerations such as these do not solve the chronological problem of when experience ceases to be indiscriminate and becomes discriminate, but they make it seem more probable that ego-organization and ego-differentiation (which ultimately culminates in definitive super-ego formation) begin and proceed more or less together. No 'precocity' is involved in the fact that anxiety crises may occur at any age, and that these may be 'proto-moral' in the sense that they stimulate ego-differentiation and initiate feelings which revive as components of later incontrovertible guilt experiences.

There is no escape from the patent fact that all hypotheses about very early infancy, like hypotheses about the primordial life of mankind, are speculative. At present we simply do not know how much mental organization may be inherited. From what we do know of the social control of murder and sex-relations in extant primitive communities, we may surmise that the child's phylogenetic heritage, if any, would predispose him to fear murderous impulses and to experience acute anxieties about Oedipal wishes. Both these predispositions would be amply reinforced by the culture pressure of the average Western family. The preservation of good relations with parents is a very practical necessity of early life. The feeling of moral goodness in adults, which Melanie Klein equates with unconscious reconciliation with parents (Waddington *et al.*, 1942, p. 87), is an ego awareness of super-ego approval which could not occur unless similar relations between parent and child had really existed in infancy. It is questionable, however, whether Money-Kyrle's 'primary morality' (1944, p. 169) is quite so primary as he supposes. As it operates in adults, it often seems to represent a post-Oedipal regressive solution of ambivalence by idealization, often obsessional in quality and sometimes highly charged with persecutory sadism and reckless masochism.

It is the earlier phases of ethical development, or protomorality, that are most controversial. As has frequently been repeated, there is general agreement among psycho-analysts that individual personal morality is established (successfully or unsuccessfully) with the post-Oedipal completion of the ground plan of mental organization and personality-pattern. This morality is by no means uniform from person to person, but, henceforward, for any given person, that which his conscience approves is moral good, and that which his conscience disapproves is moral evil. Conscience evaluation now supersedes, or considerably modifies, immediate pleasure-pain evaluation; it makes considerable use of anticipatory pleasure-pain expectations (conscious guilt nearly always includes fear of punishment), but it inherits in full the absolutism of early all-or-none experiences. The moral transvaluation of primary values may proceed to a stage at which almost all direct instinctual gratification becomes suspect and 'good' becomes chiefly disagreeable duty and self-righteous thwarting of oneself and others. Short of such extremes, most people suffer in some measure from incompatibility between their primary need and their moral standards. One or other, or both, may at any time conflict with rational adaptation to current environment.

(c) *Integrative values: total personality and mature ego standards.* It will now be evident that a 'good life' can result only in so far as the demands of instinct and of conscience can be harmonized sufficiently well to give the ego some measure of united backing in its conduct of daily life. The demand for a rational ethic of necessity is really nothing less than a demand for a third, post-moral or integrative, standard of values. A purely external standard of environmental necessity or rational cultural requirement can never suffice, because human adaptation is multi-polar and not bi-polar and mental conditions must also be taken into account. It is always a question of how far and by what means the subjective economy of the individual will allow him to accommodate himself to current conditions. Integrative valuation can be based only upon a more realistic assessment of instinctual needs, of conscience demands, and of environmental requirements. A standard of integrity is implied in Karin Stephen's discussion of 'goodness' in her correspondence with Waddington (Waddington *et al.*, 1942, pp. 78-9).

It seems quite evident, theoretically, that the relation between individual and group should be one of mutual give and take. An ego-centric life of self-expression devoted to purely individual aims is as far from the optimum balance of interests as the opposite extreme in which personal life is submerged in the pursuance of group-welfare. Neither isolationary individualism nor person-ignoring collectivism are genuinely life-promoting. The standard of psycho-social good is rather a standard of co-ordination between person and group which ensures optimal benefit to both. Integration results from the harmonization of variety which enriches life and not from the attempted imposition of uniformity which can only impoverish it. Since psychological peace and freedom depend upon sufficiently harmonious co-operation of the different aspects of the personality, world peace can presumably only be stabilized and human freedom assured by voluntary co-operation directed towards that harmonization of nations which would yield eventually a measure of world-integrity.

(7) NEGATIVE ETHICS AND POWER CONTROL

The part played by frustration and anxiety in the development of moral values helps to explain the predominantly negative character of so many ethical systems and their reliance on prohibition and fear of punishment. There can be no question of undoing the effects of evolution, of stopping human beings from developing consciences, or of doing away with anxiety and guilt. A great deal could probably be done, however, to prevent intensification of anxiety and guilt and to enable the ego to come to better terms with them. A basic problem for mankind to-day is the acquisition of more life-fulfilling habits of self-control. It is hard to see, for example, how any democracy can mature and function with maximum efficiency unless a majority of its members become capable of more effective self-control by appropriate use, rather than by inhibition or repression, of their vital capacities. Ethical conceptions of self-control have always tended to become one-sided and prohibitory. The essential test of self-control is less the ability to prevent personally or socially unacceptable behaviour than the ability to express the maximum possible energy in acceptable and life-fulfilling ways. Prohibition is only an intermediate step on the road to permissible, alternative expression, a means and not an end. The end is control by use, giving the life-enhancement which comes from integrative living, and leading to continued growth and development.

Negative morality, whether individual or group, is an authoritarian regime demanding obedience without insight and operating through fear and threat of force. It is no exaggeration to say that it is dynamized almost wholly by aggression. It is highly effective in promoting the in-turning of infantile hostility against the id and ego and its out-turning against people identified with these objects of super-ego hatred. There are few emotions more cruel and ruthless than righteous indignation. The hostile character of a negative moral regime may be self-evident or may be more or less adequately disguised as a passion for control. The latter may show itself in various forms of strict self-discipline, in over-conscientious behaviour, over-scrupulous exactitude and so forth. It may, however, find outlet in urgent attempts to manage other people, ostensibly for their own good and, in similar projective 'power' manœuvres. In short, negative morality is personal power-politics, and it is as little likely to achieve personal integrity as its international counterpart is adapted to promote world-integration.

Plato long ago realized that the people who desire power are not always those who can be trusted with it. Acton's now proverbial dictum that all power corrupts and absolute power corrupts absolutely has proved only too true. Party politics, with all their inanities, are a better safeguard of certain important types of personal liberty than single party governments. The exercise of power by men over men can diminish only if the human capacity for life-promoting self-control increases.

It is, perhaps, as well to emphasize that the technique of psycho-analysis is not a power technique. The influence the analyst acquires over his analysands through transference-relationships is often exaggerated by lay persons, but it is always fairly strictly limited. Such as it is, this influence is habitually used in ways that aim at increasing the patient's own reality-tolerance and self-control. Transference analysis is directed, in particular, to the gradual emancipation of the analysand, not to his permanent subjugation. Analysts are fallible, no one's technique is uniformly perfect, and results are always conditioned by a number of different factors, but the goal of analysis is certainly not domination by the analyst but freedom for the patient through the development of greater personal integrity and more efficient self-management. Being human, analysts are quite as liable as other people to feel the lure of power, but they are also in a much better position to appreciate how greatly the lust of power is enhanced by psychological as well as by environmental insecurity. It is common knowledge that the patients who are most tyrannical and interfering are those whose internal economy is least stable; their mental budget is so precariously balanced that they live under an unconscious threat of mental bankruptcy.

(8) The Christian Ethic of Love; the Realist Ethic of Life

The need for a more positive morality and a more vitalizing ethical code is now widely recognized. The conception of an ethic of love existed long before Christ, but there has always been agreement amongst Christians of truest insight that the essential ethic of Christianity is an ethic of love. Modern Christians are becoming increasingly alive to this fact; it is, for example, the corner-stone of Albert Schweitzer's thinking. Unfortunately, in practice, this ethic too often ceases to be a realistic charity and active fellowship, and becomes either a sadistic ethic of ruthless persecution in defence of ideals, or a masochistic ethic of pacifism and self-immolation. Not a few sincere Christians regard pacifism as the only logical conclusion to be drawn from the teaching of the Gospels. It is to Christianity that the civilized West, though not the East, owes its conviction that aggression is evil in itself. Non-recognition of aggression as a natural, pre-moral force, having its appropriate uses as well as its too frequent abuses, is, in part, responsible for the Christian failure to solve the problems of aggression (see Flugel, 1945, p. 274). By reason of its very nature, an idealistic ethic should not be expected to provide a stable solution of any profoundly real human problem.

It will be apparent, however, that there is a measure of agreement between the Christian ethic of love, as presented, for instance, by Schweitzer in the unequivocal form of reverence for life and active love, and the type of ethic of life-promotion which tends to emerge from the findings of psycho-analysis. The differences are, in the main, the inevitable differences between an idealism that must incline, in view of its origins, to be over-selective and to perpetuate the absolutism of primitive experience and the moral dichotomy, and a realism that strives to be adequately comprehensive and to correlate personal experience with objective knowledge about mental life. An integrative ethic of life-promotion which is realist will seek, like Christianity, to further libidinal dominance in personal and social life; it will do this by providing for the appropriate use of all instinctual impulses and personal intentions in ways conducive to this end. Unlike Christianity, a realist ethic will try to solve problems of aggression on the assumption that this natural force cannot be eliminated or 'rooted out' of human nature, but can only be more or less suitably employed. The same applies to the variety of human motives with which aggression is closely associated. For example, ambition and rivalry are strong incentives unlikely ever to cease to function in men and women; the desire to outdo infantile rivals has contributed to much valuable individual prowess in many fields. To a realist it will seem an impossibility that mankind should ever wholly cease to be competitive and become instead wholly co-operative; but it will seem a possibility, though not necessarily an immediate probability, that competition could be subordinated to co-operation, most effectively by using it to further integrative ends.

The differences between Christian and realist ethics could be illustrated by comparing the technique of Christian prayer with the technique of psycho-analysis, but this cannot be undertaken here. A concise account of 'The Degrees of Prayer' is given in the posthumous *Collected Papers* of Evelyn Underhill (1946, pp. 35-53). There is a striking contrast between the concentrated direction of Christian prayer to God and the 'free association' essayed by the analysand to permit the unconscious determinants of his mental life to emerge. The Jungian technique of 'amplification' (Jacobi, 1942, p. 81) is akin to some methods of meditation. A few other relevant likenesses and differences between Christian and psycho-analytic conceptions are discussed in the following paragraphs.

i. RESPECT FOR PERSONS: AS CHILDREN OF GOD; AS HUMAN BEINGS

Respect for individual persons is possibly the most enduring value contributed by Christianity to human life. The Christian reason for this respect, the sanctity of persons as children of an idealized Heavenly Father, made in His Image, tends to concentrate respect on the '*Imago Dei*' rather than on the human being as such. This tendency has often sadly impaired respect for persons in the common practice of daily life. This was not the case, however, with the historical Jesus or with the greater Saints. In regard to Christians now living, anyone reading the work of Albert Schweitzer will probably conclude that, in him, his id urge-to-live and his super-ego ideal of love are truly harmonized in his reverence for life, and issue in very practical care for persons; a great part of his life has been spent as a medical missionary in Africa. The findings of psycho-analysts fully endorse respect for life and for persons, but they endorse respect for all the life impulses and all the variety of persons.

ii. RELIGIOUS IDEALISM; HUMANE REALISM

The realist must acknowledge the positive functions of idealization and the part ideals have played in diversifying human culture and in inspiring altruistic behaviour. He must also recognize the havoc and misery wrought by the companion process of denigration and by the excesses of persecutory sadism and masochistic self-immolation that issue so readily from devotion to ideals. The psycho-analyst can afford to be a plain realist and to remain agnostic about ultimate issues, because he knows that inspiration for living is given to every human being in his very instincts. He does not need to idealize love, because he has constant evidence in his clinical work of the integrative power of libidinal impulses and their derivative interests and affections, and also evidence of the way in which destructive impulses can be employed to constructive ends. His experience of mal-adaptation and disease and of the conditions which govern therapeutic success and failure, serve to illumine for him the principles of adaptation and the conditions of mental health. The conception of optimal integration as the goal of personality development is derived, not from ideals, but from matter-of-fact inferences from the intensive study of living people.

The sovereignty of ideals in mental life may be as much an anachronism as the sovereignty of nations in the present world. Things worth living for may be worth dying for, and it is certainly true that there can be no greater test of love for another person than laying down one's life for him. But it is all too evident that the readiness of men and women to sacrifice their lives for their ideals has been shamelessly exploited throughout the ages for quite unworthy ends. All the indications suggest that the time is ripe for the transference of allegiance from ideals to more rational aims of life-fulfilment. These aims may at least be ultimately attainable, although at present they share with many ideals the character of short-term unattainability. Idealism may free one from narrow ego-centricity, but so also can personal affection and fellowship. Men and women bear responsibility for the life in themselves as well as for other people: indeed, the Christian is taught this in the parable of the talents, but does not always remember it. It is true that the most a confirmed idealist may be able to do by way of transcending his idealism is to identify his ideals with more intelligently realistic standards, but this process would itself tend to modify the idealist in a realist direction and so make for re-adaptive behaviour.

iii. PERSONAL RELEVANCE AND ORIENTATION

The deepest appeal of Christianity is to the heart of man; its respect for persons involves concern with their desires and emotions. It is this profound subjective appeal that is responsible for its continued vitality and for its several renewals. The Christian may frequently be puzzled by God and by life, but he is encouraged to believe that, whatever the trials of his daily life and the state of his human feelings, he is the beloved child of his Heavenly Father and may, therefore, rest upon the decision, 'Though He slay me, yet will I trust in Him'. The Christian doctrines of creation and redemption offer him, in addition, the conception of purpose in his own life and an orientation to the Divine Purpose. It is hardly surprising, therefore, that people disillusioned with the earlier over-optimistic humanism should tend to return to the Christian fold. But those who desire to reinstate Christian values, and consider that these alone offer guidance for personal life, forget that many other people now hold that Christianity has itself failed as completely as a too facile humanism.

It is also natural that a similar attraction to Christianity should be felt by people convinced by experience of the inadequacy of materialism and the purely objective natural sciences in respect of urgent problems of emotional and impulsive life. To such people there may seem to be no alternative to Christianity (or some other avowedly mystical religion which contrasts the 'natural' with the 'spiritual') but the narrowly sensualist doctrine of eating, drinking, and making merry, which is to them a doctrine of despair. This Hobson's choice, however, is not compulsory since better understanding of human nature offers another way out of the dilemma. This way is already attracting a number of men and women for whom the choice between idealism and simple animality is impracticable, and who feel, dimly or clearly, that another and more genuinely human choice must be possible. Popular interest in psychology is steadily increasing; Jung even regards interest in psychology as a leading characteristic of modern man. The vitality of this interest is confirmed, for example, by the high sales of psychological literature and the statistics of attendance at popular lectures (the average attendance at a recent W.E.A. psychology course was more than three times as high as the average for any other course in the same term). No psychology has so far made more basic contributions to the understanding of human nature and personal life-problems than has psycho-analysis. Infant science though psycho-analysis may be, the orientation it affords is not the blind submission of the 'good child' to the inscrutable Will of God, but adult acceptance of responsible living in accord with the insight so far attained into the natural laws of personal life.

iv. SPIRITUAL AND INTEGRATIVE VALUES

The Christian's treasure is in Heaven, and his human life in time and space is also in Eternity. Christian values are, therefore, of the spirit and not of the flesh. The sacramental view of life, however, does not deny the flesh, but requires its dedication and its use to the glory of God. This more integrative, sacramental attitude cannot very easily be maintained in partnership with Christian idealism, because it connotes the simple acceptance and enjoyment of sensual pleasures as bodily 'graces'. There is an inevitable tendency towards the attitude that such pleasures befoul the fleshly tabernacle of the spirit and have no place in the 'temple of the Holy Ghost'. The body-spirit correlation of the sacramentalist readily gives place to the body-spirit conflict of the ascetic.

How do the integrative values implicit in psycho-analysis compare with Christian 'other-worldly' and spiritual values? Psycho-analysis is definitely not 'other-worldly' but neither is it crudely materialistic nor naïvely ego-centric. It does not concern itself with ultimate issues but accepts man as it finds him, a psycho-social being, the course of whose development has endowed him with a highly organized mental life and corresponding psychological needs in addition to his primary animal requirements. Hence, the satisfaction of primary needs alone is no longer sufficient to make human life worth-while. Man lost his animal simplicity when he developed moral values. Over and above the moral values, Christians place what they call 'spiritual' values associated with ideals of Divine Love, Truth, the Beauty of Holiness, Absolute Reality, and Goodness.

The nature of these spiritual, or purely psychological, values, is liable to be obscured by their association with theological dogmas and metaphysical theories; if these associations are ignored, the cardinal spiritual values appear as idealist and absolutist versions of realist integrative values. Thus, 'Love' represents the whole range of libidinal values, *i.e.* the human realities of love, affection, and fellow-feeling, upon which the possibility of personal and social integration ultimately depends. 'Truth', as real truth, stands for the relative but constantly expanding body of human knowledge, for personal sincerity, and for the common-sense desiderata of veracity and honesty in human relationships. The 'humility' and 'obedience' required of the Christian are paralleled for the realist by the pride-deflating recognition of the givenness of life and its conditions, and the necessity for finding and complying with the natural laws upon which life-fulfilment depends. Integrative values are natural, not supernatural; they develop out of the primary values at the human level of mental organization, and they make for the optimal co-ordination of primary and derivative needs.

There is no tendency in psycho-analysis to decry the senses or to undervalue sensual enjoyment. There is only a recognition that a life of purely sensual indulgence is no longer adequate or possible for man. A worth-while life ordinarily includes a personal optimum of primary gratifications, but it usually demands other channels of expression and other forms of enjoyment as well, including a greater or lesser variety of emotional and intellectual interests. Psychological freedom is neither licence nor inhibition; it is the ability to make integrative use of instinct through the ego-organization in ways that best meet id and super-ego requirements in current circumstances. The formula for life-fulfiment is necessarily specific for each person, but individual formulas may be expected to show type resemblances.

v. OTHER-WORLDLINESS AND SPIRITUALITY; ULTRA-EGOISM AND INTEGRITY; SOME EGO MISCONCEPTIONS

Christianity is other-worldly and spiritually minded. Psycho-analysis is neither other-worldly nor supernatural in outlook, but it is intrinsically ultra-egoistic. It extends the conception of mental life and personality far beyond the narrow confines of the operative conscious and pre-conscious ego. The ego seems to have developed primarily as the agent of intelligent adaptation to the outer world. Human intelligence has now called in question the validity of moral and religious traditions. It has also

discovered that there are features about man's automatic unconscious systems of instinct-control which militate, not only against
mental health and happiness, but also against a fully objective
appreciation of external conditions themselves. The ego, therefore, has to take a further step, to which it is not yet so well
adapted, and to use its intelligence to explore subjective life and
the constitution of human nature with the same thoroughness
which it has hitherto devoted to the natural sciences. The result,
according to Freud's threefold conception of the mental constitution, is that the ego finds it is not an end in itself, but an
agent of a more comprehensive life, the total personality. It has
often been said that Freud struck the third, most shattering blow
to man's ego-centric over-estimation of himself, the first two
having been dealt by Copernicus and Darwin respectively.
Freud thus offered to mankind its third great chance to re-survey
'the place of man in nature'.

The self-importance of the ego is diminished by the extended
conception of personality, but its responsibilities are, if anything,
increased. It remains the controller of voluntary motility and
the active manager of personal behaviour and relationships,
but it has to enlarge its conceptions of management and to
apprentice itself afresh to life with a view to acquiring a more
adequate technique of multi-polar adaptation. The apprentice-
ship includes the critical revision of both traditional and revolutionary standards of value in relation to a central aim, the harmonization of the various demands made upon the ego by id,
super-ego, and external conditions.

Arguments about free-will versus determinism usually derive
from abstract conceptions which express antithetic human wishes
and are not based on evidence from psychological facts. The real
situation appears somewhat paradoxical. The validity of psychological determinism is seldom questioned by psycho-analysts, because clinical evidence re-proves from hour to hour that we are
what we have become as a result of our past history, and that
what we are now becoming is shaping our future. But, equally,
there can be no question that living is creative and that, within
limits variously circumscribed for different people, the ego
appears to have some possibilities of choice. Every decision is a
fresh decision, which may represent a new beginning, a re-
adaptation, not necessarily always predictable in advance,
although explicable after the event. It would seem that the ego

is fulfilling its proper functions when it tries to take the most reasonable decision on the evidence before it, as if it were a responsible free agent. But the sounder the internal and external reality-sense of the ego, the better will it recognize the limiting conditions of its own choices and the more likely will it be to arrive at integrative, practicable decisions. In relation to the total personality, the adequately realistic ego might well say with St. Paul, 'I live, yet not I'.

The situation of the ego and its prerogative of consciousness induce it to arrive at a number of misconceptions, most of which are not merely natural mistakes of self-ignorance, but defences against anxiety. It seems inevitable that the ego should regard itself as the personality, until evidence to the contrary is forced upon it. The major errors arising from this over-determined ego-centricity are short-sighted confusions of the means and the consequences of adaptation, its pleasure-pain and other affective indices, with the aims of instinct and the goals of personal life. Hedonism is an ego mistake of this kind. Pleasure and happiness are not aims of instinct, but conscious indices of the fact that instinct is attaining its ends, usually through the establishment of suitable relationships with appropriate objects (see pp. 170-71). This in no way implies that happiness and joy in living are not eminently desirable, but only that they are concomitants of, or signs of, mental health. Modern criticism of traditional systems of ethics, on grounds that they do not promote happiness, is warranted.

Fairbairn's proposition (1946, p. 30) that 'libido is not primarily pleasure-seeking, but object-seeking', is wholesomely corrective of hedonistic over-emphasis, but tends to encourage another error of ellipsis. It is preferable to describe the aim of instinct in full as 'object-relation-seeking' rather than to describe it in ego short-hand as 'object-seeking'. The ego is the practical conductor of instinct-object relationships and is constantly engaged in object discrimination and assessment; 'objects' therefore tend to figure largely in personology. The patient of Fairbairn who protested (Fairbairn, 1946, p. 30): 'You're always talking about my wanting this and that desire satisfied; but what I really want is a father', was fully justified; but wanting a father is ego short-hand for wanting a father to love and to be loved by, etc.; the patient wanted to re-establish a system of relationships she still needed.

Concentration on objects has its drawbacks even in persono-logy, but it is disastrous in metapsychology, where systems are all systems of dynamic object-relationships. Curiously enough, it is Fairbairn who makes the mistake of thinking that Freud's conception of mental structure is static rather than dynamic (Fairbairn, 1946, p. 36). Admittedly, Freud's later conception of mental organization is greatly to be preferred to his earlier, more mechanist 'fiction' of the psychic apparatus, but his theory of mental structure was never other than dynamic. The conception of mental organization is intrinsically a dynamic conception of energy-pattern, and this dynamism of structure is basic to the psycho-analytic conception of mental life.

The tendency of the ego to mistake means for ends is illustrated in the social sphere by the elevation of the acquisition of wealth and power to be goals of human endeavour, though they have welfare value only in so far as they can be used to provide the conditions for creative and integrative living.

Some of the commonest errors made by the ego arise, then, from a too short-sighted reality-sense, *i.e.* from the mistaking of means and consequences for ends. The reality-ego tends to regard itself as the person, instead of merely the conscious agent of the total personality; it tends to concern itself with objects as such and to forget that their personal significance is dependent upon the relations established with them; it also readily confuses pleasure and happiness with goals of living, whereas they are the result of adequate adaptation and the indices of life-fulfilment. In addition to developing better perspective in regard to its own rôle in mental life, the conscious ego has further to recognize that although the total personality is an individual focus of life, this focus or nexus (Whitehead's term) constantly interacts with other foci. Human life is psycho-social life. It is an affair of reciprocal relationships, not an affair of living for oneself alone, nor of living only for one's fellows, but of harmonizing individual and social interests. The conscious self is the responsible executive agent of the total personality, existing in active mutual relationship with other persons.

vi. ATTITUDES TO INSTINCT AND THEIR CONSEQUENCES

It can be argued that the simple endeavour of the ego to find and to accept the fullest attainable measure of personal and objective reality, and to deal with it as integratively as may be, is an exacting discipline not so far removed in practice from the Christian discipline of 'Thy Will be done'. For the would-be realist, however, the urge to life-fulfilment finds its first authoritative expression in the promptings of instinct and in the inferred laws of mental life, rather than in super-ego inspired codes of traditional morality and idealistic creeds. The pressure of instinct is, after all, the pulse of life itself, whereas the voice of conscience is all too often the voice of human prejudice and stupidity. Anyone whose respect for natural law is greater than his regard for human decree, cannot regard instinct as evil in itself, nor the advice of conscience as necesssarily good. The realist, however, will not fall into the error of idealizing instinct and contemning wholesale both morality and religion. He will respect instinct but he will also respect any integrative values which find expression in ethical codes and religious teaching. At the same time, he will not hesitate to seek the reasons for the failure of these codes and creeds, notwithstanding their positive value-content, to advance humanity farther on the road it is apparently attempting to pursue, a way of greater integrity in personal life and social organization.

The positive psycho-social values of religion may be attributed, in great part, to its salvage and redistribution of infantile energies and relationships and the possibility it offers to the individual, on the one hand, of some degree of personal, if partial, integration and, on the other hand, of some degree of effective orientation to his fellow-men and the universe in general. Christianity, in particular, offers a positive way of living inasmuch as it stresses love, the truly integrative factor in life. In practice, however, and in its historical development, Christianity has exercised too preferential a selectivity in love. It has favoured the more highly sublimated forms of love while denigrating the more primitive libidinal impulses, although these are the root and source of all the varieties of love and of all the diverse trends of human creativity. Many of the negative and life-impeding effects of religion are connected, in one way or another, with the defects of idealization-denigration as a method of solving problems of ambivalence and of severing emotional love from sensuality.

The direction of evolution may be towards an expansion of consciousness, but the implications of psycho-analysis suggest that this needs to be a balanced, or all-round, expansion which would extend ego-awareness in both super-ego and id directions.

It would be a result of better ego-assimilation of instinctual impulses and infantile relationships and their more complete utilization under positive and humane ego and super-ego control. If the race does not cease to exist in the meantime, such a process of all-round widening of the sphere of consciousness might, eventually, yield a higher proportion of adequately realistic men and women with a greater degree of mental integrity and, consequently, more intelligent and life-promoting habits of personal conduct and social organization. Utopias will always remain roseate dreams, but a saner and more gracious world than exists to-day is not merely a wish-fulfilling illusion; it is a real possibility, although it may not be an immediate probability.

(VI) CONCLUSION

It is evident that the revolt of modern man against the dead hand of traditional and supernatural authority has proved a somewhat Pyrrhic victory, in that it has resulted in a triumph of unreason and aggression. Crude materialism is, indeed, a more frustrating attitude to life than Christianity, but, humanly speaking, there must be something wrong with both the personal and social aspects of a religion which can provoke, or at least fail to prevent, such cataclysmic reactions as this century has already witnessed. It seems not unlikely that, if the religious revival desired by Christians did come about on a large scale, it would be followed at a subsequent date by a still more vigorous revolt. At present the intellect has won relative freedom; but not so the heart, whose capacities for personal love and social co-operation are still fettered by traditional modes of dealing with infantile conflicts. The fact that substitutes for orthodox religion have been found in plenty, most recently in political ideologies, is a sign that these traditional modes are still in operation. These alternatives to religion demand the focus of an ideal, whose ostensibly abstract appeal is nearly always reinforced by identification with its personal promoters and 'leaders'. Acceptance of the new ideal brings in its train all the old consequences of idealization-denigration. What is needed is not more ideals but more enlightened, realistic, and integrative standards of private and public behaviour, standards which are relevant to the psycho-social necessities and the actual conditions of world affairs.

The development of such re-adaptive standards would require modification of current attitudes towards instinct and a reassessment of 'values' ancient and modern, with a view to establishing the living conditions which would favour, rather than hamper, psychological maturation and the development of fellowship. Religions are attempts at integrative living, but the development of more stable civilizations depends upon the discovery and practice of more efficient methods of psycho-social integration than Christianity has yet achieved. In terms of life, the only practical religion of humanity would be a way of living which would promote both personal and social integration. Such a way of living could be firmly based only on realistic knowledge of man's nature and a humane, or personalist, approach to the many-sided and extremely difficult problems of social organization for human welfare.

Existentialists maintain that life is an experience to be lived, and not a problem for solution. The findings of psycho-analysis support the conception that life is simply for living, but they also show that experience raises a host of problems whose solution is likely to be found only through the fuller use of intelligence and the development of a more trustworthy subjective and objective reality-sense. But, although more knowledge is urgently required to make plain the way of integrity and to establish the principles of integrative living, it is equally true that the goal can be achieved only in so far as knowledge is applied in living and so translated into being. Hence, every personal attempt to live integratively is a direct, if minute, contribution to the raising of the psychological standard of life for all.

REFERENCES CITED IN THE TEXT

(Journal titles are abbreviated in accordance with the *World List of Scientific Periodicals* (Oxford University Press), 2nd ed. 1934. The *Collected Papers* of Sigmund Freud are cited as *C.P.*)

Abraham, Karl (1924). A short study of the development of the libido. *Selected Papers on Psycho-Analysis* (London: Hogarth Press, trans. 1927), 418.

— (1925). Character formation on the genital level of libido development. *Selected Papers on Psycho-Analysis* (London: Hogarth Press, trans. 1927), 407.

Adams, Henry H. (1947). Narcissistic equilibrium. *Int. J. Psycho-Anal.*, **28**, 107.

Adler, Gerhard (1945). C. G. Jung's contribution to modern consciousness. *Brit. J. med. Psychol.*, **20**, 207.

Adrian, E. D. (1946). The mental and the physical origins of behaviour. *Int. J. Psycho-Anal.*, **27**, 1.

Alexander, Franz (1930. Trans.). (Orig. pub. 1927.) *The Psychoanalysis of the Total Personality* (New York: Nervous and Mental Disease Publishing Co.).

— (1933). The relation of structural and instinctual conflicts. *Psychoanal. Quart.*, **2**, 181.

— (1935). The logic of the emotions. *Int. J. Psycho-Anal.*, **16**, 399.

— (1948). Development of the ego-psychology. In Lorand, *Psycho-Analysis Today* (London: Allen & Unwin), 143.

Almedingen, E. M. (1945). *Dom Bernard Clements* (London: John Lane).

Baggally, W. (1947). A generalized hedonic theory of the ego. *Int. J. Psycho-Anal.*, **28**, 179.

Balint, Alice (1945). Identification. *Yearb. Psychoanal.* (London: Imago Publishing Co.), **1**, 317.

Balint, Michael (1936). The final goal of psycho-analytic therapy. *Int. J. Psycho-Anal.*, **17**, 206.

— (1948). On genital love. *Int. J. Psycho-Anal.*, **29**, 34.

Barnes, Bishop E. W. (1947). *The Rise of Christianity* (London: Longmans, Green).

Baron, S. A. (1939). Review of Sigmund Freud's *Moses and Monotheism*. *Amer. J. Sociol.*, **45**, 471.

Bennett, E., and Slater, P. (1945). Some tests for the discrimination of neurotic from normal subjects. *Brit. J. med. Psychol.*, **20**, 271.

Berdyaev, Nicolas (1943). *Slavery and Freedom* (London: Geoffrey Bles).

Bergler, Edmund (1934). The psycho-analysis of the uncanny. *Int. J. Psycho-Anal.*, **15**, 215.

— (1935). An enquiry into the 'material phenomenon'. *Int. J. Psycho-Anal.*, **16**, 203.

Bibring, Edward (1941). The development and problems of the theory of the instincts. *Int. J. Psycho-Anal.*, **22**, 102.

Bibring, Edward (1947). The so-called English School of psycho-analysis. *Psychoanal. Quart.*, **16**, 69.

Bion, W. R. (1948). Psychiatry at a time of crisis. *Brit. J. med. Psychol.*, **21**, 81.

Blackburn, Julian (1945). *Psychology and the Social Pattern* (London: Kegan Paul).

Bowlby, John (1940). *Personality and Mental Illness* (London: Kegan Paul).

Brierley, Marjorie (1932). Some problems of integration in women. *Int. J. Psycho-Anal.*, **13**, 433.

— (1936). Specific determinants in feminine development. *Int. J. Psycho-Anal.*, **17**, 163.

Burlingham, Dorothy, and Freud, Anna (1942). *Young Children in Wartime* (London: Allen & Unwin).

Burt, Sir Cyril (1939). The factorial analysis of emotional traits. *Character & Pers.*, **7**, 238.

— (1940). *Factors of the Mind* (University of London Press).

Cadoux, C. J. (1948). *The Life of Jesus* (London: Penguin Press).

Carington, Whately (1945). *Telepathy* (London: Methuen).

Cattell, R. B. (1946). Personality structure and measurement, I and II. *Brit. J. Psychol.*, **36**, 88, 159.

Collingwood, R. G. (1944). (Orig. pub. 1939.) *An Autobiography* (London: Penguin Press).

Confessions of St. Augustine, The (trans. Pusey, 1930) (London: Medici Society).

D'Arcy, Father M. C. (1946). *The Mind and Heart of Love* (London: Faber & Faber).

Dark, Sidney (1946). *The Passing of the Puritan* (London: Skeffington).

Deutsch, Helene (1946). *Psychology of Women*. Vol. 1, *Girlhood* (London: Research Books).

Dollard, John (1939). Culture, society, impulse, and socialization. *Amer. J. Sociol.*, **45**, 50.

— et al. (1939). *Frustration and Aggression* (Yale University. London: Kegan Paul, 1944).

Dorsey, John M. (1943). Some considerations on psychic reality. *Int. J. Psycho-Anal.*, **24**, 147.

Ehrenwald, Jan (1942). Telepathy in dreams. *Brit. J. med. Psychol.*, **19**, 313.

— (1944). Telepathy in the psychoanalytic situation. *Brit. J. med. Psychol.*, **20**, 51.

— (1947a). *Telepathy and Medical Psychology* (London: Allen & Unwin).

— (1947b). Exploring telepathy. *J. Amer. Soc. psych. Res.*, October.

Emmet, D. M. (1945). *The Nature of Metaphysical Thinking* (London: Macmillan).

Eysenck, H. J. (1947). *Dimensions of Personality* (London: Kegan Paul).

Fairbairn, W. R. D. (1944). Endopsychic structure considered in terms of object-relationships. *Int. J. Psycho-Anal.*, **25**, 70.

— (1946). Object-relationships and dynamic structure. *Int. J. Psycho-Anal.*, **27**, 30.

Federn, Paul (1926). Some variations in ego-feeling. *Int. J. Psycho-Anal.*, **7**, 434.

— (1928). Narcissism in the structure of the ego. *Int. J. Psycho-Anal.*, **9**, 401.

Federn, Paul (1936). Zur Unterscheidung des gesunden und krafthaften Narcissismus. *Imago*, **22**, 5.

— (1938). The undirected function in the central nervous system. *Int. J. Psycho-Anal.*, **19**, 173.

— (1943). Psychoanalysis of psychoses. *Psychiat. Quart.*, **17**, 3, 246, 470.

Fenichel, Otto (1931). The pre-genital antecedents of the Oedipus conflict. *Int. J. Psycho-Anal.*, **12**, 141.

— (1946). *The Psychoanalytic Theory of Neurosis* (London: Kegan Paul).

Ferenczi, Sandor (1916). Stages in the development of the sense of reality. *Contributions to Psychoanalysis* (Boston: Badger).

— (1926). The problem of acceptance of unpleasant ideas. *Int. J. Psycho-Anal.*, **7**, 312.

Flugel, J. C. (1945). *Man, Morals and Society* (London: Duckworth).

— (1948). 'L'Appétit vient en mangeant': some reflexions on the self-sustaining tendencies. *Brit. J. Psychol.*, **38**, 171.

Fordham, Michael (1945). Professor C. G. Jung. *Brit. J. med. Psychol.*, **20**, 221.

Frank, S. B. (1946). *God With Us* (London: Jonathan Cape).

Freed, Lan (1948). *Social Pragmatism* (London: Watts).

French, T. M. (1942). Some psychoanalytic applications of the psychological field concept. *Psychoanal. Quart.*, **11**, 27.

Freud, Anna (1937. Trans.). (Orig. pub. 1936.) *The Ego and the Mechanisms of Defence* (London: Hogarth Press).

Freud, Sigmund (1912). Contributions to the psychology of love. *C.P.* (1925), **4**, 203.

— (1913). The pre-disposition to obsessional neurosis. *C.P.* (1924), **2**, 122.

— (1914). On narcissism, an introduction. *C.P.* (1925), **4**, 30.

— (1915a). Instincts and their vicissitudes. *C.P.* (1925), **4**, 60.

— (1915b). The unconscious. *C.P.* (1925), **4**, 98.

— (1917). Mourning and melancholia. *C.P.* (1925), **4**, 152.

— (1922a). (Orig. pub. 1920.) *Beyond the Pleasure Principle* (London: Hogarth Press).

— (1922b). (Orig. pub. 1921.) *Group Psychology and the Analysis of the Ego* (London: Hogarth Press).

— (1922c). Dreams and telepathy. *C.P.* (1925), **4**, 408.

— (1923). The infantile genital organization of the libido. *C.P.* (1924), **2**, 244.

— (1924a). The economic problem in masochism. *C.P.* (1924), **2**, 255.

— (1924b). The passing of the Oedipus complex. *C.P.* (1924), **2**, 269.

— (1924c). The loss of reality in neurosis and psychosis. *C.P.* (1924), **2**, 277.

— (1925). On negation. *Int. J. Psycho-Anal.*, **6**, 367.

— (1927). (Orig. pub. 1923.) *The Ego and the Id* (London: Hogarth Press).

— (1928). (Orig. pub. 1927.) *The Future of an Illusion* (London: Hogarth Press).

— (1929, Trans. rev. ed.). (Orig. pub. 1927.) *Introductory Lectures on Psycho-Analysis* (London: Allen & Unwin).

Freud, Sigmund (1930a. Trans. 4th ed.). (Orig. pub. 1905.) *Three Contributions to Sexual Theory* (New York: Nervous and Mental Disease Publishing Co.).

— (1930b). (Orig. pub. 1929.) *Civilization and Its Discontents* (London: Hogarth Press).

— (1932a. Trans. rev. ed.). (Orig. pub. 1899.) *The Interpretation of Dreams* (London: Allen & Unwin).

— (1932b). Female sexuality. *Int. J. Psycho-Anal.*, **13**, 281.

— (1932c). Libidinal types. *Int. J. Psycho-Anal.*, **13**, 277.

— (1933). *New Introductory Lectures* (London: Hogarth Press).

— 1936). (Orig. pub. 1926.) *Inhibitions, Symptoms and Anxiety* (London: Hogarth Press).

— (1937). Analysis terminable and interminable. *Int. J. Psycho-Anal.* **18**, 373.

— (1939). *Moses and Monotheism* (London: Hogarth Press).

Fromm, Erich (1949). *Man for Himself* (London: Routledge & Kegan Paul).

Fulton, J. F., and Nachmansohn, D. (1943). Acetylcholine and the physiology of the nervous system. *Science*, **97**, 569.

Glover, Edward (1932a). On the aetiology of drug addition. *Int. J. Psycho-Anal.*, **13**, 298.

— (1932b). Medico-psychological aspects of normality. *Brit. J. Psychol.*, **23**, 152.

— (1932c). A psycho-analytic approach to the classification of mental disorders. *J. ment. Sci.*, October.

— (1933a). Review of Melanie Klein's *Psycho-Analysis of Children. Int. J. Psycho-Anal.*, **14**, 119.

— (1933b). The relation of perversion-formation to the development of reality-sense. *Int. J. Psycho-Anal.*, **14**, 486.

— (1935). A developmental study of obsessional neurosis. *Int. J. Psycho-Anal.*, **16**, 131.

— (1938). A note on idealization. *Int. J. Psycho-Anal.*, **19**, 91.

— (1939). The psycho-analysis of affects. *Int. J. Psycho-Anal.*, **20**, 299.

— (1943). The concept of dissociation. *Int. J. Psycho-Anal.*, **24**, 7.

— (1945). Examination of the Klein system of child psychology. *The Psychoanalytic Study of the Child* (London: Imago Publishing Co.), **1**, 75.

— (1947a). *War, Sadism and Pacifism*, 3rd ed. (London: Allen & Unwin).

— (1947b). *Basic Mental Concepts* (London: Imago Publishing Co.).

Glover, James (1926). The conception of the ego. *Int. J. Psycho-Anal.*, **7**, 414.

Hadham, John (1944). *God and Human Progress* (London: Penguin Press).

Hardcastle, D. N. (1935). A suggested approach to the problems of neuro-psychiatry. *J. ment. Sci.*, April.

Harrison, Jane E. (1908). *Prolegomena to the Study of Greek Religion* (Cambridge University Press).

Hartmann, Heinz (1939a). Ich-Psychologie und Anpassungsproblem. *Int. Z. Psychoanal. u. Imago*, **24**, 62.

— (1939b). Psycho-analysis and the concept of health. *Int. J. Psycho-Anal.*, **20**, 308.

— (1948). Psychoanalysis and sociology. In Lorand, *Psycho-Analysis Today* (London: Allen & Unwin), 326.

Hartmann, Heinz, and Kris, Ernst (1945). The genetic approach in psycho-analysis. *The Psychoanalytic Study of the Child* (London: Imago Publishing Co.), **1**, 11.

Hendrick, Ives (1945). Work and the pleasure principle. *Yearb. Psychoanal.* (London: Imago Publishing Co.), **1**, 95.

Hobhouse, L. T. (1915). *Morals in Evolution* (London: Chapman & Hall).

Hodges, H. A. (1944). *Wilhelm Dilthey: an Introduction* (London: Kegan Paul).

Hollitscher, Walter (1943). On the concepts of psychological health and illness. *Int. J. Psycho-Anal.*, **24**, 125.

Hopkinson, A. W. (1946). *Mysticism: Old and New* (London: Nisbet).

Horney, Karen (1926). The flight from womanhood. *Int. J. Psycho-Anal.*, **7**, 324.

— (1932). The dread of woman. *Int. J. Psycho-Anal.*, **13**, 348.

— (1933). The denial of the vagina. *Int. J. Psycho-Anal.*, **14**, 57.

— (1946). *Our Inner Conflicts: a Constructive Theory of Neurosis* (London: Kegan Paul).

Hügel, Baron F. von (1909). *The Mystical Element of Religion as Studied in Saint Catharine of Genoa and Her Friends*, 2 vols. (London: Dent).

Huxley, Julian (1944). *On Living in a Revolution* (London: Chatto & Windus).

Huxley, T. H., and Huxley, Julian (1947). *Evolution and Ethics 1893–1943* (London: Pilot Press).

Isaacs, Susan (1939). Criteria for interpretation. *Int. J. Psycho-Anal.*, **20**, 148.

— (1945). 'Notes on metapsychology as process theory': some comments. *Int. J. Psycho-Anal.*, **26**, 58.

Jacobi, Jolan (1942). *The Psychology of C. G. Jung* (London: Kegan Paul).

Jones, Ernest (1913). Hate and anal erotism in the obsessional neurosis. *Papers on Psycho-Analysis*, 3rd ed. (London: Ballière, Tindall & Cox, 1923), 553.

— (1920). Recent advances in psycho-analysis. *Papers on Psycho-Analysis*, 3rd ed. (London: Ballière, Tindall & Cox, 1923), 40.

— (1922). A psycho-analytic study of the Holy Ghost. *Essays in Applied Psycho-Analysis* (London: Hogarth Press, 1923), 415.

— (1924). The classification of the instincts. *Brit. J. Psychol.*, **14**, 256.

— (1929). Fear, guilt and hate. *Int. J. Psycho-Anal.*, **10**, 383.

— (1933). The phallic phase. *Int. J. Psycho-Anal.*, **14**, 1.

— (1936). Psycho-analysis and the instincts. *Brit. J. Psychol.*, **26**, 273.

— (1937). Love and morality. *Int. J. Psycho-Anal.*, **18**, 1.

— (1942). The concept of a normal mind. *Int. J. Psycho-Anal.*, **23**, 1.

— (1946). A valedictory address. *Int. J. Psycho-Anal.*, **27**, 7.

— (1948). The psychology of religion. In Lorand, *Psycho-Analysis Today* (London: Allen & Unwin), 315.

Jung, C. G. (1923). *Psychological Types* (London: Kegan Paul).

— (1928). *Two Essays in Analytical Psychology* (London: Ballière, Tindall & Cox).

Klein, Melanie (1932). *The Psycho-Analysis of Children* (London: Hogarth Press).

— (1948a). *Contributions to Psycho-Analysis 1921–1945* (London: Hogarth Press).

Klein, Melanie (1948b). The early development of conscience in the child. In Lorand, *Psycho-Analysis Today* (London: Allen & Unwin), 64.

Kris, Ernst (1947). The nature of psychoanalytic propositions and their validation. In *Freedom and Experience*: Essays presented to Horace M. Kallen (Cornell University Press).

Kulovesi, Irgo (1931). Psychoanalytische Bemerkungen zur James-Langeschen Affekttheorie. *Imago*, **17**, 392.

Landauer, Karl (1938). Affects, passions and temperament. *Int. J. Psycho-Anal.*, **19**, 388.

Latourette, K. S. (1946). *A History of the Expansion of Christianity*. Vol. VII, *Advance Through Storm*, A.D. *1914 and After* (London: Eyre & Spottiswoode).

— (1949). *The Prospect for Christianity* (London: Eyre & Spottiswoode).

Lee, H. B. (1939). A critique of the theory of sublimation. *Psychiatry: J. Biol. Path. Interpers. Rel.*, **2**, 239.

— (1940). A theory concerning free creation in the inventive arts. *Psychiatry: J. Biol. Path. Interpers. Rel.*, **3**, 229.

Leuba, J. H. (1925). *The Psychology of Religious Mysticism* (London: Kegan Paul).

Levy-Suhl, Max (1946). The rôle of ethics and religion in psycho-analytic theory and therapy. *Int. J. Psycho-Anal.*, **27**, 110.

Lewin, K. (1939). Field theory and experiment in social psychology: concepts and methods. *Amer. J. Sociol.*, **44**, 868.

Lewis, C. S. (1942). *The Screwtape Letters* (London: Geoffrey Bles).

— (1947). *Miracles* (London: Geoffrey Bles).

Linton, Ralph (1947). *The Cultural Background of Personality* (London: Kegan Paul).

Loewenstein, R. (1940). The vital or somatic instincts. *Int. J. Psycho-Anal.*, **21**, 377.

Lorand, Sandor (1948). Comments on the correlation of theory and technique. *Psychoanal. Quart.*, **17**, 32.

— edit. (1948). *Psycho-Analysis Today* (London: Allen and Unwin).

Mackinder, Dorothy (1946). *Silver Fountains* (London: Macdonald).

MacMurray, John (1935). *Reason and Emotion* (London: Faber & Faber).

Mannheim, Karl (1943). *Diagnosis of Our Time* (London: Kegan Paul).

Mauriac, François (1946). *A Woman of the Pharisees* (London: Eyre & Spottiswoode).

McCulloch, Joseph (1946). *Medway Adventure* (London: Michael Joseph).

McDougall, William (1920). *The Group Mind* (Cambridge University Press).

— (1922). *Social Psychology*, 17th. ed. (London: Methuen).

Michaels, J. J. (1945). The concept of integration in psychoanalysis. *J. nerv. ment. Dis.*, **102**, 54.

Middlemore, Merell P. (1941). *The Nursing Couple* (London: Hamish Hamilton).

Milner, Marion (1945). Some aspects of phantasy in relation to general psychology. *Int. J. Psycho-Anal.*, **26**, 143.

Moberly, Sir Walter (1949). *The Crisis in the University* (London: S.C.M. Press).

Money-Kyrle, R. E. (1944). Some aspects of political ethics from the psycho-analytical point of view. *Int. J. Psycho-Anal.*, **25**, 166.

Morley, Iris (1946). *Nothing but Propaganda* (London: Peter Davies).

Mumford, Lewis (1944). *The Condition of Man* (London: Secker & Warburg).

Murray, R. (1943). *The Good Pagan's Failure* (London: Hollis & Carter).

Myers, Sir Charles S. (1945). The comparative study of instincts. *Brit. J. Psychol.*, **36**, 1.

Needham, Joseph (1943). *Time: the Refreshing River* (London: Allen & Unwin).

Newman, Cardinal J. H. (1890). *Apologia pro Vita Sua* (London: Longmans, Green).

Niebuhr, Reinhold (1941). *The Nature and Destiny of Man.* Vol. I, *Human Nature* (London: Nisbet).

— (1943). *The Nature and Destiny of Man.* Vol. II, *Human Destiny* (London: Nisbet).

Nunberg, Hermann (1932). *Allgemeine Neurosenlehre auf psychoanalytischer Grundlage* (Berne: Hans Huber).

Oldfield, R. C., and Zangwill, O. L. (1942–3). Head's concept of the Schema and its application in contemporary British psychology. *Brit. J. Psychol.*, **32**, 267; **33**, 58, 113, 143.

Payne, Sylvia (1935). A conception of femininity. *Brit. J. med. Psychol.*, **15**, 18.

— (1946). Notes on developments in the theory and practice of psycho-analytical technique. *Int. J. Psycho-Anal.*, **27**, 12.

Pear, T. H. (1948). Perspectives in modern psychology. *Brit. J. Psychol.*, **38**, 158.

Perls, F. S. (1947). *Ego, Hunger and Aggression* (London: Allen & Unwin).

Peto, Endre (1946). The psycho-analysis of identical twins. *Int. J. Psycho-Anal.*, **27**, 126.

Pfister, Oscar (1949. Trans.). (Orig. pub. 1944.) *Christianity and Fear: a Study in History and in the Psychology and Hygiene of Religion* (London: Allen & Unwin).

Philpott, S. J. F. (1942). Unconscious mechanisms in religion. *Brit. J. med. Psychol.*, **19**, 292.

Reik, Theodor (1941). Aggression from anxiety. *Int. J. Psycho-Anal.*, **22**, 7.

Rhine, J. B. (1948). *The Reach of the Mind* (London: Faber & Faber).

Richardson, Canon Alan (1947). *Christian Apologetics* (London: S.C.M. Press).

Riviere, Joan (1936a). A contribution to the analysis of the negative therapeutic reaction. *Int. J. Psycho-Anal.*, **17**, 304.

— (1936b). The genesis of psychical conflict in early infancy. *Int. J. Psycho-Anal.*, **17**, 395.

Russell, Bertrand (1931). *The Scientific Outlook* (London: Allen & Unwin).

— (1946). *History of Western Philosophy* (London: Allen & Unwin).

— (1948). *Human Knowledge: its Scope and Limits* (London: Allen & Unwin).

— (1949). *Authority and the Individual* (London: Allen & Unwin).

Sackville-West, V. (1943). *The Eagle and the Dove* (London: Michael Joseph).

De Saussure, R. (1939). Identification and substitution. *Int. J. Psycho-Anal.*, **20**, 465.

Schmideberg, Melitta (1938). Intellectual inhibition and disturbances in eating. *Int. J. Psycho-Anal.*, **19**, 17.

Schweitzer, Albert (1933). (Orig. pub. 1931.) *My Life and Thought: an Autobiography* (London: Allen & Unwin).

— (1946). *Civilization and Ethics*, 3rd ed. (London: Adam & Charles Black).

Shand, Alexander (1914). *The Foundations of Character* (London: Macmillan).

Sharpe, Ella (1946). From 'King Lear' to 'The Tempest'. *Int. J. Psycho-Anal.*, **27**, 19.

Sherrington, Sir Charles (1940). *Man on his Nature* (Cambridge University Press).

Simmel, Ernst (1945). Self-preservation and the death instinct. *Yearb. Psychoanal.* (London: Imago Publishing Co.), **1**, 143.

Smuts, Jan C. (1926). *Holism and Evolution* (London: Macmillan).

Spearman, Charles (1927). *The Abilities of Man* (London: Macmillan).

Strachey, Alix (1941). A note on the use of the word 'internal'. *Int. J. Psychol-Anal.*, **22**, 37.

Strachey, James (1934). The nature of the therapeutic action of psychoanalysis. *Int. J. Psycho-Anal.*, **15**, 127.

— (1939). Preliminary notes upon the problem of Akhenaten. *Int. J. Psycho-Anal.*, **20**, 33.

Taylor, A. E. (1945). *Does God Exist?* (London: Macmillan).

Temple, William (1944). *The Church Looks Forward* (London: Macmillan).

Thomson, Godfrey H. (1946). *Some Recent Work in Factorial Analysis and a Retrospect* (University of London Press: pamphlet).

Thouless, Robert H. (1948). Psychological research and experimental psychology. *Brit. J. Psychol.*, **39**, 97.

Toynbee, Arnold J. (1948). *Civilization on Trial* (Oxford University Press).

Tyrrell, G. N. M. (1945). *The Society for Psychical Research* (London: S.P.R. pamphlet).

— (1946). *The Personality of Man* (London: Penguin Press).

Underhill, Evelyn (1913). *The Mystic Way* (London: Dent).

— (1927). *Man and the Supernatural* (London: Methuen).

— (1946). *Collected Papers*, edit. Lucy Menzies (London: Longmans, Green).

Van der Waals, H. G. (1948). Heredity and psycho-analysis. *Int. J. Psycho-Anal.*, **29**, 41.

Vann, Gerald (1944). *The Heart of Man* (London: Geoffrey Bles).

Vernon, M. D. (1947). Different types of perceptual ability. *Brit. J. Psychol.*, **38**, 79.

— (1948). The development of imaginative construction in children. *Brit. J. Psychol.*, **39**, 102.

Waddington, C. H. (1941). *The Scientific Attitude* (London: Penguin Press).

— (1944). Life from a new angle. In *This Changing World*, edit. J. R. M. Brumwell (London: Routledge), 39.

— (1947). Science and belief. *Int. J. Psycho-Anal.*, **28**, 123.

— *et al.* (1942). *Science and Ethics* (London: Allen & Unwin).

Waelder, Robert (1936). The problem of freedom in psycho-analysis. *Int. J. Psycho-Anal.*, **17**, 89.

Weiss, Edoardo (1934). Bodily and mental pain. *Int. J. Psycho-Anal.*, **15**, 1.

— (1935). Todestrieb und Masochismus. *Imago*, **21**, 396.

Wells, H. G. (1944). The illusion of personality. *Nature, Lond.*, **153**, 395.

— (1945). *Mind at the End of its Tether* (London: Heinemann).

Werfel, Franz (1942). *The Song of Bernadette* (London: Hamish Hamilton).

Westermarck, Edward (1906–1908). *The Origin and Development of the Moral Ideas*, 2 vols. (London: Macmillan).

White, Amber Blanco (1949). *Ethics for Unbelievers* (London: Routledge & Kegan Paul).

Whitehead, A. N. (1929). *Process and Reality* (Cambridge University Press).

Wisdom, J. O. (1943). Determinism and psycho-analysis. *Int. J. Psycho-Anal.*, **24**, 240.

— (1947). *The Metamorphosis of Philosophy* (Cairo: Al-Maaref Press).

Witcutt, W. P. (1943). *Catholic Thought and Modern Psychology* (London: Burns, Oates & Washbourne).

Wolters, A. W. (1943). Some biological aspects of thinking. *Brit. J. Psychol.*, **33**, 176.

— (1945). The concept of mental maturity. *Nature, Lond.*, **156**, 494.

Young, Kimball (1946). *A Handbook of Social Psychology* (London: Kegan Paul).

— (1947). *Personality and Problems of Adjustment* (London: Kegan Paul).

Zilboorg, Gregory (1938a). Some observations on the transformation of instincts. *Psychoanal. Quart.*, **7**, 1.

— (1938b). The sense of immortality. *Psychoanal. Quart.*, **7**, 171.

— (1939a). The fundamental conflict with psycho-analysis. *Int. J. Psycho-Anal.*, **20**, 480.

— (1939b). Sociology and the psychoanalytic method. *Amer. J. Sociol.*, **45**, 341.

— (1943). *Mind, Medicine and Man* (New York: Harcourt, Brace).

— (1944). A response. *Psychoanal. Quart.*, **13**, 93.

— Waelder, R., and Menninger, K. A. (1945). Present trends in psychoanalytical theory and practice. A symposium. *Yearb. Psychoanal.* (London: Imago Publishing Co.), **1**, 79.

INDEX

Abraham, K., 25-8, 32, 64, 74, 81, 132, 190, 192-3
Abreaction, 43, 54
Absolutism, 273-4, 282
Abstinence, 35
Activation, 108-10
Acton, Lord, 281
Adams, H. H., 267
Adaptation, 19, 77, 97, 100-101, 106, 143, 166-71, 185-8, 194, 275, 284; endopsychic, 100-101; modern, 148; multi-polar, 19, 106, 133, 248, 288; to reality, 37, 41, 99-101; social, 179
Adler, A., 163, 200
Adler, G., 230
Adrian, E. D., 117
Aetiology, 80-83, 132
Affect(s), 108; and ego development, 49-55; ego-experiences, 44; Federn's views on, 54-5; indices of conditions in the psyche (subjective reality), 50, 55, 170; and instinct, problems of definition and classification, 44-9; layering and compounding of, 45; primary, 48, 52, 58, 136; primitive, intensity of, 259; relative neglect of, in theory, 43-4; repressed, 54; significance of, for psycho-analytical technique and therapy, 55-6; in theory and practice, 43-56
Affection, 59, 178, 192-3, 258, 284, 287
Affectivity, 44, 46-7, 52
Affirmation, world and life, 247
Aggression (Aggressivity), 27-9, 31, 35, 37, 41, 111, 120, 132, 136, 139, 167, 172-3, 177-8, 196, 226, 230, 249, 253, 256, 280, 282; and conscience, 138, 167, 172; domestication of, its preventive and auxiliary uses, 258, 259-67; interaction of, relations with, libido, 31, 41; relation to anxiety, 35-6, 57-8, 136
Agnosticism, 233
Agriculture, 270

Akhenaten, 209
Alexander, F., 32-3, 52, 133-4
Almedingen, E. M., 217, 220
Alternation(s): of content and dissatisfaction, 176; of feelings, 51-2; of gratification and frustration, 127; of love and hate, 27, 78; of mood, 77, 176; of projection and introjection, 37, 39, 58; of relationship to patients, 93
Altruism, 139, 284
Ambivalence, 27, 52, 56, 63-4, 78, 82, 101, 128, 176, 211, 219, 249, 263, 278, 291
'Ambivert', 188
American Institute of Mathematical Statistics, 241
Ampère, 157
'Amplification', 283
Anger, 59, 265
Anglican Church, 202
Anglo-Catholicism, 205
Animism, 68, 81, 100, 128, 200, 234, 245
Ann Arbor (Mich., U.S.A.) Research Centre for Group Dynamics, 117
'Anschauung', mechanistic, 154
Anthropology, 150, 152, 166, 208, 210
Anxiety(ies), 33-7, 40-41, 46, 48, 56-8, 60, 64, 82, 85-6, 112, 127, 136, 163, 171, 174-6, 222, 245, 252, 254, 259, 266, 269, 275, 277-8, 289; and aggression, 35-6, 57-8, 136, 259, 277; castration, 26, 34, 37, 85; feminine, 37, 86; masculine, 37, 85; mastery of, 24, 37, 41-3, 58, 266; separation, 34, 82
Archetypes, 149, 163, 184, 229, 231-232, 243-4
Aristotle, 199
Art (artists), 152, 162, 195, 199, 270-272
Artefact, intellectual, 204
Asceticism, 173, 198, 214, 286
Atheism, 234
Atonement, 195